Fast Track to CAE

Alan Stanton
Susan Morris

Longman

Tests by Jane Allemano and Peter Sunderland

Teacher's Book

Pearson Education Limited
Edinburgh Gate, Harlow
Essex CM20 2JE, England
and Associated Companies throughout the world

© Alan Stanton and Susan Morris 1999

The right of Alan Stanton and Susan Morris to be identified as authors of this Work has been asserted by them in accordance with the Copyright, Designs and Patents Act 1988

First published in 1999

This edition published in 2003

ISBN 0 582 82773 6

Set in Slimbach Book 9.5/12pt

Printed in Spain by Graficas Estella
Project Managed by Helena Gomm

Acknowledgements

We are grateful to the following for permission to reproduce copyright material:

the editor, *Focus* magazine for an extract used as tapescript based on the article 'Going underground' by Catherine Ormell in *FOCUS* September 1994; News International Syndication for an extract used as tapescript based on information in the article 'Things could get ugly' by Christopher Goodwin from *THE SUNDAY TIMES STYLE* magazine 28.1.96, © Christopher Goodwin/The Sunday Times, London 1996; Guardian Newspapers Ltd for extracts used as tapescript from the article 'Sins of the father and saving graces' by Liz Hodgkinson in *Society* column *THE GUARDIAN* 11.12.91, a slightly adapted article 'Awful wedded husbands' by Laura Matthews from *Women* column *THE GUARDIAN* 14.7.93, an extract based on the article 'Coral Seas of destruction' by Paul Olding in *THE GUARDIAN* 4.5.95, an extract from the article 'Guilty of Nomadism' by Nicola Gregory, *end piece* in *THE NEW INTERNATIONALIST* December 1992, 'The best medicine' by Thomas Quirke in the *OBSERVER MAGAZINE* 1993; Newspaper Publishing plc for an extract used as tapescript from the article 'Telling the truth about lies' by Angela Neustatter in the *INDEPENDENT ON SUNDAY* 10.5.92; the author, Ed Leibowitz for an adapted extract used as tapescript from his article 'Dream On' in the *TELEGRAPH MAGAZINE* 31.8.96; Consumers' Association for an extract adapted from "Time for a change?" published in *WHICH?* June 2002; The Driving Standards Agency for an extract adapted from *The Official Theory Test for Car Drivers*; Guardian Newspapers Limited for extracts adapted from "A camel, a kiss … but no wedding ring" by Sophie Campbell published in *THE OBSERVER* 25th August 2002 © Sophie Campbell 2002, "Stark realities" by Steven Morris published in *THE GUARDIAN* 24th August 2002 © The Guardian 2002, and "Polishing your CV can turn your flaws into strengths" by Karen Hainsworth published in *THE GUARDIAN* 31st August 2002 © Karen Hainsworth 2002; Guy Marks for an extract adapted from his article "Zambia: a land where eagles dare" published in the *FINANCIAL TIMES* 13th–14th January 2001; Independent Newspapers (UK) Limited for an extract adapted from "Master the art of being effective" by Marcus Field published in *INDEPENDENT ON SUNDAY: Reality Magazine* 27th May 2001; News International Newspapers Limited for an extract adapted from "Hedge against the rising street crime threat" by Paula Hawkins published in *THE TIMES* 24th July 2002 © Paula Hawkins/Times Newspapers Limited, London 2002; and Telegraph Group Limited for extracts adapted from "Softly softly" by Daisy Bridgewater published in *TELEGRAPH MAGAZINE* 13th April 2002, "Open house policy" by Jo Denbury published in *TELEGRAPH MAGAZINE* 23rd March 2002, and "Under the influence" by Dinah Hall published in *TELEGRAPH MAGAZINE* 22nd June 2002 (all © Telegraph Group Limited 2002).

In some instances we have been unable to trace the owners of copyright material and we would appreciate any information that would enable us to do so.

Sample OMR answer sheets are reproduced by permission of the University of Cambridge Local Examinations Syndicate.

Contents

Introduction to the course

The *Fast Track to CAE* course comprises a Students' Book, two class cassettes, an Exam Practice Workbook and this Teacher's Book, which contains advice on using the course, answers to the exercises in the Students' Book, tapescripts and photocopiable tests.

The course is complemented by *CAE Practice Tests Plus* by the same authors. This contains five complete practice tests in the format of the CAE examination. They may be used towards the end of the preparation course for timed exam practice, to ensure your students know exactly what to expect in the exam. The With Key edition contains an annotated Answer Key explaining why answers are right or wrong, as well as tapescripts.

KEY FEATURES

Fast Track to CAE provides students with comprehensive, graded preparation for the Certificate in Advanced English examination.

Graded Training

The early units of the course provide a graded introduction to each exam task. In Unit 2, for example, the multiple matching Listening task (Part 4) has only five options to choose from, instead of eight as in the exam. The gapped text Reading task (Part 2) is not introduced until Unit 6, after a lot of preparatory work has been done on coherence and cohesion in previous units. However, the actual listening and reading texts are at CAE level from the start.

Exam Overview

The **Exam Overview** at the front of the Students' Book gives information about each of the five Papers in the exam, and the skills each question aims to test. You can use this to familiarise students with the exam and introduce the goals of the course. There are cross-references to the relevant task types in the units, so that students can immediately get an idea of what a task involves. The **Exam Overview** can be used for reference throughout the course.

Exam File

Regular **Exam File** boxes provide key information about particular exam task types as they are introduced in the unit. They explain what the candidate has to do, give useful advice on tackling the task, and warn students of any possible pitfalls. You can use the **Exam Files** to introduce each new task type.

Language Bank

For the CAE student, vocabulary is possibly more important than grammar. Students need to learn the appropriate language for speaking and writing in the form of lexical phrases. Most Writing and Speaking sections in *Fast Track to CAE* have a **Language Bank** which contains task-specific phrases and sentences for students to use, including conversational 'gambits' for discourse management and linking expressions for writing. The **Language Banks** do not aim to be fully comprehensive, but they provide enough language to get students started and are a useful resource. To encourage students to look at the **Language Banks** and actually use the language that is provided, it is a good idea to check comprehension and, in Speaking sections, to model intonation before pairwork. You can tell students to tick off each expression as they use it.

Grammar Notes

The approach to grammar in *Fast Track to CAE* is inductive. Students are asked to analyse examples of grammatical patterns, often taken from the Reading and Listening texts, and answer questions on form and use. They then practise the forms through a variety of exercise types. The Language Study sections in each unit are cross-referenced to **Grammar Notes** at the back of the book, which give detailed explanations of the points covered. Encourage students to refer to these notes when doing the exercises. They will find help and advice which is directly relevant.

Spelling and punctuation

Spelling and punctuation may be tested in Part 3 of Paper 3, as well as being important for Paper 2, Writing. Therefore, *Fast Track to CAE* pays special attention to developing accuracy in these areas. In addition to notes on grammar, the reference section at the back of the Students' Book contains useful reference tables pulling together the most important rules of spelling and punctuation.

Pronunciation

The pronunciation points covered in this book are word stress (Unit 2), weak forms (Unit 3), elision – disappearing sounds (Unit 6) and assimilation – changing sounds (Unit 11). The aim of the pronunciation sections is not only to help improve students' pronunciation but also to improve their listening skills. Elision and assimilation are features of connected speech which can easily lead to difficulties in comprehending listening texts. For this reason, **Pronunciation** sections often precede **Listening** sections in the units and examples of the pronunciation point can be found in the recordings.

ORGANISATION OF THE STUDENTS' BOOK

There are 14 units in the Students' Book, each loosely based around a theme. Units are divided into sections, providing practice activities for each Paper in the exam, together with grammar presentation and practice, and vocabulary development work. To maintain interest and motivation, the sequence of sections varies from unit to unit. Each unit contains one or more of the following sections.

Speaking

Each unit starts with a Speaking activity illustrated with visual material. This introduces the theme of the unit and often leads into the work in the next section. Although the tasks are not always in precise exam format, the skills practised are always relevant to the requirements of the Speaking Test. In addition, there is usually a second Speaking section which provides training for a specific part of the Test. Advice on how to simulate exam procedures in the Speaking sections is given in the unit Teaching Notes. A sample script is included in the Overview of the exam on page 11 of this Teacher's Book.

The exam-related Speaking tasks in *Fast Track to CAE* focus on opinion gap rather than information gap tasks, as the latter feature only occasionally in the revised exam. This means there is no need for students to hide their pictures from each other.

In addition to the Speaking sections offering exam-related training, there are many other opportunities for class, group and pair discussion in response to reading and listening tasks.

Listening

The majority of units have two Listening sections, so that the course provides plenty of practice in all Paper 4 task types. As in the exam, the recordings contain a variety of accents. There is usually a preparatory task to introduce the topic and get students thinking about what they are going to hear. This stage provides an opportunity to pre-teach key vocabulary which you think students may not know. In some units, key vocabulary is pre-taught, for example through matching exercises or a quiz. There is almost always a follow-up activity, which often serves as a comprehension check as well as allowing students to respond personally to the ideas in the recording.

Reading

In order to do well in the CAE Reading Paper, it is vital that candidates are fast and efficient readers, able to use appropriate reading skills for the task in hand. In *Fast Track to CAE*, there are preparatory activities in the Reading sections which aim to train students in the skills they need to tackle the different types of reading

comprehension tasks effectively. These skills include skimming and identifying main ideas, highlighting key words in question and texts, and scanning to locate the relevant part of the text where the answer to a question is most likely to be found. This Teacher's Book supplies annotated answers to the exam tasks, which will help you to maximise the learning and training potential of the activity.

Follow-up activities include vocabulary search, where students have to look for expressions in the text, and analysis of style and register. These exercises aim to show students how any text can be used as a resource for adding to their store of language. You should encourage students to have their vocabulary notebooks with them at all times, so that they can add words they meet in the book.

There is always an opportunity for students to respond to the text on a personal level, and, very importantly, to put to immediate use some of the vocabulary they have looked at in order to express their ideas.

Vocabulary

The Vocabulary sections in each unit focus on areas such as phrasal verbs, collocation, idiomatic expressions and word formation, which are extremely important for the CAE exam. They often have a learner training aim. For example, students are shown how to work out the meaning of new phrasal verbs by looking at the literal meaning of the main verb (Unit 2), or by looking at the particle (Units 5 and 7). In Unit 3, students are encouraged to take a key word ('career') and record as many words as they can that collocate with the key word.

The Teaching Notes in this Teacher's Book often include suggestions for vocabulary extension activities. The Longman *Language Activator* is recommended for many of these activities. This is a unique type of productive dictionary that helps learners to put their own ideas into words, as well as understanding the ideas of others.

Language Study

Each unit has one or more **Language Study** sections. Earlier units review grammar points which students have already covered, but still tend to have problems with, such as use of modals and tenses. Also reviewed are areas typically tested in Paper 3, Part 2 (structural cloze) and Part 3 (unnecessary word), such as articles or prepositions. Later units introduce advanced aspects of familiar grammar areas as well as new grammatical items such as emphatic structures which are important at advanced level if students are to express themselves with increased sophistication.

Each **Language Study** section is cross-referenced to the **Grammar Notes** at the back of the book, and you should encourage students to refer to the notes when analysing examples of the structure and when doing the practice exercises.

Language Study sections always include opportunities for students to use the language in less controlled and more personalised contexts. The grammatical areas studied in each unit are also relevant to the Writing task in that unit. There are cross-references from the Writing sections to relevant Language Study sections.

English in Use

One or more of the six tasks in Paper 3 is practised in each unit. As all the questions in Paper 3 are based on a text, there is usually a preparatory task which encourages students to read the text through to the end before starting to do the task itself – this is a very important strategy which will help students avoid various traps set by the examiners! To help you turn a testing exercise into a teaching and learning activity, this Teacher's Book provides detailed guidance on right and wrong answers.

Writing

There is one, sometimes two, Writing sections per unit, providing practice in all the task types that occur on Paper 2. The five **Steps to Writing** guide students through the stages of **Task interpretation**, **Selecting and summarising** (for Part 1 tasks which involve reading input) or **Generating ideas** (for Part 2 tasks), **Layout and Organisation**, **Writing** with appropriate structures and vocabulary, and **Evaluating and editing** their own work.

In this Teacher's Book there are model answers for each of the writing tasks set in the Students' Book. These model answers would receive high marks in the exam, and will help to give you an idea of what your students should be striving to achieve. However, it is important to remember that, provided the task is achieved, there may be other equally good ways of answering the questions. Each student's answer must be judged on its own merits, not by the extent to which it resembles a model answer.

Exam Practice sections

There are **Exam Practice** sections after Units 5, 10 and 14. They contain Reading and Use of English questions in exact exam format. The three sets of Exam Practice Pages follow the sequence of Papers 1 and 3, and between them cover all the task types on these two papers. You can use them to give timed practice of task types that have been introduced or as class tests.

GENERAL HINTS ON PREPARING STUDENTS FOR THE CAE

It is important that your students realise that no coursebook, however good, can get them through the exam on its own. In addition to working through *Fast Track to CAE*, students should read as much English as possible outside class, to give themselves further practice in the skills they need for the exam, such as skimming rapidly for the main ideas and scanning for information. They should also listen to English whenever they can e.g. on the radio and TV or in films, to get used to hearing different accents and the way intonation patterns reflect attitudes and feelings. To encourage them to read newspapers and magazines, and listen to or watch English language programmes or films, you could allocate a regular weekly slot in which selected students in turn present a summary of an interesting article or film they have read or seen that week.

Overview of the Certificate in Advanced English

The Certificate in Advanced English (CAE) is an advanced language qualification intended for those who want to use English for professional or study purposes. The emphasis is very much on real-world tasks.

CAE is recognised by a majority of British universities for English language entrance requirements.

The examination consists of five Papers.

Reading	1 hour 15 minutes
Writing	2 hours
English in Use	1 hour 30 minutes
Listening	45 minutes approximately
Speaking	15 minutes approximately

The five Papers total 200 marks, with each Paper contributing 40 marks to the total after weighting. A candidate's overall grade is based on the total score achieved in all five Papers. It is not necessary to pass every Paper in order to pass the exam.

PAPER 1 READING
(1 hour 15 minutes)

Format

Paper 1 consists of four parts. Each part contains a text with comprehension questions. The total number of questions is 45–50. The texts range in length from 500 to 1,200 words. They may be taken from newspapers, magazines, journals, non-fiction books, leaflets etc.

Answering

Candidates indicate their answers by shading in the correct lozenge on an answer sheet, which is then marked by an Optical Mark Reader (OMR).

Marks

One mark is given for each correct answer to the multiple matching tasks. Two marks are given for each correct answer to the multiple choice and gapped text tasks.

Part	Task type and focus	Number of questions	Task format
1	Multiple matching: Reading for main ideas and specific information.	12–16	A text preceded by multiple matching questions.
2	Gapped text: understanding text structure.	6 or 7	A text from which paragraphs/sentences have been removed and placed in jumbled order after the text.
3	Multiple choice: detailed understanding of text.	5–7	A text followed by four-option multiple choice questions.
4	Multiple matching: reading for main ideas and specific information.	16–22	As Part 1 but longer, and often consisting of several short pieces.

PAPER 2 WRITING

(2 hours)

Format

The Writing Paper has two parts and candidates have to complete two writing tasks. Part 1 is a compulsory question. In Part 2, candidates choose from four tasks.

Answering

Candidates write their answers on separate answer paper.

Marks

Each question carries equal marks.

Assessment

Each question is marked on a scale from 0–5. There is a **general impression** mark-scheme that applies to all questions and refers to general features such as:

- the effect on the target reader
- natural and accurate use of language
- use of a wide range of vocabulary and grammatical structures
- choice of relevant material to complete the task with no omissions
- use of a variety of cohesive devices
- clear and consistent organisation of material

The general impression mark scheme is used in conjunction with a **task-specific** mark scheme, focusing on criteria relevant to each particular task. These include relevance (content required for task achievement), range of structure, vocabulary and presentation, and register. Examiners refer to the individual mark schemes while marking scripts.

Each paper is marked independently by two trained examiners and the scores added together to provide the total mark for this paper.

Part	Task type and focus	Number of tasks and length	Task format
1	Transactional letter, formal or informal; situationally-based or similar writing task.	one (or two) compulsory task(s) 250 words	Guidance given by rubric and input text (possibly visual material, diagrams).
2–5	Situationally-based letter, newspaper or magazine article, leaflet, information sheet, review, memo or similar.	four tasks from which candidates choose one writing task 250 words	Guidance given in rubric.

PAPER 3 ENGLISH IN USE
(1 hour 30 minutes)

Format

The Paper contains six parts and a total of 75–80 questions. Each task is based on a short text.

Answering

Candidates indicate their answers by shading in the correct lozenge on an answer sheet, which is then marked by an Optical Mark Reader (OMR).

Marks

One mark is given for each correct answer. Because Parts 2 and 4 (structural cloze and word formation) are fairly open-ended, the mark scheme used by examiners may be modified to include additional correct answers.

Part	Task type and focus	Number of questions	Task format
1	Multiple choice cloze: an emphasis on lexical items.	15 (1–15)	A modified cloze text with 15 gaps, followed by 15 four-option multiple choice questions.
2	Open cloze: an emphasis on structural words testing control of structural features of the language.	15 (16–30)	A modified cloze text containing 15 gaps.
3	Error correction, either by identifying unnecessary words *or* correction of spelling and/or punctuation.	16 (31–46)	A text with one error in most lines.
4	Word building: forming words in context with base word given.	14 (47–61)	Two gapped texts each 115–130 words.
5	Register transfer: understanding style and register.	13 (62–74)	A gapped target text to be completed using information from an input text.
6	Discourse cloze: emphasis on coherence and cohesion.	6 (75–80)	A text of 250–265 words with gaps at phrase or sentence level, followed by a list of options with three distractors.

PAPER 4 LISTENING

(45 minutes approximately)

Format

Paper 4 contains four parts with a total of 30–40 questions. The texts in Parts 1, 3 and 4 are heard twice. The text in Part 2 is heard once only. Recordings will contain a variety of accents corresponding to standard variants of English native speaker accent, as well as non-native speaker accents conforming to the norms of native speaker accents.

Text types

Text types may be taken from the following:

Monologues: announcements, radio broadcasts, telephone messages, speeches, talks, lectures

Conversations/interviews: announcements, radio broadcasts, telephone messages, interviews, meetings

Answering

Candidates transfer their answers to an answer sheet, which is then marked by an Optical Mark Reader (OMR).

Marks

One mark is given for each question. Because Parts 1 and 2 are fairly open-ended, the original mark scheme may be modified to include additional correct answers.

Part	Task type and focus	Number of questions	Task format
1	Sentence completion or note completion: understanding specific information.	8–10	Informational monologue of approx. 2 minutes.
2	As Part 1.	8–10	Monologue of approx. 2 minutes heard once only.
3	Multiple choice *or* extended sentence/note completion *or* matching ideas with speakers: understanding gist, specific information, opinions and attitudes.	6–12	4 minutes approx.
4	Multiple matching *or* three-option multiple choice: identifying speaker, topic, context, function, opinion and information.	10	Series of five extracts of 30 seconds each, 3 minutes in total.

PAPER 5 SPEAKING

(15 minutes approximately)

Format

The standard format is two candidates and two examiners. One examiner acts as both interlocutor and assessor and asks questions or provides instructions to the candidates. The other acts as assessor and does not intervene.

Assessment

Candidates are assessed on their performance throughout the test. They are not assessed in relation to each other but according to the following criteria:

• Grammar and vocabulary (accuracy and appropriacy):

candidates are expected to know enough grammar and vocabulary to produce accurate and appropriate language to meet the task requirements without continual pauses to search for words and phrases.

• Discourse management: examiners are looking for evidence that candidates can express themselves coherently in connected speech.

• Pronunciation: examiners assess the production of individual sounds, appropriate linking words, and the use of stress and intonation to convey the intended meaning.

• Interactive communication: this refers to the candidate's ability to interact effectively with the interlocutor and the other candidate through appropriate use of conversation strategies such as turn-taking, initiating and maintaining interaction. Candidates may if necessary ask for clarification.

Part	Task type and focus	Length of part	Task format
1	Social interaction: giving/asking for personal information.	3 minutes	The interlocutor encourages candidates to give information about themselves.
2	Individual long turn: expressing opinions and attitudes at length.	3–4 minutes in total	Each candidate talks uninterruptedly for approx. 1 minute in response to visual prompts. Each candidate is then invited to comment briefly on what the other has said (approx. 20 seconds).
3	Collaborative task: negotiating an outcome; problem solving.	3–4 minutes	Candidates talk to each other in response to visual or written prompts.
4	General discussion: summarising, reporting; developing ideas.	3–4 minutes	Candidates report on their decisions, and continue the discussion with the examiner by discussing wider issues.

Paper 5: What the interlocutor says

You may like to give students an idea of how the interlocutor introduces the different parts of Paper 5.

Part 2 (3–4 minutes)

(The script below is based on the activity in Unit 4, Speaking 2, Students' Book page 53.)

Interlocutor: In this part of the test I'm going to give each of you the chance to talk for about a minute. You will each see two pictures showing people with different hobbies. I'd like you to compare and contrast your pictures, saying what kind of skills are required by each activity, who might be attracted by them, and what the advantages and disadvantages of each might be.

Don't forget, you have about one minute for this.

(Candidate A), would you like to tell us about your pictures now, please?

...

Thank you. (Candidate B), would you like to tell us about your pictures now, please?

...

Thank you. Now, would you like to look at each other's pictures again and say if you agree with what has been said?

You only have a very short time for this, so don't worry if I interrupt you.

...

Part 3 (3–4 minutes)

(The script below is based on the activity in Unit 5, Speaking 2, Students' Book page 65.)

Interlocutor: Now, I'd like you to discuss something between yourselves, but please speak so that we can hear you.

Your school or college has decided to buy a work of art to display in the reception area. A committee has been set up to choose what to buy, and these four pieces have been shortlisted.

Talk to each other about the pieces and decide which one you would like your school to buy.

You have three or four minutes for this.

...

Thank you.

Part 4 (report the outcome, develop the discussion)

Which work of art have you chosen?

Did you find it easy or difficult to make your choice?

Do you like going to art galleries?

Do you think public art is important? Should the state support art in the community?

etc.

Making an impression

This unit provides an introduction to some of the key skills and strategies students will need to master in order to perform successfully in the Certificate in Advanced English exam.

SPEAKING 1 (page 8)

The Speaking activity serves as a lead-in to Listening 1, encouraging students to think about the issues discussed in the listening text.

1 Talk about photographs.

In Paper 5 of the CAE exam, students are required not only to describe pictures, but also to comment on and react to them. The aim of the photographs is to prompt students to use the language of description combined with the language of speculation. First, check that students understand the words and phrases listed. You could ask them to decide which are positive and which are negative. Refer students to the **Language Bank** for useful expressions they can use in their discussion. You could discuss one of the photos as a class to practise the language, before letting students work in pairs.

Photo 1 shows a group of punks standing outside a pub, one of whom has hair which has been dyed bright pink. Another is wearing a kilt over his jeans and a third is wearing army camouflage trousers. All are wearing heavy leather jackets with metal studs.

Photo 2 shows a young man wearing glasses, looking at his computer. He might be described as a 'computer nerd'. A nerd is a colloquial expression for someone who is extremely interested in computers, and also rather boring and unfashionable.

Photo 3 shows two teenagers cycling. Both have dark hair. The boy is wearing a red checked lumberjack shirt and jeans; the girl is wearing a denim top and shorts.

Photo 4 shows a good-looking man, with blue eyes and blond wavy hair. He is wearing an open-necked shirt. He is conventionally good-looking and appears very self-confident, if not arrogant.

2 Compare impressions.

This can be done in groups or as a whole class.

LISTENING 1 (page 9)

The aim of the Listening activity is to introduce students to the Part 4 multiple matching task in Paper 4 and encourage them to think about how to approach it.

Note: This is not a true exam level task, as there are only four speakers instead of five.

1 ▭ Listen for gist.

Play the recording once all the way through.

TAPESCRIPT

Speaker 1, Aengus: Mm, how do I assess people? I suppose I look at how they dress. <u>I like to dress smartly most of the time, not very smart, smart casual I suppose you'd call it.</u> I'd wear smart trousers and a blazer and a tie for school, cream trousers as well, but I don't like dressing **really** smartly like a business man, I don't like wearing suits. So I suppose I'd have to look at how they dressed, and then I'd probably, I might look at their hair or their face next. It depends if it was a man or a woman.

I'm not really influenced by people's accents. I don't mind if they don't talk proper English. I'm sure I don't talk proper English all the time. But, no, *I think it depends on what you talk about.* If someone rabbits on about nothing all the time, then I don't like that. I like being able to chat to someone friendly, without them telling you their life story.

Speaker 2, Margaret: Well, when I first meet people I suppose I used to think, oh, they are of a certain type. But because of the number of people I meet in my work as a hairdresser, <u>I don't think anyone should ever judge on first impressions because it can totally lead you up the wrong path.</u> I also don't think that people should have to change the effect they have on others. I'm sure that people can, but again I don't think they have to. People should take you as you are but *some people fit into different circumstances, I'm sure, much more easily. They have a way of changing to fit in with people.* I don't think I could do that but I'm sure some people can.

I don't think you should judge anyone by the way they speak. It shouldn't make any difference. I don't find any accents particularly irritating. I think being Scottish you have to accept, people had to accept me when I moved to England. I had to change, not to change the way I speak, but I had to slow down my tone quite considerably when I first came to England – to make myself understood. Otherwise, it was 'Pardon?' all the time.

Speaker 3, Joe: I don't mind the new look, like with my daughter's friends, but sometimes if they look really dirty, it bothers me. But no, the changes in style or something like that don't bother me too much.

I'm not influenced by the way people speak, not at all, but I might be by the way they behave, yes, <u>... some people are very quiet and stand-offish and that makes you back off a little bit, so I'm more comfortable with outgoing people.</u>

I was born and raised in Brooklyn and I used to have trouble with the southern accent from down in the South. I don't know why, *it used to irritate me, but it doesn't as I'm getting older.* Maybe it was when I was younger and it was a different climate back then. I don't know, perhaps I didn't like Country and Western at the time or something.

Speaker 4, Barbara: <u>I try not to judge people by the way they look, but it's very difficult not to judge a book by its cover.</u> I think on initial contact, you do tend to judge them – not to judge them exactly, but see what they are wearing. That's the first thing that you notice about them, or how they carry themselves more.

I think I'm probably influenced by accents. I think that if somebody has a different accent, it's a way of kind of making conversation – commenting on their accent – and it gives you something, a base to talk about. But I don't think I make an effort to speak in a particular way.

But my accent has definitely changed. When I first went to the States, I was in my early twenties and when I got a job *it was very often difficult for people to understand me because of my accent,* so you have to start using certain expressions so that people can understand you. Otherwise, it becomes a problem, and it also brings attention to the fact that you are different, and you don't always want that.

ANSWERS

Speaker 1: dress, hair, face
Speaker 2: tries not to judge
Speaker 3: the way people behave
Speaker 4: the way people look and their accent

2 Pre-teach vocabulary.

Check understanding of the expressions, which are ones students will find helpful for the multiple matching task in Exercise 3.

ANSWERS

Expressions which are colloquial are: *rabbit on, stand-offish, back off.*

Other expressions from the tapescript which you could pre-teach are:
Country and Western = a style of American music
Brooklyn = one of New York City's five boroughs
judge a book by its cover = form conclusions based on external appearance

3 📠 Multiple matching task.

You could play the recording section by section and check answers after each section, thus narrowing down the options. Ask the students what words and expressions in the tapescript gave them the answers.

ANSWERS

(See underlined and italicised words in the tapescript.)
Speaker 1: G, C
Speaker 2: D, F
Speaker 3: A, H
Speaker 4: B, E

4 Task analysis.

This is an opportunity for students to discuss and analyse the features of the task.

ANSWERS

Tips which apply specifically to this task:
- Getting the answers right can depend on hearing a few key words. (See underlined and italicised words in tapescript.)
- Paying attention to the speaker's tone of voice and stress patterns can help identify his/her attitude to the subject.

▶▶ *Extension activity*

Dictate these statements from the tapescript or write them on the board.
1 You shouldn't judge people on first impressions.
2 It's difficult not to judge a book by its cover.
3 People should take you as you are.

Students work in groups and decide if they agree or disagree with them. Tell them to support their opinions with examples from their own experience. Groups can then report back briefly to the class.

VOCABULARY (page 9)

Connotation

1 Encourage students to use dictionaries to help them decide which words have positive and negative connotations if they are not sure.

We recommend the Longman *Language Activator*, which is specially designed to show learners how to choose the correct word or phrase for a given context, as well as how to use the words productively in their own writing and speech. Another suitable alternative would be the Longman *Dictionary of Contemporary English*.

ANSWERS

1 self-confident (positive) / arrogant (negative)
2 aggressive (negative) / assertive (positive)
3 friendly (positive) / familiar (negative)
4 trusting (neutral) / gullible (negative)
5 mean (negative) / tight-fisted (negative) / thrifty (neutral)
6 fussy (negative) / meticulous (positive) / careful (positive)

2 Students complete the sentences.

ANSWERS

1 gullible   4 fussy
2 meticulous   5 tight-fisted = someone who doesn't
3 assertive   like spending money

1 Making an impression

▶▶ *Extension activity*

Discuss different ways that students can record the vocabulary they will learn during this course. One approach is to select words they think they will be able to use and note them down in a notebook under topic areas, such as **Describing people**, together with example sentences showing the way they are used.

Tell the students to choose and note down adjectives and expressions from **Students' Book** pages 8–9 which they could use to describe:

• a best friend of theirs
• a teacher they have had who they liked/disliked
• a boss/line manager they have had
• their favourite family member.

Next, tell them to write a statement about one of these people, which they should be prepared to justify to a partner or group. E.g:

My best friend is the most easy-going person I know. (She never gets upset, . . .)

My sister needs to be a bit more assertive. (Sometimes I think she lets other people boss her around. For example, last week . . .)

Students explain their statements to a partner or group.

READING (page 10)

Exam File: Parts 1 and 4, Multiple matching

Go through the introduction in the **Exam File** with the class.

Note: The first and fourth text in Paper 1 are both multiple matching texts and the test focus is the same. However, the first text is usually shorter than the fourth text (600–800 words compared with 900–1200 words), and there are usually fewer questions.

The aim of the exercises in this section is to take students step by step through a procedure for tackling the text in Part 1.

1 Skim and summarise.

It is a good idea to skim a reading text before dealing with the questions, in order to get an idea how it is organised and what it is about. Knowing where to find the key information in a text will help students skim more effectively. They can complete the summary by reading only those parts of the text indicated in the bullet points. There is a lot to read on Paper 1 of the CAE exam so these reading skills are absolutely vital. Set a time limit of four minutes for the task.

ANSWERS

Connaught School / east London / need to build their confidence or control their behaviour / express their feelings and identify their mistakes / role-play / put the theory to practical use / offer assertiveness training as part of the curriculum / serious problems can be revealed

2 Guess meaning from context.

Students need to understand these words to do the multiple matching task in Exercise 3. If the words are new, encourage them to try to work out the meaning from the context. They can then check by matching them with the meanings given. Guessing meaning from context is an important skill, as students are bound to come across words they don't know in the exam and they need to develop strategies for dealing with them.

ANSWERS

1 C   2 G   3 F   4 A   5 B   6 H   7 D   8 E

3 Multiple matching task.

1 Students scan the text and underline the names given. Explain that doing this first will help them locate rapidly that part of the text where they are likely to find the answer to the questions.

2 Tell students to highlight the parts of the text where they find the answers. This is in preparation for Exercise 4.

ANSWERS

1 C   2 B   3 A   4 D   5 A   6 C   7 B   8 A   9 D
10 D

4 Task analysis.

Students compare their answers. The aim is to make students aware how multiple matching questions summarise and paraphrase the language of the text.

ANSWERS

Question 2: ... recognised a problem...
Text: I needed to do something about it. (lines 30–31)
Question 3: ... to try a difficult way out of her problem ...
Text: She ... decides ... to confront the boy – the toughest course of action. (lines 53–55)
Question 4: ... people's behaviour can't always be changed for the better.
Text: ... you will not necessarily be able to change their behaviour. (lines 108–109)
Question 5: ... practice to get things right.
Text: Third time lucky, armed with a better technique ... (lines 78–79)

14

Question 6: ... hard to deal with a brother's insults.
Text: He winds me up, calls me fat ... It really gets me down. (lines 21–22)
Question 7: her problem is different ...
Text: Most of the pupils ... need to build their confidence. But not all of them. Nadia, 12, is there to control a hot temper. (lines 24–28)
Question 8: ... feels resentful when she is forced to submit.
Text: ... inside she's seething with anger. (lines 4–5)
Question 9: ... importance of combining theory and action.
Text: ...success ...depends on how well students understand the theory and can put it to practical use. (lines 92–95)
Question 10: ... limits of what she can do.
Text: ... a child would then need extensive counselling beyond a teacher's scope. (lines 126–128)

5 **Vocabulary search: phrasal verbs.**

Students read the text and find the phrasal verbs. One of the aims of this kind of exercise is to encourage them to make a habit of identifying and recording useful vocabulary from the articles they read.

ANSWERS

1 end up
2 do something about
3 speak up
4 put somebody down
5 go through

▶▶ Extension activity

The Reading text uses both direct and indirect speech, which is typical of feature articles in newspapers and magazines. You could focus on this as follows.

1 Tell the students to underline all the reporting verbs in the text, and list all the alternative verbs they can find for
• *say* (admit, confess, rant, state, shout, insist, stress)
• *ask* (plead)
• *answer* (reply).

2 Ask which verbs
a) describe the purpose of what is said (*admit, confess, insist, stress*)
b) describe the way in which it is said (*rant, shout* = speak loudly; *plead* = suggests a certain tone of voice).

3 Ask students what tense the verbs are in (present tense). What does this suggest? (the words were spoken only a short time ago – this is a recent report) Does Ms Hordyk still believe that assertiveness training is 'not a solution to every problem'? (yes – indicated by use of present tense).

4 Write these words on the board:
whisper, complain, announce, claim, apologise
Elicit more to add to these.
Read out these sentences, and ask students to supply the best reporting verb orally.
1 'I'm sorry I'm late,' he . . .
2 'You never bring me flowers any more!' she . . .
3 'Please keep your voices down, the others are trying to sleep,' he . . .
4 Taxes are to be increased, the Prime Minister . . . today.
5 'I knew absolutely nothing about the affair,' the President . . .

6 **Group/class discussion: response to the text.**

This is an opportunity for students to respond to the ideas in the article they have read. If the discussion is carried out in groups, tell them to appoint a group 'secretary' who will report the main points of the discussion to the rest of the class. If this is done on a regular basis, it will provide useful practice for Part 4 of the Speaking Test.

LANGUAGE STUDY 1 (page 12)
Meaning: present and future

1 Analysis.

One of the main difficulties with modal verbs is that the same verb can have more than one meaning. But the two main divisions suggested here – between the theoretical possibility that something is true (degrees of likelihood) and real ability or opportunity to act – can help students distinguish between key functions. Students should work in pairs. Refer them to the Notes on **Students' Book** pages 197–198 before checking as a class.

ANSWERS

1 a. ability b. ability c. impossibility
2 a. possibility b. permission c. lack of ability
3 a. permission b. probability/possibility c. possibility = unenthusiastic suggestion
4 a. obligation b. assumption c. duty
5 a. assumption/deduction b. request
6 a. assumption/deduction b. negative obligation; assumption

! *don't have to / must not*

ANSWERS

a. = expresses lack of obligation
b. = expresses prohibition / strong advice

1 Making an impression

Past time reference: *could, would*

2 Analysis.

Students match the examples with their meaning and answer the questions.

> **ANSWERS**
>
> 1 a., e.
> 2 c.
> 3 d.
> 4 b.
> a. was able to
> b. was allowed to
> c. used to
> e. Were you able to ...?

3 Analysis.

The aim is to elicit the rule that *could* is only used for general ability in the past, not for specific examples of ability. Refer students to the Notes on **Students' Book** page 197 if necessary.

> **ANSWERS**
>
> 1 ... I was able to/managed to get a lift home with a friend.
> 2 Peter was able to/was allowed to borrow his father's car last Saturday ...
> 3 Yesterday I was able to/managed to finish / succeeded in finishing my homework by eight o'clock.

Note: *Managed to* indicates that something was achieved with difficulty.

4 Practice.

This exercise is designed to practise the modal verbs in a personalised context. Students should compare their sentences in pairs. Encourage them to find out as many details as possible from their partners. This will be useful practice for Part 1 of the Speaking Test.

Modals + perfect infinitive

5 Presentation.

1 Tell the students to read the dialogue and highlight the modal verbs. Invite suggestions on who the speakers are, what the situation is and how they feel.

> **SAMPLE ANSWER**
>
> A couple have invited several people to a dinner party. Two of the guests haven't turned up yet. The couple are trying to work out why. They are worried and disappointed.

2 🎞 Pronunciation: weak forms.

Students listen to the dialogue. The aim is to help them identify unstressed words which are easy to miss, often causing misunderstanding when listening to native speakers.

One of the results of using weak forms is that different words sound the same. For example, unstressed *have* and *of* sound the same. *Have* can sometimes sound the same as *a* or not be heard at all. Listening more carefully will not necessarily help but a good knowledge of grammar is useful. It is possible for students to work out, from their knowledge of grammar, that the word they hear must be *have*, regardless of what it sounds like. Encourage students to use their knowledge of grammar and vocabulary to support their listening skills.

> **TAPESCRIPT**
>
> See Students' Book.

! *needn't have done / didn't need to*

> **ANSWERS**
>
> Jane hurried unnecessarily. Sam didn't hurry.

6 Practice.

Students read the letter and discuss how they would respond in groups. They should appoint a secretary to report their solution to the class.

7 Pair/group discussion.

This activity draws on the issues raised in the Reading text on page 11 and gives students an opportunity to refer the concepts to their own experience.

LISTENING 2 (page 14)

> **Exam File: Part 1, Sentence completion**

Introduce the task type by going through the advice in the **Exam File** with the class.

1 Introduce the topic.

The aim of this ranking activity is to introduce the topic of the Listening.

2 Pre-teach vocabulary.

The italicised words are needed for the Listening task. Students can discuss the statements in pairs or as a class.

3 Sentence completion task.

1 Students can do this preparation activity in pairs. It is important to train them always to read through the task before they listen.

2 🔲 Play the recording. Students listen and write the answers. They should check their answers on the second hearing.

TAPESCRIPT

Presenter: Does the way you look affect your career chances? Jeff Biddle and Daniel Hamermersh of the University of Texas wanted to find out, and their research seems to indicate that your personal appearance does affect the amount you earn. A study they conducted, based on <u>7,000</u> people, showed that on average good-looking people earned <u>15%</u> more than those considered less attractive. These findings applied to jobs such as bricklayers, factory workers and telephone sales personnel. 33% of employers admitted that looks were important for construction work. 66% thought a mechanic should have a good appearance.

They also studied a group of <u>lawyers</u> over a fifteen-year period. At the beginning of the research project, Biddle and Hamermersh selected a group of students at a top American law school. They showed photos of the students to a panel of people who were asked to rate the attractiveness of each student on a scale from one to five. They followed their careers and discovered that the lawyers that had been rated unattractive by the panel earned less in later years than those who were better-looking. Better-looking lawyers also <u>tended to get promoted</u> more quickly to partnerships in law firms. Biddle and Hamermersh also discovered that <u>clients expected better-looking lawyers to perform better and more effectively</u> when appearing in court.

Traditionally, of course, it was accepted that certain jobs, such as working on hotel reception and being an air-stewardess, required an attractive appearance. And in an area such as modelling it is essential. But now there is a reaction against this. People are beginning to object, in the workplace at least, to the inbuilt advantage that being attractive seems to bring. In the USA, cases of legal action are being brought on the basis of <u>discrimination</u> based on appearance. Nowadays when people are dismissed from their posts because of particular aspects of their appearance, such as being overweight, their response is to bring and win cases for unfair <u>dismissal</u>. They are also being awarded large sums in compensation.

And the town of Santa Cruz in California has introduced legislation to prohibit discrimination against people who are ugly. A new law there forbids discrimination against anyone based on <u>physical characteristics</u>. This means anyone who is short or tall, hairy or bald, skinny or obese. As a city councillor said, the only judgement when it comes to employment is whether or not someone can <u>do the job</u>.

ANSWERS

(See underlined words in the tapescript.)

1	7,000	6	discrimination
2	15%	7	dismissal
3	lawyers	8	physical characteristics
4	promotion	9	do the job
5	clients		

4 **Group discussion.**
Have groups appoint a secretary to report back to the class.

ENGLISH IN USE (page 15)

Exam File: Part 1, Multiple choice cloze

The exercises in this section introduce students to the concept of collocation – the way two or more words frequently occur together – which is extremely important for Paper 3 of the CAE exam. Go through the advice in the **Exam File** with the class. Make sure students understand they should always record phrases and sentences, not just individual words.

Explain that most of the collocations in this section have been taken from the Reading and Listening texts which students have dealt with in the unit.

Encourage students to use a dictionary such as the Longman *Language Activator* to check their answers.

Fixed expressions

1 Students complete the sentences.

ANSWERS

1	boring	3	sound	5	breakfast
2	tidy	4	lodging	6	western

Adjective/noun collocations

2 Students cross out the adjectives which do **not** collocate with the nouns.

ANSWERS

1 preliminary (investigations/findings)
2 pale (complexion/face)
3 blonde (hair)
4 good-looking (man/woman)
5 boiling (water)
6 self-confident (of a person only, not a thing)

Verb/noun collocations

1 Students cross out the nouns which do **not** collocate with the verbs.

> **ANSWERS**
>
> 1 a fault (be someone's fault; the engine has a fault)
> 2 a fee (charge/demand/negotiate a fee)
> 3 a prize (win a prize/gain first prize)

2 Students cross out the verbs which do **not** collocate with the nouns.

> **ANSWERS**
>
> 1 pull   2 win   3 turn

4 Students choose the correct option to complete the sentences.

> **ANSWERS**
>
> 1 B   2 A   3 D   4 D   5 C   6 A   7 A   8 A   9 C

LANGUAGE STUDY 2 (page 16)

Tense review: Present perfect simple/continuous

Refer students to the Notes on **Students' Book** page 198. This is a rapid review of an area of grammar that students are familiar with, but still prone to making mistakes with. The review is intended to prepare students for the activity in Speaking 2, and for the Writing task.

1 Analysis: present perfect/past simple.

The aim is to revise the different uses of these tenses, paying special attention to time adverbials.

> **ANSWERS**
>
> Time adverbials:
> 1 a. all my life
>   b. all my childhood
> 2 a. always
>   b. when I was younger
> 3 a. the first time / ever
>   b. the first time / last year
> 4 a. just
>   b. two days ago
> 5 a. for three years, ever since I left school
>   b. for three years after I left school
>
> We use the present perfect to talk about an action that started in the past and is unfinished / has just finished.
>
> We use the past simple to talk about a completed action that started and finished in the past.

2 Analysis: present perfect simple/continuous.

The aim is to show when there is little difference between the two forms and when there is a significant difference.

> **ANSWERS**
>
> The present perfect simple and continuous are practically interchangeable when talking about an action/state that began in the past and continues in the present. The difference is one of emphasis: the present perfect simple focuses on the result of an action while the present perfect continuous focuses on the activity
>
> The present perfect simple, but not the continuous, is used when the activity is complete/finished, as in 3b and 4b.

3 Analysis: stative versus dynamic verbs.

The aim is to show that stative verbs do not normally occur in continuous tenses (unless the meaning has changed in some way).

> **ANSWERS**
>
> These are stative verbs and cannot usually be used in a progressive form.

4 Practice.

Students underline the most suitable tense.

> **ANSWERS**
>
> 1 have been staying (emphasis is likely to be on activity)
> 2 has received (*he's going to take it* indicates this has to be present perfect tense; *receive* cannot be used in the continuous with a single noun: compare *Peter has been receiving lots of job offers*)
> 3 have you been teaching? (emphasis is likely to be on activity)
> 4 had (time adverbial *as a child* indicates completed activity)
> 5 have you been doing? (emphasis is likely to be on activity)
> 6 wrote (*two weeks ago* indicates competed activity); haven't received (*yet* is typically used with present perfect in British English)

5 Practice.

Students correct the sentences. Ask them to explain why the sentences are wrong. They should have no difficulty with this after working through Exercises 1–4.

ANSWERS

1 I passed all my exams a year ago. (definite time marker)
2 I received your letter yesterday. (definite time marker)
3 It's the first time I have visited this museum. (period of time up to now)
4 I have heard that you have lived/been living in England for a year now. (unfinished time period)
5 I have worked in this company for two years./I started working in this company two years ago.
6 I have only studied/been studying this subject for one month. (unfinished time period)
7 We haven't seen each other for a long time. / It's been a long time since we last saw each other.
8 I have known Veronique for three years. / It's three years since I got to know Veronique.

SPEAKING 2 (page 16)

Exam File: Part 1, Social language

Go through the advice in the **Exam File** with the class so that students know what is expected of them.

1 Preparation.

Students list questions. Circulate and check the grammar as they are working.

2 Role-play.

Draw students' attention to the **Language Bank**. Allow 4 minutes for this activity.

3 Evaluation.

Student C evaluates the other two students' performance on the basis of the criteria given. Refer students to the **Language Bank**.

WRITING (page 17)

This section provides students with an overview of the types of writing they are likely to meet in the exam, and explains what the examiners are looking for when they mark exam answers.

Exam File: Part 2, Formal letter

Go through the advice in the **Exam File** with the class.

1 Introduction to writing task types.

When discussing questions 1–5, emphasise the close relationship between target reader, reason for writing and tone/register. Point out that using the wrong tone or register can result in failing to achieve the intended result.

This is an opportunity to compare the conventions of English with those of the students' own language.

ANSWERS

Question 5
notes and messages: very informal, no fixed rules about layout
informal letters: see example on Students' Book page 18
formal letters: see example on Students' Book page 19
leaflets: see Students' Book Unit 11 page 152, Unit 13, page 179
articles: see **Exam File**, Students' Book Unit 4, page 54
reports: see **Exam File**, Students' Book Unit 6, page 80
reviews: see **Exam File** and example, Students' Book Unit 5, page 68

2 Analysis of writing samples.

In this exercise students analyse samples of writing for effectiveness, applying the criteria applied by CAE examiners.

ANSWERS

Text 1
Notice.

This is aimed at persuading college students to vote for the writer. It gives quite a lot of information. She tells us three things about herself, describes two things she has already done and says what she wants to do next but she doesn't say what she has done in her second year. She also says where you can meet her (but she doesn't say when). The tone is positive, determined and business-like.

Text 2
Notice.

You might wonder why the last flatmate left and why she emphasises that she is tolerant. The information is relevant but it does not say what the rent is or when and how you can find Charlotte. There is not much information about the flat itself and it comes at the end – there is more information about Charlotte.

Text 3
Informal letter.

The sentences are rather short and simple. Kirsty doesn't make herself, her family or her town sound very interesting.

Text 4
Formal letter.

The letter contains all relevant information and is in the correct style. References could have been included, but are not vital here.

3 Writing task.

The **Steps to Writing** take students through the stages they should follow in order to produce a successful piece of writing in the given time (1 hour in the exam).

1 Making an impression

Step 1 Task interpretation

Emphasise that it is vital to read the task instructions very carefully. Marks are often lost through not following the instructions correctly. Tell the students to highlight the key words in the instructions which tell them about the text type required, the target reader and reason for writing.

Step 2 Generating ideas

Having understood the task, the next step is for students to decide what they want to say.

Tell students to highlight the words in the instructions that indicate what information they need to include.

They should use these as headings and make notes under each heading. Let them do this individually, then compare notes in pairs. Point out that the information does not have to be true.

ANSWERS

full details of education and interests
the subject you wish to pursue
why you would be a suitable recipient of the grant

Step 3 Layout and organisation

Tell students that it will save a lot of time in the exam if they plan their answer carefully before they actually start writing. The next step is to map out a paragraph plan and decide the best order to put the information in. Refer students to Text 4 again if necessary.

ANSWERS

Four paragraphs in all.
Paragraph 1: Short introduction: why you are writing
Paragraph 2: Outline education and interests. Give details of subject you want to study.
Paragraph 3: Reasons why you think you are suitable for grant (relevant experience, benefits for your studies etc.)
Paragraph 4: Ending

Step 4 Write

1 A good range of structures, and good use of cohesive devices such as link words, are among the marking criteria applied by examiners. Encourage students to suggest different ways of combining the example sentences.

POSSIBLE ANSWERS

1　I am responding to your advertisement in *Away from Home* which offers / offering grants to young people to study abroad.
2　I am a modern languages student at Hull University, and am in my final year. / I am a final year modern languages student at Hull University.
3　I am doing a thesis on Cervantes and/so would welcome the opportunity to do further research in Spain.

2　Students are now ready to write their letter. Refer them to **Language Study 2** on page 16 (present perfect tense).

MODEL ANSWER

Dear Sir or Madam

I have seen the Lonsdale Trust advertisement in the May edition of 'International Student' magazine and I would like to apply for one of the grants that the Trust is offering.

I am twenty-two years old and for the last eight months I have been studying English at a college in Oxford. Before I came to England I studied for three years at Heidelberg University in Germany. My course was in English Language and Literature and I specialised in Irish playwrights of the early twentieth century. I have started, but not yet completed, a thesis on that topic. Because I am interested in drama I have taken the opportunity, while living in England, to get involved in amateur dramatics and I have appeared in two productions.

I would very much like to spend about four months in Ireland, mainly in Dublin, to develop my interest in Irish theatre both through study and, I hope, in a practical way. I am sure that I will be able to make my stay in Ireland as fruitful as my time in England has been.

If you would like to interview me I am available at any time up to the end of May, but in the first week in June I have some important exams to take. I have attached to this letter the names, telephone numbers and addresses of the principal of the school where I am now studying, and the secretary of my local amateur dramatic society. They are both willing to give me a reference if you require one.

I look forward to hearing from you.

Yours faithfully

Step 5 Evaluate and edit

Point out that checking what you have written is an important part of the writing process. Students should always check their writing when they have finished. Go through the writing checklist on page 214 with the class. Tell them to use it as a reference for this last stage every time they do a written task.

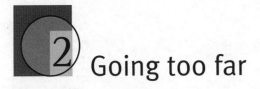

2 Going too far

SPEAKING (page 20)

The topic of Speaking leads into and helps prepare for the Listening task.

1 Talk about photographs.

Students work in pairs. Each student should choose two photos and talk about them, using the questions as a guide, while the other student listens carefully. This activity provides each student with the opportunity to speak uninterruptedly for a minute or so, as in Part 2 of the Speaking Test (the 'long turn'). Refer them to the **Language Bank** on page 21.

Photo 1 shows someone tightrope-walking over a canyon.
Photo 2 shows a stunt rider riding though flames on a motorbike.
Photo 3 shows a skydiver on a snowboard above a desert landscape.
Photo 4 shows a bunjee jumper throwing himself off the jumping platform, which is visible in the background.

2 Compare impressions.

When each student has finished, their partner should comment on what the other has said, as in Part 2 of the Speaking Test. They also have the opportunity to add a further brief comment of their own.

▶▶ *Alternative procedure*

Treat the Speaking activity as a conventional pair, group or class discussion activity.

3 Extension of the discussion.

Students can discuss the questions in pairs or groups, then report their conclusions briefly as a class.

LISTENING 1 (page 21)

Part 1, Sentence completion

1 Preparation.

In the exam, students have about one minute to read the task before they listen. Allow more time in the classroom situation.

Encourage students to work out the meaning of any unknown vocabulary themselves. It should not be necessary to pre-teach any other vocabulary from the tapescript.

2 🖭 Sentence completion task.

Play the recording. Let students check their answers on the second hearing.

TAPESCRIPT

Presenter: We've all encountered them, haven't we? Those madcap people who take their lives in their hands and indulge in wild and wonderful exploits. Have you ever asked yourself the question: Are people who chase after risks different from everyone else? Well, it looks as though science may have come up with some sort of answer. It's being suggested that risk seekers might actually have a different brain chemistry from those who adopt a more ordered approach to their lives.

So what exactly goes on in the bodies and brains of people who get high on thrills? Well, psychologists recently conducted an investigation of trainee parachutists before, during and after their first jump. When they carried out an analysis of all the data they had collected, they discovered that there was an eight-fold increase in adrenaline levels during the jump – adrenaline, as you know, is a hormone in our bodies – and that another hormone, which is called noradrenaline, had increased by 150 per cent.

As you probably know, it's adrenaline that's at work in situations of fear and tension, where the body needs to prepare itself for self-defence. What adrenaline does is to increase the heart-rate and blood pressure. Sugar molecules are released to produce energy in the muscles. Those are the effects of adrenaline. What noradrenaline does is to stimulate the brain's pleasure centres. This is thought to be the reason for the good feeling experienced by risk-takers.

Apparently, not everybody reacts in this way, in fact people differ considerably in the way they react to stimuli. There are those who really want to have intense excitement, and others who find the difficulties of everyday life more than enough to cope with. It seems that these two different reactions correspond to the distinction made between extroverts and introverts. In terms of the way the brain operates, extroverts have slow waves, indicating low levels of excitement in the brain. In contrast, introverts have fast waves indicating high excitement. They react quickly and strongly to quite mild stimuli, and don't feel the need to do dangerous things in order to feel excited.

This is contrary to what you would expect. You might have thought that extroverts would show signs of high excitement, but they don't. It seems that extroverts have a slow-acting nervous system, which means that they do not respond quickly to stimuli. That is why they have to go in search of high-risk activities in order to achieve a higher degree of excitement.

The psychological justification for this is that the brain tries to maintain the highest level of alertness. If it is too high or too low, we try to modify it, consciously or unconsciously, and choose environments that are either relaxing or exciting.

3 **Discussion: comprehension check.**

The question is designed to check full understanding of the concepts in the Listening text. Elicit the main points of the text. The surprising thing is that extroverts apparently require a lot of stimulation.

4 **Pairwork.**

When students have finished, ask how many extroverts and how many introverts there are in the class, through a show of hands.

READING (page 22)

Exam File: Parts 1 and 4, Multiple matching

The Reading introduces students to the type of text they will meet in the fourth part of Paper 1, which often consists of several sections on a similar theme. Go through the advice in the **Exam File** with the class. The exercises take the students step by step through a procedure for tackling this task type.

Notes on the text:
reading music: studying music at university
Clifton Suspension Bridge: a bridge spanning a high gorge in Bristol in the West of England
Baffin Island: in the north of Canada

1 **Skim and summarise.**

Set a time limit for the skimming task, to discourage students from reading every word.

There may be disagreement about the answers to 1.2. Encourage students to point to phrases in the text that justify their choice. One of the aims is to present vocabulary.

2 **Multiple matching task.**

Tell students to highlight the relevant phrases or sentences in the texts while doing the multiple matching task. When they have finished, ask them to justify their answers by reading out the parts they have highlighted.

3 **Vocabulary: guess meaning from context.**

Students can do these exercises in pairs. Make sure they look at the context.

10 If you *take no notice of something*, you disregard and ignore it.
11 If you *join the ranks of* an organisation, you *become a member*. *Ranks* is a military term (ranks of soldiers). The comparison is with joining the army.
12 If you *rake over* something, you *examine it in great detail*.

4 Vocabulary search: collocation.

Make sure students look back at the text rather than simply guessing. Encourage them to use a dictionary for the second part of the exercise. The Longman *Language Activator* is specially designed to help learners expand their vocabulary.

ANSWERS

1 earn 2 receive 3 await 4 take
Other verbs that collocate with the same nouns:
1 have / gain
2 give / serve
3 go on / put on / stand
4 avoid / run

5 Group/class discussion.

Groups of about four are appropriate for this task. Have them appoint a group secretary to report back.

▶▶ *Alternative procedure*

You could organise a semi-formal debate of one of these statements, and have students prepare their arguments in advance for homework. Choose a chairperson, and two speakers to speak for and against the 'motion'. Each speaker should have a seconder who will add any further points. When the speakers have presented their arguments, the debate is thrown open to the 'floor'. Finish by taking a class vote.

LANGUAGE STUDY 1 (page 25)
Review of relative clauses

1 Analysis.

This section deals with defining clauses and non-defining clauses as both subject and object clauses. Refer students to the Notes on **Students' Book** page 199 before confirming their answers to the questions.

ANSWERS

b. another hormone, which is called noradrenaline,
c. high risk activities that provide them with the excitement which they need.
d. the shock which he needed
1 b. = non-defining relative clause
2 a., c., d = defining relative clause

3 c., d., a
4 c. (the excitement they need) and d. because the relative pronoun is the object of the clause
5 b.

2 Practice: subject vs. object clauses.

For the practice exercises, let students work in pairs and discuss the reasons for the choices they are making. Having to justify their answers to each other will help to raise their level of grammatical awareness.

ANSWERS

1 who = subject of relative clause
2 (that / whom) = object of relative clause
3 which / that = subject of relative clause
4 (which / that) = object of relative clause

3 Practice: defining vs. non-defining clauses.

Again this is best done in pairs so that students can discuss the reasons for their choices.

ANSWERS

2 Mount Asgard, which is on Baffin Island, was the scene of the most famous BASE jump of all.
4 Her mother, whose advice Sarah did not take, was against the marriage.

4 Analysis: prepositions in relative clauses.

This exercise deals with the use of prepositions in relative clauses.

ANSWERS

a. The building *in which* I work is fifty storeys high.
b. The Neckar Valley, *through which* we'll be driving, is very beautiful.
c. The day *on which* they got married was Saturday.
d. The travel agent *from whom* I bought my holiday gave me free insurance.
1 The relative pronoun *where* can be used in sentence a. The relative pronoun *when* can be used in sentence c.
2 c.

5 Practice.

This exercise gives practice in adding information to sentences using relative clauses.

ANSWERS

2 His evening classes, which he went to twice a week, were the most important thing in his life.
3 The year when / in which he started university was 1905.

4 The hotel where / in which my parents spent their honeymoon is going to be demolished.

5 The museum, to which the guide referred, is well worth a visit. / The museum which / that the guide referred to is well worth a visit. (This could be either defining or non-defining.)

6 Martin Ford, who you lent your notes to / to whom you lent your notes, has passed his exams with flying colours.

7 Jack Brown, who we were talking about yesterday, has just got married.

VOCABULARY (page 26)

Phrasal verbs

1 Presentation.

Go through the explanation of *metaphorical* with the class.

2 Practice.

ANSWERS

1 chickened out	4 root out
2 trigger off	5 throw it in
3 iron out	6 duck out of

LISTENING 2 (page 26)

Exam File: Part 4, Multiple matching

Go through the advice in the **Exam File** with the class.

1 Preparation.

Let students work in pairs to list words associated with each option. Then compare as a class.

ANSWER

The use of quotation marks for 'politician' suggests that the speaker isn't actually a politician, although he/she may think of him/herself as one.

Notes on the text:
You might like to explain the following words and concepts before playing the recording.

a Victorian eccentric (Speaker 2): Queen Victoria ruled Britain from 1838 to 1901. An eccentric is someone (usually a man) with strange ideas and behaviour. To be an eccentric was considered interesting.

weird and wacky: (Speaker 5): both words mean very strange and unusual. Putting them together strengthens the meaning.

2 Multiple matching: Task One.

TAPESCRIPT

Speaker 1: I once had *a neighbour* who was obsessed with making mechanical devices. He once made a very small gun firing tiny bullets which he used to shoot wasps and flies – not very accurately, I might say. He also tried to build his own helicopter in his garage, but by the time he had finished it was too big to get through the garage door. I doubt if it would have flown anyway.

Speaker 2: I think it was called 'Wild Food' or something like that – it was quite old, *published about 1900,* I think and it was by this man, a typical Victorian eccentric, I suppose, whose ambition was to eat every kind of living creature, including things you would never dream of eating like crocodiles and tigers, and he would travel round the world with rod and gun catching and eating anything that moved. Of course, it was easier to do that then because you didn't have protected species and that sort of thing.

Speaker 3: One of my *uncles* had this peculiar way of speaking. He used to jumble his words up, putting the wrong endings on some words and the wrong beginnings on others so you couldn't follow what he was saying, although it sounded very convincing. Sort of like this . . . People thought he did it deliberately to make them laugh, and in fact he used to appear in comedy films and on television. He made quite a lot of money out of it, but my father said he had never heard him speak normally.

Speaker 4: *A friend of mine once told me about this man he knew* who grew nothing but garlic. No other vegetable at all, just all these different varieties of garlic from France, Spain and Italy. He used to sell it and make quite a lot of money out of it, and he ate a lot of it as well. In fact, he put it in everything he cooked and even used to treat his guests to ice-cream with garlic sauce.

Speaker 5: Once, *at a party* I was at, he actually came up and talked to me, you know, this chap who always wears these very strange clothes and stands for Parliament whenever there's an election and gets about fifteen votes. He was telling me about his ideas, which were really weird and wacky. He has his own party, and one of their policies was to give people an extra vote if they owned a cat or a dog.

Task analysis.

Elicit the key words that gave students the answers. Ask how accurate their predictions in Exercise 1 were.

ANSWERS

(See underlined words in the tapescript.)
1 D   2 C   3 E   4 A   5 B

3 **Multiple matching: Task Two.**

ANSWERS

(See italicised words in the tapescript.)
1 B   2 D   3 C   4 E   5 A

Task analysis.

Elicit the key words that gave students the answers.

▶▶ *Extension activity*

Discuss the following questions as a class.

What kind of behaviour is considered unconventional or eccentric in the students' countries? How do people react to such behaviour?

Can they describe anyone with an unusual hobby?

LANGUAGE STUDY 2 (page 27)

Tense review: Narrative tenses

1 **Analysis.**

This section focuses on the past continuous, past simple and past perfect simple and continuous, which are the four tenses we need for narratives. Refer students to the Notes on **Students' Book** pages 199–200 before confirming their answers to the questions.

ANSWERS

- We use the *past simple* tense to recount the main events of a narrative in chronological sequence.
- We use the *past continuous* tense for interrupted acts or for background activities in narratives.
- We use the *past perfect* tense to refer to a past event that happened earlier than another past event.

2 📼 **Pronunciation.**

The aim of this exercise is to show that it can be difficult to hear the difference between the past simple and past perfect but that this may not always matter very much.

Tapescript

1 I'd sent the parcel when I got your fax.
2 By their late twenties, his friends had settled down to respectable jobs.
3 He read the documents before the meeting started.
4 Jack lived in Spain for many years before he returned to England.
5 We'd hardly had time to get over our surprise, when there was more good news.
6 He'd appeared in many films by the age of 25.

ANSWERS

(See underlined words in the tapescript.)
The past perfect is used to make it clear that one event happened prior to another, as in Sentence 1.
When a time marker makes the sequence clear, the past perfect is not necessary, as in Sentences 3 and 4.
The past perfect is preferred with expressions with *by*, as in Sentences 2 and 6.
In Sentence 5 it is optional.

3 **Practice.**

1 Students put the verbs into the correct tense. Tell them to read the story to the end before trying to fill in any of the gaps.

ANSWERS

1 walked	7 put	13 was
2 had not visited	8 got	14 could not
3 had grown	9 unlocked	15 Was I imagining
4 had been raining	10 had locked	16 did I hear
5 was	11 stepped	
6 was getting	12 noticed	

2 Students finish the story in groups. Have each group read out their ending and choose the best.

4 **Extension: write a news article.**

This activity can be set as a written task for homework if preferred.

WRITING (page 28)

Exam File: Part 1, Formal letter

Go through the advice in the **Exam File** with the class. This introduces them to the Part 1 Writing task type, which always involves processing up to 400 words of reading input.

Writing task

Students read the writing task and follow the **Steps to Writing**. These take them through the stages they should follow to produce a successful piece of writing in the time allowed (1 hour in the exam).

Step 1 Task interpretation
Tell the students to highlight the key words in the instructions which tell them about the text type required, the target reader and reason for writing. These will determine what is the appropriate register and tone.

ANSWERS

text type:	letter
target reader:	newspaper editor
purpose:	to set the record straight and complain about bad reporting
register, tone:	formal; adopting a cool, objective tone while making sure that the facts speak for themselves will probably be more effective than being angry and 'ranting'
begin:	Dear Sir or Madam (as the name of the addressee is not known)
end:	Yours faithfully (this is the correct form if the letter begins Dear Sir)

Step 2 Selecting and summarising

Tell students to highlight key words in the instructions that make clear what information must be included. Explain that when marking Part 1 papers, examiners look for specific items of information that must be included for 'task achievement'. It is vital to include all the relevant information from the reading input, or marks will be lost.

Let students work individually or in pairs to find the discrepancies between the two input texts, then compare as a class.

ANSWERS

Article	Reality
teenager	21
first year student	final year student
happened at 2.30 a.m.	happened at 11.30 p.m.
verbal abuse	one pulled out a knife
Tom provided description	Lucy provided description

Step 3 Layout and organisation

Remind students that planning before they start writing is a more effective use of time in the exam than writing the whole piece and then writing it out again neatly, which is what many candidates do.

Step 4 Write

Before writing their own letter, students do the two tasks: combining sentences and adding linking expressions. Discuss the possible answers as a class.

ANSWERS

1 I would like to point out a number of inaccuracies in your recent article, 'Local hero', which describes an incident (that) my friend Lucy Hebden was involved in/involving my friend . . .
2 Firstly, Lucy is not a first year student. In fact, she is in her final year. Secondly, she left her friend's party at 11.30 p.m., not at 2.30 a.m.

Refer students to **Language Study 1** and **2** on Narrative tenses and Relative clauses, and the **Language Bank**. They should use the language sections to check their grammar. The **Language Bank** is a useful resource of words and expressions they can use in their writing.

MODEL ANSWER

Dear Sir or Madam

I have read the article entitled 'Local hero' in last Monday's edition of The Echo, which describes an incident involving my friend Lucy Hebden, and I am writing to complain about the factual inaccuracies in it. I have some personal knowledge of what happened because I was present when Lucy made her statement to the police on the night of the incident.

First of all, I would like to point out that Lucy is 21 and not a teenager, as stated in your article. Secondly, Lucy is not a first year student but is in her final year. In addition, the incident happened at 11.30 p.m., not 2.30 a.m. We are extremely concerned that your reporter could not get such simple details right.

However, these are minor inaccuracies compared with the serious omissions and misinterpretations in the article. According to your article, Lucy was the victim of verbal abuse, whereas what actually happened was that one youth threatened her with a knife, making the incident far more serious than you suggest. Furthermore, Mr Bradley, who you call a 'hero', offered Lucy very little assistance. In fact, he never even got out of his car! And it was Lucy, not Mr Bradley, who gave all the information to the police. His role was therefore much less 'heroic' than you suggest.

I would be grateful if you could print a correction as soon as possible, and I hope that in future you will make sure your articles report the facts more accurately.

Yours faithfully

Step 5 Evaluate and edit

For this step, you could ask students to exchange their work with a partner. Each student should evaluate their partner's work, using the Writing checklist on page 214, and write comments and suggestions for improvement.

ENGLISH IN USE 1 (page 30)

Exam File: Part 4, Word formation

This is an introduction to the word formation task in Paper 3, intended to alert students at a very early stage to the importance of recording words together with their related forms. The students will probably be familiar with the task type from First Certificate. For the CAE exam, students have to fill in a total of 15 gaps in two short texts and not 10 gaps in one text, as in FCE.

Go through the advice in the **Exam File** with the class.

1 Presentation.

This section shows the different types of changes that students have to make to words in the word formation task.

ANSWERS

1 realisation	3 choose	5 skilfully
2 confidential	4 applaud	6 disappear

2 Practice.

The words are all ones students have come across in the unit. Encourage them to use dictionaries if they are not sure.

ANSWERS

1 behaviour	4 strengthen	7 disapproved
2 advise	5 acceptable	8 unintelligible
3 practical	6 irresponsibly	

PRONUNCIATION (page 30)

Word stress

There is a lot of evidence which suggests that native speakers depend heavily on the correct stress pattern to identify a word. A wrong stress pattern can more easily cause misunderstanding than a wrongly-pronounced individual sound. Although English does not have a regular word stress pattern, it is possible to make useful generalisations which can help students, particularly with regard to the effect of affixes on the base word.

1 Tell the students to read the sets of words and mark the stress using a square or a circle. Then play the recording and let them check their answers themselves.

TAPESCRIPT

See Students' Book.

ANSWERS

The suffixes in set 1 do not change the stress of the base word.
The suffixes in sets 2 and 4 change the stress to the penultimate syllable.
The suffixes in set 3 are stressed. These suffixes are all of French origin.
Set 5 contains examples of shifting stress where the stress is on a different syllable in each word.

Set 1
o O	o Oo
attract	attractive
behave	behaviour
dismiss	dismissal

Set 2
O o o	o o O o
legislate	legislation
o O o o	o o oO o
discriminate	discrimination
contaminate	contamination

Set 3
O o o	o o O
voluntary	volunteer
engine	engineer
O o	o O
laundry	laundrette

Set 4
O o	oOo
atom	atomic
magnet	magnetic
O o o	o O o
strategy	strategic

Set 5
Oo o	oOo o	o ooOo
origin	original	originality
O oo	o O o o	O oo o
advertise	advertisement	advertiser

2 Proceed as above.

TAPESCRIPT

See Students' Book.

ANSWERS

	O o		o O
1 a.	survey	b.	survey
	O o		o O
2 a.	discount	b.	discount
	o O		O o
3 a.	permit	b.	permit
	o O		O o
4 a.	refill	b.	refill
	O o		o O
5 a.	rebels	b.	rebel

27

ENGLISH IN USE 2 (page 31)

Exam File: Part 3, Error correction

This is an introduction to the error correction task in Paper 3, and alerts students to the type of errors they should look out for.

Introduce the task type by going through the advice in the **Exam File** with the class.

1 Let the students work in pairs to identify the extra wrong words in the sets of sentences. Then discuss the answers as a class.

ANSWERS

1 Articles
1 the   2 ✓   3 a   4 the
For explanations, see Grammar Notes, Students' Book page 00.

2 Prepositions
1 ✓
2 for (You *pay for* a purchase e.g. a meal, ticket, holiday. But you *pay* a bill.)
3 for
4 to (*Reach* does not require a preposition. Compare *get to* a destination.)

3 Phrasal verbs
1 for (You *set off for* a destination, but you *set off at* a particular time.)
2 up (One of the meanings of *show up* is *appear*.)
3 ✓
4 of (The explorers had nearly run out of food would be correct – *of* needs to be followed by a noun.)

4 Auxiliary verbs
1 ✓
2 been (*Been* suggests a passive, but *arrive* cannot be used in the passive as it is intransitive.)
3 be
4 been (*Been living* would be correct = present perfect continuous.)

5 Relative and personal pronouns
1 he
2 who
3 ✓
4 it
For explanations, see Grammar Notes, Students' Book page 199.

6 Familiar and unfamiliar phrases
1 lots (The correct phrase is *lots of.*)
2 ✓
3 better (The correct phrase is *We had better*. The correct sentence contains a present simple to refer to the future.)
4 to (Here, *use* is a verb meaning *make use of*.)

2 Students read the text and underline the extra wrong words. You can point out that in the exam, there will be sixteen lines with potential errors.

ANSWERS

1 to (A modal verb cannot be followed by a *to*-infinitive.)
2 a (The indefinite article can only be used with singular countable nouns.)
3 who (To identify the unnecessary relative pronoun, you have to read the whole sentence carefully.)
4 be
5 up (*Speak up* means *speak more loudly* or *say what you really mean*.)
6 he (The relative pronoun replaces the subject in the relative clause, so it is not necessary to repeat the subject.)
7 for
8 was
9 it (same type of mistake as 6 above)
10 had (The past perfect is not the right tense here.)
11 if (*Even if* is a conjunction that introduces a subordinate clause – there is no subordinate clause here.)
12 the (wrong use of *the* with a general concept noun)

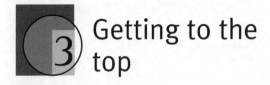

3 Getting to the top

SPEAKING 1 (page 32)

1 Talk about photographs.

Have students work in pairs according to the instructions in the Students' Book, which follow the format of Part 2 of the Speaking Test (see **Overview of the CAE** page 11). Alternatively, deal with this activity as a pair/group or whole class discussion.

Photo 1 shows the sculptor Antony Gormley with two of his sculptures. One of his most controversial works is the Angel of the North, a giant sculpture with aeroplane wings just off the A1 in Tyne and Wear. It was commissioned by Gateshead council and cost them £800,000. It is reputedly the largest sculpture in the UK. He has exhibited some of his other works at the Tate Gallery.

Photo 2 shows an aerial view of a luxurious mansion in Beverley Hills. The house belongs to Aaron Spelling, a famous and successful Hollywood producer who was born the son of poor Jewish immigrants in Dallas, Texas.

Photo 3 shows elevated tramlines in Florida, an achievement in the field of engineering.

Photo 4 shows the actor Jack Nicholson at the Academy Awards, with the Oscar he had just won for his role in *One Flew Over The Cuckoo's Nest*.

2 Ranking activity.

Students decide individually which three achievements would be important to them, then compare in pairs. Refer students to the **Language Bank** during the discussion stage. Ranking activities of this type often come up in Part 3 of the Speaking Paper.

LISTENING 1 (page 33)

Exam File: Part 4, Multiple matching

Go through the advice in the **Exam File** with the class. This is a reminder of how to approach this task type.

1 Pre-teach vocabulary.

Check understanding of the expressions listed. You may need to explain the following items:

mint: a factory where money is produced, hence the expression *making a mint* i.e. making a lot of money
outback: the Australian word for the *countryside*, far away from cities
station: the Australian word for *farm*.

Emphasise how important it is to be aware that words may have more than one meaning. Students should always listen for confirmation of which meaning it is in the context, or they may be misled.

---

2 ▭ Multiple matching: Task One.

Warn students that in this task, there is one option that doesn't fit at all.

TAPESCRIPT

Speaker 1: At that time I didn't have a proper job. I was doing some research and I had a small income from writing articles for magazines and that was it. But one day, it was in May, *I got a call* from a producer and he said, 'Do you want to do a programme for us?'

Well, it was an entirely new thing, there wasn't a lot of interest in my subject at that time – it was just before things started to get really exciting. That helped a lot later on, of course. Of course, I jumped at the opportunity, and we decided to call it 'The Sky Tonight'.

Well, it's been on for over forty years now, every Friday at 11 p.m. It's been my life. If I hadn't been given that chance . . .

Speaker 2: A friend of mine said, 'You really must put some money in that company. If you do you will become rich beyond the wildest dreams of avarice.' Well, the funny thing is that I could easily understand what the company was doing because it was a transport company, and at the university where I work (still!) I do a course in transport economics – that's my speciality – so I could see it was a good buy, a golden opportunity. But I hesitated. I wish I hadn't. Talk about a *missed opportunity*! The shares rocketed. After three years, the price had increased twenty times.

Speaker 3: I was working in Australia in the early seventies, on a cattle station in the outback. I enjoyed it a lot, and I was thinking of buying my own place because land was quite cheap there – I could really see a future for myself. But then I got a phone call from my family in England and, you know, they said that they needed me back there because my father was getting too old to run things by himself, and with the experience I had gained in Australia I'd be able to take over. So I came back.

Things are OK here. We do all right, although I'll always regret not buying a place in Australia. I might have had a huge ranch out there. I often dream about that.

Speaker 4: Well, one night about ten years ago I was working late in the office with a colleague who said to me, 'You know, they won't pay us for all this extra work we're doing. We'll never make any money here. We could do better by ourselves.' So that was how it started.

We left, invested all the money we had and borrowed an enormous amount, and we set up our own magazine. We hired some good people to write for us while <u>the two of us looked after the finance and administration</u>.

Now, as you know, it is one of the leading titles in its field, and the one we used to work for went bust years ago. I've absolutely no regrets. *We're making a mint – the money is just pouring in.*

Speaker 5: It was something that I really wanted to buy because I already had <u>several others from the same school</u>. Of course, I had to bid for it, and the price kept going up and up – it was getting astronomical. I've always gone to <u>auctions</u> with a definite price limit, which I never exceed. You've got to have that sort of self discipline. So when it went past my limit I dropped out of the bidding and I lost it, although it went for a price only very slightly above my limit. If only I'd gone on for a bit longer – *I've been regretting it* for ten years! But it's on the market again – the auction is next week and *this time* I'm not going to miss it . . .

ANSWERS

(See underlined words in the tapescript.)

1 E   2 C   3 F   4 D   5 B

Elicit the words that gave students the answers. Discuss the potential traps students might have fallen into.
Speaker 4: The words *magazine* and *leading title* were potentially misleading, suggesting the answer 'a writer'. The rest of the text points clearly to the answer 'company director'.
Speaker 5: The words *astronomical* and *rocket* could suggest the answer 'astronomer', but in fact both words are used metaphorically here.

3 🎧 **Multiple matching: Task Two.**

ANSWERS

(See italicised words in the tapescript.)

1 C   2 F   3 E   4 B   5 A

Elicit the words that gave students the answers.

4 🎧 **Discussion: response to the text.**

This is an opportunity for students to respond personally to the content of the tapescript.

LANGUAGE STUDY (page 34)

Wish/If only

1 Analysis.

Make sure that students realise that *wish/if only* have the same grammar, so there is one set of patterns to learn, not two. Point out that there is a mismatch between

tense and time. The past tense after *I wish/If only* refers to present time not past time. The reason is *that I wish/If only* does not refer to how things are but how we would like them to be. Students may need a lot of explanations and examples.

ANSWERS

c. Fact: I didn't study very hard at school.
d. Fact: We don't have a very big house.
e. Fact: I'm not rich.
f. Fact: Mark is not at the beach.
g. Fact: I can't/don't spend much time with my children.
h. Fact: My neighbours make a lot of noise.
i. Fact: Ann's husband doesn't have a very good job.
j. Fact: I am leaving tomorrow.
k. Fact: I have to go to work on Monday.

1
• in the past: a, b, c
• now: d, e, f, g, h
• in the future: i, j, k
We use past tense and past perfect to show hypothetical meaning.
2 We can use *was* or *were*. *Were* is the subjunctive, and is more formal.

Pronunciation point: When we say *If (only) I were . . .*, *were* is unstressed.

2 Error correction.

Refer students to the Notes on **Students' Book** pages 200–201 to check their answers.

ANSWERS

Sentences 1, 3 and 6 are incorrect.
1 I wish I *had* my own flat.
3 I wish you *had* your own flat.
6 I wish I *could* give up smoking.

3 Practice.

Students need to pay particular attention to tenses because the tenses they need are not in the prompt sentences. This exercise highlights the tense/time difference.

ANSWERS

1 I wish / If only I had worked harder at school.
2 I wish I had seen the Statue of Liberty when I was in New York.
3 I wish / If only I didn't have to go to an interview tomorrow.
4 I wish / If only I wasn't so bad at Maths.
5 Sally wishes she didn't have to go to the dentist's next week.
6 I wish / If only I hadn't got married so young.
7 I wish I could drive.
8 I wish my sister would stop pestering me to help her with her homework.

Regret

4 Analysis: patterns after regret.

Regret is more commonly followed by a gerund than by an infinitive. When it is followed by an infinitive it is usually in fixed phrases such as *I regret to inform you that . . .* .

ANSWERS

1
Structures that follow the verb *regret*: noun, gerund, noun clause.
The action comes before the feeling of regret.

2
The feeling of regret comes first.
You would expect to find this type of sentence in written English.

5 Practice: *regret* + gerund or infinitive.

This exercise contrasts the gerund after *regret* and the infinitive after *regret*.

ANSWERS

1 I regret to have to inform you that you have not won the Lottery, as your ticket is a forgery.
2 I (deeply) regret what I said. / I do apologise, I regret saying that.
3 I regret leaving [town] so soon. / I regret not having stayed longer in [town].
4 I regret giving up my previous job.

6 Practice.

Students complete the sentences so that they are true for them. They can compare their answers in pairs, and give further details.

! *regretfully* / *regrettably*

ANSWERS

a. = sadly, with regret
b. = it is to be regretted that . . .

Mixed conditional sentences

7 Analysis: revision of conditionals.

This section revises students knowledge of zero, first, second and third conditionals as a preparation for work on mixed conditionals. Encourage students to look at each clause separately and to make connections between tense and meaning.

ANSWERS

1
a. present tense + zero conditional
b. present tense + first conditional
c. past simple + second conditional
d. past perfect + third conditional
2
b. is likely to happen
a. is generally true
d. is contrary to fact or unreal
c. is unlikely to happen

8

1 Analysis: mixed conditionals.

Students may only be familiar with first, second and third conditionals but many other types are possible. The key to understanding is to analyse the time and tense of each clause separately.

ANSWERS

1
a. past + past
b. present + past
c. present + past
d. past + present
e. present + past
2 A comma is used when the *if* clause comes first, but not when it comes second.

2 Pronunciation.

The grammar of conditional sentences can be obscured when they are spoken because of the use of weak forms. Key grammatical words such as *have* and *had* may be difficult to hear. (But note that when *have* and *had* are the main verbs and not auxiliaries, they will be pronounced in their strong form.) Initial *h* in *he*, *his*, *him*, *her* and *hers* may also disappear.

It is important that students hear how conditional sentences are really pronounced in normal English speech, however difficult they may sound. The solution to the problem of understanding is not for students to listen more carefully but to use their knowledge of grammar to work out what they must have heard.

TAPESCRIPT

Note: Unstressed words are in italic. Apostrophes indicate 'swallowed' words.
a. If 'e'd stayed in Australia, he might've bought 'is own farm.
b. He'd be a rich man if 'e'd bought shares in the company.

> c. If I didn't have family responsibilities, I could've spent a year travelling round the world.
> d. If 'e'd gone to college, 'is job prospects 'd be better.
> e. If I knew the answer, I'd've told you last week.

9 Error correction.

Despite the great variety of conditional sentences, some combinations of tenses are clearly wrong. Only two out of the eight sentences here are wrong, although students are likely to think that more are incorrect. This exercise is useful preparation for the error correction task in Paper 3 (Part 3).

ANSWERS

Sentences 3 and 5 are incorrect.
3 If you had been there, you would have seen us.
5 You would be able to finish earlier if you had started earlier.
Sentence 2 is a correct polite request / offer. A secretary, or member of staff might say this.

10 Practice.

Students complete the sentences. Encourage them to be as imaginative as possible. Let them compare their sentences in pairs or as a class.

▶▶ Extension activity

Write the following descriptions of past events on cards. Divide the class into groups and give each group a card. Ask them to speculate on how things would/could/might have been different, better or worse if they hadn't happened. Tell them to appoint a secretary to note down their ideas. Set a time limit. Then let each secretary read out their ideas, without mentioning the event itself. The rest of the class should try to identify the event.

1 The German engineer Benz invented the internal combustion engine in 1885.
2 Scientists discovered DNA in the 1950s.
3 The computer was invented by the American Howard Aiken in 1944.
4 Women in many countries gained the vote in the 20th century.

READING (page 36)

Exam File: Part 3, Multiple choice questions

This section introduces students to a useful strategy for dealing with multiple choice questions. Go through the advice in the **Exam File** with the class.

1

1 Prediction.

The aim of this exercise is to get students to think about the topic before they start reading. This will help them to read with greater understanding.

2 Skim for gist.

Refer students to **Students' Book** Unit 1 page 10 for advice on how to skim a text. Set a time limit of maximum 5 minutes to encourage them not to read in detail yet.

ANSWERS

1 Psychologists have identified 'hot regret' which is fleeting and 'wistful regret' which is long lasting.
2 Wistful regret.
3 Education.
4 People don't regret events that seem to be beyond their control.

2 Vocabulary: guess meaning from context.

The aim of this exercise is to show students ways of using the context to work out the meaning of words they may not know. Emphasise that they shouldn't spend long trying to work out the meaning the first time they meet a new word: words are often repeated and paraphrased in later parts of a text, so that by the time they have read the whole thing, they will probably be able to figure it out. They should also be content with an approximate guess.

ANSWERS

1 think about and evaluate, draw conclusions
2 went wrong, failed
3 failure to act
4 long range perspective
5 unavoidable
6 very important / significant
7 mentioned

3 Multiple choice questions.

Discuss the example. Tell students to continue, following the advice in the **Exam File**.

ANSWERS

2 A The fear is that it will pull us down the slippery slope of depression and despair. (lines 28–30)
3 C But psychologists say that regret is an inevitable fact of life. "In today's world . . . (lines 31–33)
4 D But a growing body of research suggests that wistful regret may figure more prominently in people's lives over the long term. (lines 69–73)
5 C Asked to describe their biggest regrets, participants most often cited things they failed to do. (lines 74–76)

! *Linking ideas: concession*

The aim here is simply to help students understand a structure that they might find difficult. They do not need to be able to produce this type of structure. Refer students to the Notes on **Students' Book** page 205.

ANSWERS

a) Although regrettable actions might be troubling initially, when people . . .
b) Regrettable actions might be troubling initially, but when people . . .
The adjective now follows the noun it describes.

4 **Group/pair discussion: response to the text.**

This is an opportunity for students to relate the concepts in the text to their own lives.

VOCABULARY (page 38)

Collocation

1 The aim of this exercise is to encourage students to see that any reading text can be used to help them develop their vocabulary.

ANSWERS

1
Verb	+ Noun
follow	*a career*

Adjective	+ Noun
different	*career*

Noun	+ Noun
career	*path*

2
Verb + Noun
sacrifice / pursue / launch a career
Adjective + Noun
a successful / political career
Noun + Noun
career strategy / prospects / choice / developments
Noun + Preposition + Noun
a career in film / publishing / medicine / as an actor

2 Students write sentences about themselves. Point out that the best way of remembering words is to use them in sentences. Writing sentences that are true for you is a way of making them more memorable.

3 Students note down other useful collocations. Emphasise that this is something they can do with any text they read.

Style and register

These exercises provide good practice for Paper 3, Part 5 in which students are required to transfer information from one text to another written in a different register.

4 **Matching task.**

ANSWERS

1 C   2 D   3 B   4 A

5 **Rewrite a text in a different register.**

ANSWERS

1 dropped out of
2 set up
3 handled/looked after
4 looked after/handled
5 a mint
6 go up
7 went bust
8 pretty low
9 fancied
10 taking over
11 jumped at
12 Talk about luck.

LISTENING 2 (page 39)

Exam File: Part 2, Note completion

Go through the advice in the **Exam File** with the class.

1 **Topic discussion.**

The aim is to get students thinking about the topic of the Listening, which will help them with the Listening task.

2 📼 **Note completion task.**

Tell the students to try to answer all the questions the first time they listen, but play the recording again if they want to check their answers.

3 Getting to the top

TAPESCRIPT

Presenter: Those of us working on the Holiday Special Programme know that many of our student listeners are always on the lookout for that holiday with a difference, something that won't cost a fortune, will be interesting and maybe useful in terms of future jobs, and might even bring in some much-needed cash. We've got some ideas for you today that could well be worth following up.

Have you ever wanted to see your name up in lights or at least on the big screen at the local cinema? Ever thought about being a film extra? There's a demand for people of all shapes, sizes and ages for walk-on parts in the many films that are now being produced around the country. <u>Previous experience is not essential,</u> and you get paid – <u>about seventy pounds a day is the going rate</u> – so just <u>five days' work would get you three hundred and fifty pounds</u>. Costumes are provided and so is free food from the film caterers.

So if you see your future in films or simply want a fun way to spend the vacation, contact 797 8641 for further details. <u>Remember it doesn't matter if you haven't done it before</u>, but they do ask you to fill in a questionnaire with all your personal details, and <u>it helps if you have got extra skills. Can you ride, swim, play a musical instrument? These extra things will give you a better chance.</u>

If you're looking for something more conventional, but like most students want to travel and see a bit of the world, what about looking after kids? The Nanny Agency is looking for enthusiastic men and women, eighteen and over, for posts in Australia and New Zealand. If you've got <u>three months or more to spare</u>, you get free board and lodging provided by the host family and <u>the flight paid for as well. Getting there (and back) won't cost you anything.</u> They'll be young kids for you to supervise, and you'll have to provide your own pocket money. But just think, you'll have had an expenses-paid trip down under for at least twelve weeks, and the chance to make some new contacts. Phone 556 7854 for further details. The Nanny Agency is waiting for your call.

<u>Good at languages?</u> Then another way of getting some travel cheaply is to be a tourist guide. Europe Explorer is looking for group leaders, <u>aged twenty plus</u>, preferably twenty-two or three, to take groups of tourists round <u>European cities</u>. Travel from London with the group and cope with any problems that come up. Show people round and help them have a good time.

This is a demanding job. It requires bags of initiative and the hours are long. But you'll see lots of cities, and it'll look great on your CV.

To recap then, our three suggestions are film extra – the best paid of all the jobs considered, nanny in Australia or New Zealand, and <u>tourist guide in Europe</u>.

ANSWERS

(See underlined words in the tapescript.)
1 (previous) experience   5 flight
2 £70   6 languages
3 skills   7 20
4 3 months/12 weeks   8 Europe

3 Discussion: response to the Listening.

PRONUNCIATION (page 39)

Weak forms

1 Recognition of weak forms.

Certain words, such as the prepositions *to, for, from, of, at* and also *that* and *to* + infinitive have two pronunciations – weak and strong. Getting this right will make an enormous difference to students' pronunciation, especially to their rhythm.

Let students try to fill in as many of the gaps as they can before listening to check.

ANSWERS

1 Those *of* us working on the Holiday Special Programme know that many *of* our student listeners *are* always on the lookout *for* that holiday with *a* difference, something *that* won't cost *a* fortune.

2 Have you ever wanted *to* see *your* name up in lights or at least on the big screen *at* the local cinema? There's *a* demand *for* people *of* all shapes, sizes and ages *for* walk-on parts.

2

1 Recognition of weak forms.

In each short dialogue there is a contrast between the weak and strong form of the same word.

ANSWERS

(Strong forms are underlined.)
1 A: Where are you <u>from</u>?
  B: I'm from South America.
2 A: How long are you planning to <u>stay</u>?
  B: I'll stay as long as I need to.
3 A: Who's the present <u>for</u>?
  B: It's for Peter.
4 A: What's your sweater made <u>of</u>?
  B: I think it's made of wool. What about <u>yours</u>?
5 A: Did you see <u>that</u> Western that was on TV last night?
  B: Yes, it's one of my favourite films.
6 A: Which job have you applied <u>for</u>?
  B: I've applied for the one that's well-paid!

2 Pair practice.

Monitor students carefully. It is not an easy exercise.

34

SPEAKING 2 (page 40)

Introduce students to the task type by going through the advice in the **Exam File** with the class. (Marking criteria for the Speaking Test are given in the Exam Overview, **Teacher's Book** page 10.)

1 Select and rank.

Students work in pairs for the ranking activity. Refer them to the **Language Bank** and make sure they use at least some of the expressions given. You could tell them to tick off each expression as they use it.

To simulate exam conditions, you could set them a time limit of 3–4 minutes.

Picture 1 shows two people wearing breathing apparatus, sitting in the cockpit of a jet.
Picture 2 shows a skydiver.
Picture 3 shows a clapperboard, used in making films.
Picture 4 shows a yacht.
Picture 5 shows someone having a piano lesson.

2 Report decisions.

In Part 4 of the Speaking Test, the two candidates report back to the examiner, summarising their decision and the reasons for it. To simulate exam conditions, this exercise could be done by putting pairs into groups of four, with each pair taking turns to play the roles of candidates and examiners. Set at time limit of 3–4 minutes for each pair of 'candidates'.

If you prefer, treat this as a class discussion at this stage.

ENGLISH IN USE (page 41)

Introduce students to the task type by going through the advice in the **Exam File** with the class.

1 Preparation.

The aim of the exercise is to show students how important it is to look at overall meaning as well as grammar when doing this type of exercise.

ANSWERS

2 B   3 C

2 Reading for gist.

Emphasise how important it is to read the text first in order to get an overall understanding of the meaning. The aim of having students answer the question is to check understanding of the main idea of the text.

ANSWER

People who are considered attractive have more self-confidence.

3 Task.

Tell students to look backwards and forwards in the text to find links which will indicate where the missing phrases belong. Elicit what links helped them when you check answers as a class.

ANSWERS

1 E (*More or less attractive* links back to the *Western ideal of beauty.*)
2 F (This answer is indicated by the use of emphatic *do* in the first part of the sentence, and the words *No doubt part of the explanation . . .* in the next sentence – i.e. the explanation for why people *tend to think that someone with good looks is confident and socially adept.*)
3 A (The grammar suggests a relative clause is needed here.)
4 D (The reference to *the attractive children's behaviour* in the next sentence shows this has to be D not G.)
5 C (The verb *judge* can only be followed by an infinitive or *as.*)

WRITING (page 42)

Go through the advice in the **Exam File** with the class to remind students how to approach a Part 1 task which involves reading input.

Writing task

Students read the writing task and follow the **Steps to Writing**.

Step 1 Task interpretation
Remind students to highlight key words in the task for this Step.

ANSWERS

text type:	letter
target reader:	customer services department of a holiday company
purpose:	to complain and ask for compensation
register/tone:	formal
begin/end:	Dear Sir or Madam / Yours faithfully

3 Getting to the top

Step 2 Selecting and summarising

Remind students to highlight those parts of the instructions that make clear what information must be included. When marking Part 1 papers, examiners look for specific items of information that must be included for task achievemen. Marks will be lost if relevant information from the reading input is not included. For this task, students must include information that explains why they are dissatisfied.

ANSWERS

1 The points to complain about are: cost/hotel amenities/hotel staff/airport transfers.

2

Advertisement	Reality
bargain price	lots of extra charges
three swimming pools	one, dirty
moderately priced restaurants	restaurants very expensive
in beautiful gardens	next to motorway flyover
helpful staff	badly dressed, impolite
close to beach	miles away
local airport	200 km away
budget cars	expensive

Step 3 Layout and organisation

ANSWERS

Paragraph 1: Introduce yourself and reason for writing; general expression of disappointment and reference to misleading advertisement
Paragraphs 2/3: specific complaints: what the advertisement said versus the reality
Paragraph 4: Sum up situation and request compensation

The best order for the points in paragraphs 2/3 is probably:
Cost: 'bargain' price vs. extra charges, expensive restaurants, expensive car hire
Hotel amenities and staff: one swimming pool, long way from beach, air-conditioning not working properly, empty fridge, poor staff
Airport transfers: distant airport

Step 4 Write

Students combine the sentences and add the linking expressions. Check as a class before students start writing their own letter.

Refer students to Language Study page 34 (regret) and the **Language Bank**.

ANSWERS

1 I have just returned from a holiday in Florida (which was) organised by your company. Regrettably, the holiday did not meet my expectations. It was supposed to be a dream holiday, but (in fact) it turned out to be a nightmare.
2 but / In addition / and / Although / What is more

MODEL ANSWER

Dear Sir or Madam

I have just returned from a holiday in Florida, which was arranged by your company. Regrettably, the holiday did not meet my expectations. It was supposed to be a dream holiday, but in fact it turned out to be a nightmare. I feel that your company should accept responsibility, as much of the information in your advert was misleading or inaccurate.

First of all, your advertisement offered a bargain price. It failed to mention all the extra charges which were not included. It stated that there was a choice of moderately priced restaurants, but in fact they were very expensive. It offered budget rate car hire but, as it turned out, only expensive cars were available.

As regards the hotel amenities, there was only one swimming pool, not three as claimed in your advertisement, and it was very dirty. The hotel was not 'close' to the beach, but at least two miles away. In addition, the air conditioning didn't function properly and the fridge in my room was always empty. To make matters worse, the staff were rude and unhelpful, as well as badly dressed. On top of everything else, we were promised convenient transfers to and from the local airport, but, in fact, the airport was 200 kilometres away. I was exhausted before the holiday even started.

As compensation for what I have suffered, I feel that I am entitled to a full refund. I would be grateful if you would reply by return of post, letting me know what you propose to do.

Yours faithfully

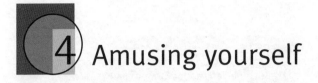

4 Amusing yourself

SPEAKING 1 (page 44)

1 Interpret cartoons.

Cartoon 1 shows a man hanging by his fingertips from a window ledge of a tall building, with a phone in his free hand. He is saying 'I'll hold,' meaning 'I'll wait'. The humour is in the double meaning of *hold*, which also refers to holding on to the window ledge.

Cartoon 2 shows a woman arriving at her desk at 9.20. The message on her computer screen reads 'What time do you call this?' The reference is to the importance that computers now have in our lives.

Cartoon 3 shows a security guard watching a closed circuit TV screen, while a pickpocket is removing money from his back pocket. The image on the screen he is watching is of himself and the pickpocket.

2 Pair discussion.

ANSWERS

Joke 1 relies on one of the words having a double meaning. *Coach* means *a bus* and *a trainer*.
Joke 2 relies on displacement. The punchline shows that the speaker is as mad as his brother.
Joke 3 relies on displacement: the doctor, who is supposed to be supportive, is as unsympathetic as everyone else.
Joke 4 relies on a double meaning. *Fowl* means a bird, *foul* means an illegal tackle in football.
Joke 5 depends on the contrast between the bizarre question and the literal, matter-of-fact answer.

▶▶ *Extension activity*

Ask students if they know any jokes they would like to tell. It may be best to let them work in groups before choosing one joke to tell the whole class.

VOCABULARY 1 (page 45)

Homophones

1 Introduction/analysis.

Practice with homophones is a good way to revise advanced students' pronunciation of English phonemes. Note that the words described as homophones here are homophones in Southern British Standard pronunciation but not necessarily in other varieties of English.

ANSWERS

1	roar	raw
2	taut	taught
3	meet	meat
4	sea	see
5	write	right
6	site	sight
7	weigh	way
8	brake	break
9	pear	pair
10	heir	air
11	herd	heard
12	through	threw

2 📼 Practice.

TAPESCRIPT

1	soar	saw
2	walk	work
3	mood	mud
4	choose	chews
5	hall	whole
6	lip	leap
7	real	reel
8	wonder	wander
9	role	roll
10	bear	beer
11	born	borne
12	advise	advice
13	lose	loose
14	life	live

ANSWERS

1, 4, 7, 9 and 11 are homophones.

Words with more than one meaning

3 Vocabulary: homonyms

Students will need to use dictionaries for this task. The aim is to pre-teach some of the vocabulary which students will meet in the reading text in the next section (**Students' Book** page 47).

ANSWERS

1 *nature* = character
2 *bear a relationship to* = be similar to
3 *light* = something that is not too serious or difficult to understand
4 *founder* = person who established something
5 *butt* = person that other people make jokes about
6 *setting* = the metal that holds a stone in a piece of jewellery
7 *tackle* = try to take the ball from the other members of the team

4 Amusing yourself

8 *background* = behind the main thing that you are looking at
9 under *observation* = watched continuously by someone
10 *degree* = qualification awarded to someone who has successfully completed a course of study at a university

READING (page 46)

Exam File: Part 1, Multiple matching

Go through the advice in the **Exam File** with the class.

1 Pre-teach vocabulary.

Note: Subversive appears in the multiple matching questions, not the text. Don't try to pre-teach other vocabulary at this point.

ANSWERS

1 E   2 C   3 D   4 B   5 A

2 Skim and summarise.

1 Tell the students that an introduction generally gives an overview of the main ideas which will be developed in the rest of the text. The sentence completion exercise helps students to summarise these ideas and serves as a comprehension check.

ANSWERS

1 Plato believed that humour was malevolent and should be avoided by civilised people.
2 Sigmund Freud's view was that humour can be a way of avoiding conflict with others.
3 Recently, psychologists have emphasised the valuable role of humour in social interaction.

2 This exercise encourages students to predict where they will find the information they will need to do the multiple matching task.

3 Multiple matching task.

Tell students to highlight those parts of the text that give them the answers. When they have finished, let students compare their answers and justify them with reference to the text. Then check as a class.

ANSWERS

1 D . . . comedians adopt humour early in life . . . (lines 78–79)
2 A Historically, humour has often been seen in a very negative way . . . (lines 1–2)
   Modern psychology, however . . . (line 8)
3 C Remarks or actions that people would often not see as very funny are sometimes found quite hilarious in a group setting, (lines 65–66)
4 B Group loyalties, political opinions and ethnic background all influence the way a joke is received and how funny people find it. (lines 35–37)
5 D The professional comic is thought by psychoanalysts to be an angry person whose skills enable him to channel his aggression in a socially acceptable and productive manner. (lines 93–96)
6 C Studies of persuasion have revealed that humorous people are perceived as being more likeable and this in turn enables them to have greater influence. (lines 42–44)
7 D . . . who lacked the confidence themselves to go against accepted values in the way that most humour requires (lines 84–86)
8 B . . . the punch line bears an unexpected relationship to the opening part of the story. (lines 22–23)
9 A . . . it meant trying to give yourself a sense of superiority by making fun of other people and he taught that only people of lesser worth did this. (lines 4–7)
10 D The professionals tackle taboo subjects without inhibition and this gives them considerable social value. (lines 87–89)
11 C It was found that dealers with the more light-hearted attitude were able to get a significantly higher price for the painting. (lines 49–51)

4 Guess meaning from context.

You could also ask students to explain the following expressions:

the sting is in the tail (line 39) = the nasty part is in the punchline

corny old joke (line 23) = silly, not sophisticated

ANSWERS

1 incongruity: when two things do not go together and seem out of place
2 rebound on: show something negative about the joke-teller
3 lose face: feel humiliated
4 make/win concessions: persuade someone to give you something, a lower price for example
5 hilarious: very funny
6 standing: reputation, how highly people regard you
7 cope with: manage
8 defiance: show no fear or respect

5 **Group/class discussion: response to the text.**

Tell students to read Section C again in preparation for this discussion. Elicit:

a) in what situations humour can be helpful (when buying and selling, when opening a conversation with a member of the opposite sex, in conversations with friends)

b) how and why humour is helpful (it establishes a relaxed, non-threatening atmosphere)

Then tell them to work in pairs or groups and think of experiences in their own lives which support or disprove these ideas.

LANGUAGE STUDY 1 (page 48)

Reference

This section focuses on how pronouns can be used to link phrases, sentences and paragraphs. It is useful practice for Paper 1, Part 2 (gapped text) and Paper 3, Part 6 (discourse cloze). Refer students to the Notes on **Students' Book** page 204 before confirming their answers to the questions.

1 **Analysis.**

ANSWERS

1 humour
2 make fun of other people
3 laughter
4 Freud's analysis of humour
5 an essential incongruity
6 the perception they are more likeable
7 remarks . . . are found hilarious in social settings

2 **Analysis.**

ANSWERS

1 The experiment in which trained psychology students impersonated salesmen.
Humour is a useful tool to use when you are trying to persuade someone.
2 The effect known as 'social facilitation'.
You are able to increase your influence by being funny.

Conjunction

3 **Analysis.**

This exercise shows how conjunctions and other linking words make connections between ideas and sentences. It is also relevant to Paper 3, Part 6 (discourse cloze). Refer students to the Notes on **Students' Book** page 208 before confirming their answers to the questions.

ANSWERS

1 a. while . . . also
  b. For example,
  c. however
2 Three, also/another
3 See Notes **Students' Book** page 208.

! *be to* + **infinitive**

The time reference is to future time, either seen from a point in the past or in the present. This structure suggests that something is inevitable or definitely planned.

VOCABULARY 2 (page 48)

Word formation

1 **Presentation.**

The aim here is to show that the prefix *in–* is not always negative.

ANSWERS

1
invaluable = very valuable
2
1 Yes   2 Yes   3 Yes   4 No

Opposites
1 Your help has been valueless / of no value.
2 The island is uninhabited.
3 This liquid is non-flammable.
Note: inflammable/flammable both mean *able to catch fire easily*.
4 This sculpture is worthless / valueless / of no value / not worth anything.
Note: worthless is possible in 1, but very insulting.

Idiomatic expressions

2 **Practice.**

Let students work in pairs to think of paraphrases for the expressions given.

POSSIBLE ANSWERS

1 look serious
2 put my make-up on
3 come
4 confront / deal with
5 in person / in real life
6 made an effort to appear cheerful
7 seems irrational

▶▶ *Extension activity*

You could extend Exercise 2 into a dictionary-based activity to include idiomatic expressions based on other parts of the body. Students will find the Longman *Language Activator* or the *Dictionary of Contemporary English* useful for this.

Write the following parts of the body on the board.

HEAD   EAR   EYE   NOSE   HANDS

Divide the class into groups. Each group should note down as many idioms or phrases as they can think of that include the words. Set a time limit. Then tell the students to check their ideas in the dictionary. Ask who got the most expressions right.

Tell them to add the idioms they like best to their vocabulary notebooks, under a relevant topic area.

Remind them to include example sentences, preferably related to themselves and their own experiences.

LISTENING 1 (page 49)

Exam File: Part 1, Note completion

Go through the advice in the **Exam File** with the class.

1 **Topic discussion.**

This prepares students for the ideas and vocabulary that they will hear.

2 **Preparation.**

Predicting, even incorrectly, is a valuable way of preparing the mind for a listening comprehension task.

3 📼 **Note completion task.**

Emphasise to students that there is a word limit for this type of task, and they should write no more than three words as directed.

TAPESCRIPT

Presenter: Do you like laughing? Well, most of us do, don't we? But have you ever thought that laughter might be good for you? There's evidence that seems to show that it is. More than a hundred medical and psychological studies seem to indicate that a good sense of humour works as an excellent 'immunity medicine', increasing resistance to disease. According to these studies, the ability to see the funny side of things improves both physical and psychological well-being. Laughter helps to relax the body by reducing blood pressure and tension in the muscles, as well as helping to control stress, so a person who can laugh at life suffers less illness and has better health.

If you think this sounds like a recipe you'd like to follow, you could visit a Laughter Clinic. And what, you might wonder, goes on there? The usual start to a session is breathing exercises. Clients are then invited to picture the last time they were happy and try to re-create that feeling. They are encouraged to smile. Apparently even simulated smiles improve mood. People are then split into groups and asked to recount an amusing incident, a humorous story or joke. It's even better if it's something that has happened to them recently. The aim is to make the others laugh. Next there could be a whole class discussion on how humour can be used to enhance relationships. Tape-recordings of someone enjoying a good laugh end the session.

For their homework, students might be told to choose a fixed time every day to think of something funny and laugh about it for at least two minutes. They also know how they should start the day – by standing in front of a mirror and laughing at their reflection. Apparently, these activities help train people to appreciate laughter and the lighter side of life.

The medical profession as a whole still needs to be convinced. People who run the clinic obviously take a different approach. They agree that laughter may not solve life's problems, but it does put people in a better position to tackle them.

ANSWERS

(See underlined words in the tapescript.)

1 sense of humour
2 laughter
3 breathing exercises
4 make others laugh
5 tape-recorded laughter
6 something funny
7 a mirror
8 unconvinced / sceptical

---

4 **Group activity.**

Invite students to comment on the ideas suggested in the recording: do they think they are likely to work?

Groups of at least four, possibly six, would be best for the group activity. Give students some time to prepare first. (They could do this for homework.)

5 **Group/class discussion.**

Students discuss the sayings and work out what they mean.

LANGUAGE STUDY 2 (page 50)

Prepositions followed by gerund

1 Analysis and practice.

The rule that a verb form following a preposition must be a gerund is a very powerful one and can help students avoid a lot of mistakes. Be prepared to explain that *to* is sometimes a preposition and sometimes part of the infinitive.

Refer students to the Notes on **Students' Book** page 202.

ANSWERS

When a verb follows a preposition it must take the *-ing* form.
2 by telling
3 without visiting
4 of learning
5 from driving/getting
6 of becoming / about being
7 with getting/becoming
8 to selling
9 of being/getting

Verbs followed by gerund and/or infinitive

2 Analysis.

Some verbs are always followed by gerunds and never by infinitives and some are always followed by infinitives and never by gerunds. It is important that students learn the most common verbs in each category. There are lists in the Notes on **Students' Book** page 202.

The notes students have to complete offer a useful rule of thumb which will help them to understand why an infinitive or gerund is used. However, as with all rules in English, there are exceptions, as the practice exercises show.

ANSWERS

- The *to-infinitive* frequently looks forward: the action of the verb in the infinitive form happens after the action of the main verb.
- The gerund indicates either:
a) an action or state prior to the action of the main verb,
or
b) the general idea of activity.

3 Practice: gerund or infinitive.

To do this exercise, students must know which verbs take the gerund and which take the infinitive. Tell them to check their answers by looking at the lists of verbs in the Notes if necessary.

ANSWERS

1 not to rehearse   2 to lend   3 selling   4 to change
5 being recognised   6 driving   7 to help   8 making

4 Analysis.

The verbs which can be followed by both the infinitive and the gerund with little difference in meaning will cause few difficulties for students. But *forget*, *stop* and *try* can be confusing. Ask students questions such as: What did he stop? Why did he stop?

For *remember*, ask: Which happened first – doing the action/having the experience or thinking about the action/experience?

For *try* ask: Did he succeed? Was it easy to do? Was it successful?

ANSWERS

1 a. He was writing and then he stopped.
   b. He stopped first and then he began to write.
2 a. He saw John first and then he remembered.
   b. He remembered first and then he bought the card.
3 a. Describes a goal (which may have been impossible to do)
   b. Describes a course of action (which may not have led to success but was easy to do)

5 Practice.

This exercise contains examples of all the different uses of the gerund and infinitive that have been described so far.

Make sure that students read the text to the end before filling in the gaps. When they have finished, tell them to check their work in pairs and discuss any differences. Tell them to refer to the Notes.

ANSWERS

1 to think	5 to lock	9 walking/to walk
2 to bring	6 switching off	10 going
3 buying	7 locking	11 checking
4 to put	8 worrying	12 to go

Gerund and infinitive nominals

6 Analysis and practice.

This section contrasts sentences beginning with gerunds, infinitives and introductory *It*. When reading, it is very important to be able to identify the subject of a sentence rapidly. The aim of the practice exercise is to show that the subject can consist of a very long clause.

Refer students to Notes on **Students' Book** page 203.

ANSWERS

Sentences 4 and 6 can be rewritten beginning with *It*.
4 It's no use wishing someone else would come along and make your dreams come true.
6 It's really important to me to be able to help other people in my job.

7 Analysis.

The rule of thumb introduced in Exercise 2 is helpful here.

ANSWERS

1 The *to*-infinitive is impossible in 1b. because the infinitive looks forward to something in the future. The event in question happened in the past.
2 The *-ing* form is impossible in 2b. because the gerund doesn't give the idea of future intent. If I have an ambition, I am thinking of the future.

8 Practice.

POSSIBLE ANSWERS

1 . . . go for a long walk in the countryside.
2 . . . listening to classical music.
3 . . . to make sure you get a good night's sleep.
4 . . . joining a club . . .

LISTENING 2 (page 52)

Exam File: Part 3, Multiple choice questions

Introduce students to this task type by going through the **Exam File** with the class.

1 Pre-teach vocabulary.

ANSWERS

1
1 D   2 C   3 A   4 B   5 E   6 F
2
1 shutter   2 shoot   3 wind   4 load

2 🔊 Multiple choice questions.

TAPESCRIPT

Man: When I was growing up, I became fascinated by visual images, whether in paintings or photographs or advertisements. What you saw in these images was the real and not the real world both at the same time. What you saw was what the person making the image had chosen to create. I enjoyed painting classes at school and from those I learnt a lot about composition – how to put together a picture, how to balance the different shapes and how to create mood through the use of colour.

Interviewer: I see, but how exactly did you become interested in photography? You might have just stuck to painting.

Man: Well, what really got me started on photography was when I got my first camera – a gift from an uncle who had moved on to something better. It was fairly simple. Basically, you pointed it at the subject, pressed the shutter and hoped for the best. It produced prints, small black and white ones, and you could only get good results when shooting out of doors when the light was good.
In my teens, I got my second camera, which was more complex. It took a variety of lenses – wide-angle, macro, zoom and so on. You had to adjust the focus manually and take account of the lighting attachment. There were some obvious disadvantages – the equipment was expensive. I bought more and more extra pieces of equipment, bit by bit, whenever I could afford them. And you needed a strong bag to carry all the bits and pieces around. You had to be extremely organised too, when taking photographs, and a lot of spontaneity was lost because of the time it took to get everything ready.

Interviewer: It sounds like a lot of trouble, all those bits and pieces . . .

Man: Oh yes, it was. But on the other hand, as a learning process, it was invaluable. That was the best thing about it. I learnt the basic techniques, such as how a camera operates, how important the light is, what effect is produced by using different lenses and how fed up people can get if you want to take their picture but have to fiddle around with the equipment. A bonus for me was that the school gave me great support. There was a darkroom where I learnt all about developing the pictures I'd taken, and we had a flourishing Camera Club run by a keen non-professional. We also put on exhibitions of our work, which provided us with a clear purpose in taking photos.

Interviewer: One thing I've always wanted to ask is, is it better to take slides or prints? What do you think?

Man: People often ask me that. There's advantages and disadvantages to both, and in some ways it all comes down to personal taste. I prefer slides myself – slides allow you to get greater contrasts of dark and light in the frame. A major disadvantage for most people is that you need to be able to project them, and for this a large screen is most effective. <u>This and a good projector do not come cheap. There is no point in taking slides if you don't have this equipment.</u> Handy-sized portable slide projectors are now on the market, so these do allow you to carry around your slides to show to friends. But if this is your main aim, then prints are the best bet. They are so easy to pass around and people can look at them together.

Interviewer: But you've been describing how things used to be when you started. Isn't it a lot easier now, with more modern equipment?

Man: It certainly is. Cameras have moved on a lot these days, so everything is much, much easier now for youngsters taking it up. For a reasonable price, you can get a camera that does virtually everything for you – loads the film, winds it on and rewinds, adjusts the focus automatically and has different lenses and flash built in. And uses colour too. <u>You just point and press. Except that the good photographer doesn't. The successful photographer is one who decides first what the final image should look like and then works out what is needed to get it. You have to decide what the important element in</u> the photo is. Is it a close-up of an individual, an impressive landscape, a permanent record of a group? You set up your photograph according to what you want to achieve, taking account of background, colours and the composition of the image.
I'd recommend photography as a hobby to everyone. There's nothing easier than taking a photo, and if you want to make sure that every photo is a good one, then learning the technical side of cameras will improve the results you get. Joining a camera club is a good idea for young photographers. They can combine learning about technique with the companionship of meeting like-minded enthusiasts, who can give them valuable advice.

ANSWERS

(See underlined words in the tapescript.)
1 B   2 A   3 B   4 A   5 C   6 B

---

3 **Vocabulary: intensifying adverbs.**

ANSWERS

1 fairly   2 obvious   3 extremely   4 major   5 virtually

SPEAKING 2 (page 53)

Exam File: Part 2, Describe and compare

Introduce students to this task type by going through the **Exam File** with the class.

---

1 **Talk about photographs.**

Give students a few minutes to prepare answers to the questions individually before putting them into pairs or groups.

To simulate exam conditions, you could have students work in groups of three or four rather than pairs. Students C and D can play the role of the examiners, and time each 'candidate'. They can also invite each candidate to comment on what the other has said (Exercise 2) and lead the discussion in Exercise 3, by asking each candidate the questions supplied.

Photo 1 shows a young couple playing chess outdoors in a park.
Photo 2 shows an elderly man building a model boat.
Photo 3 shows young women in an aerobics class.
Photo 4 shows two people hill-walking. They are wearing hiking boots and shorts and carrying rucksacks on their backs.

2 **Compare opinions.**

In the exam, the second candidate has about 20 seconds to respond as directed by the examiner. Tell the students that it is perfectly all right for students to disagree with each other in the Speaking Test as long as they justify their points of view.

3 **Extension of the discussion.**

See Exercise 1 above.

WRITING (page 54)

Exam File: Part 2, Article

Before going through the **Exam File**, ask students to suggest what they think are the main features of articles written for newspapers or magazines. Elicit the ways that article writers try to attract and hold the readers' interest. Students then read the **Exam File** to compare.

Step 1 Task Interpretation

ANSWERS

text type:	article for a magazine
target readers:	teenagers, people in their early twenties (a teens and twenties readership)
purpose:	to inform and entertain the reader
register/tone:	informal

Step 2 Generating ideas

Tell the students it is always best to write about a topic they know something about. Find out if any students share similar interests and hobbies, and tell them to work in pairs for this step. They will be able to help each other with ideas and vocabulary.

Step 3 Layout and organisation

1 Emphasise that the plan given is just a suggestion – it is not the only way to organise the article.

2 The aim is to give students ideas they can use for their own writing.

POSSIBLE ANSWERS

Put yourself in the picture – photography
Adventures on water – canoeing / sailing
Going down in the world – pot-holing
Sounds interesting! – playing an instrument
A winter sport guaranteed to raise your temperature – skiing / snowboarding

Step 4 Write

Before starting to write their own article, students compare the two opening paragraphs and decide which is more appropriate to the task.

ANSWER ·

Paragraph A is more suited to the target audience. Asking a question is a good way to attract the readers' interest and make them want to read on. The tone is livelier and more appealing.

Point out to students that it is also important to bring an article to an effective close, rather than simply stopping mid-paragraph. One way to do this is to refer back to something that was mentioned in the first paragraph, to round off the text. Another way is to ask a question or make a comment that summarises the content in a sentence. You could refer students to the article in Unit 3, **Students' Book** page 37, which offers a good example of using a question to round things off. See also the model answer below.

MODEL ANSWER

Put yourself in the picture
Have you ever considered taking up photography? If not, why not? Photography can provide you with hours of enjoyment both indoors and out of doors – and you don't have to be an expert to do it! All you need is a camera, some free time and a little creativity.

Getting started
To start with, any camera will do. You don't need to buy expensive equipment. I started when I was fifteen with a very basic camera I got for my birthday. What you should do is get a book on basic photographic skills – there are plenty of good ones – and see what results you get. If you are pleased with the results, you can take things further.

Moving on
As you get better, you will want to invest in better equipment, but don't be put off! This doesn't mean you have to spend a fortune. You can buy excellent second-hand equipment through specialist magazines, which means the cost won't mount up too much.

Taking off
The next challenge that you will face is learning how to develop your own photos. This means mastering a lot of new skills and finding somewhere that can be used as a dark room. But it's worth it in the end to get complete control over the final photo. A very good tip is to join a club. You'll get plenty of advice from fellow enthusiasts. And it's a great way of meeting people! So what are you waiting for? Why not start today?

ENGLISH IN USE 1 (page 55)

Exam File: Part 3, Error correction

Go through the information in the **Exam File** with the class. The aim of this section is to revise the basic rules for the use of commas in English.

1 Analysis: features of sentences.

The aim of this exercise is two-fold: first, to remind students that a complete sentence must contain at least a subject and a verb; second, to let them experiment with ways of combining ideas into a sentence. You could point out that incomplete sentences are often used e.g. in adverts, brochures and leaflets to achieve specific effects, but these effects depend upon people knowing the correct punctuation rules.

Elicit possible sentences and put them on the board, but don't check them until students have worked through the rest of the exercises.

POSSIBLE ANSWERS

Two years ago I went to Hollywood, home of the stars, to study acting because I wanted to get a job as an actor.
I wanted to get a job as an actor, so two years ago I went to Hollywood, home of the stars, to study acting.

2 Analysis: commas in sentences with introductory elements.

ANSWERS

(Adverbial) elements at the beginning of a sentence are separated off by a comma.

3 Analysis: commas in sentences with inserted elements.

ANSWERS

1
Inserted elements (i.e. elements containing extra, non-essential information) in a sentence, either adverbial or adjectival, are separated off with commas.
2
Example a. is a general statement of fact.
The use of commas in example b. gives additional information about Susan and Ann. If this clause is removed, the sentence still makes sense.

4 Analysis: commas in a list.

ANSWERS

Commas are used here because items are being listed.

5 Practice.

ANSWERS

Stand-up comedian Basile has appeared on prime time television, he's been heard on over 450 radio show and he's played some of the biggest clubs across the United States. However, comedy was not Basile's first career choice. This native New Yorker, who now lives in North Carolina, played semi-professional football before attending law school. In his final year, needing a break from the stress, he took a year off to pursue stand-up comedy. That was nine years ago. Since then Basile has used his wit, improvisation skills and voice impersonations to build a fast-paced, high-energy show. "My act is always on the edge," he says. "I never take it too seriously. I try to touch the inner child of every person. From the beginning to the end, you're not sure of what's going to happen." No matter where he performs across the country, Basile says he's always looking for the same response from his audience. "I'm not like one of those comedians who stand there with their hands in their pockets and get polite applause for witty remarks. I don't want that. When people are roaring with uncontrollable laughter, that to me is what comedy is all about."

6 Review Exercise 1.
Discuss students' answers to Exercise 1.

ENGLISH IN USE 2 (page 56)

Exam File: Part 1, Multiple choice cloze

1 Discussion: introduction to the topic.
For this exercise, divide students into groups of at least four students.

2 Read for gist.
Make sure students do read to the end before choosing from options A, B, C or D. The question gives students a reason for reading. Check their answer before they do the multiple choice exercise. Students have a strong tendency to start choosing the answers straightaway, but this should be discouraged, as it is not the best way to tackle the task.

ANSWERS

According to the article, watching TV makes teenagers more prone to crime and drug taking.

3 Multiple choice cloze.
Students select the best word for each gap from the options given. Tell them to try this individually, then discuss their choices with a partner.

To make this a learning rather than a testing activity, encourage them to use a dictionary when they are uncertain, rather than simply telling them the answer. The Longman *Language Activator* is designed to help learners make the right choice of word for a given meaning and context.

ANSWERS

1 A
2 D
3 B
4 D
5 A
6 B
7 B (*Survey* is the only item that collocates with *participate in*.)
8 D (Only *paint* collocates with *picture* in this context – it has a figurative meaning here.)
9 B (Option A requires the preposition *from*. Option C doesn't make sense in the context. Option D doesn't collocate: you can *finish school*, but not *stop school*.)
10 D (Option D is the only verb that can be followed by *as*.)

4 Response to the text.
This can be done in groups of four, or as a whole class.

 Creativity

SPEAKING 1 (page 58)

The Speaking activity introduces the theme of the unit, creativity. The questions in Exercises 1 and 2 should prompt students to discuss how far creative talent is innate and how far it can be learned or developed.

1 Class/group discussion.

Prompt students with questions such as:

What is a blockbuster? (a best-seller, usually aimed at the mass market)
What type of plot, setting, characters do blockbusters typically have? (often either romance or politics, with rich and powerful characters.)
Describe a best-seller you know.
Do you think you can be **taught** how to write a best-seller?
How important is technique and understanding of the mechanics of the task?
What about writing a film script? Painting a picture?

2 Group discussion.

Have students appoint a group secretary and prepare a list of proposals for encouraging creativity either a) at school or b) in the workplace. Set a time limit, then compare their suggestions as a class.

E.g.: (schools)

Project work to encourage pupils to find information for themselves; abolish exams; non-compulsory lessons . . . etc.

LISTENING 1 (page 58)

Exam File: Part 2, Note completion

Remind students about this task type by going through the **Exam File**.

1 Preparation.

Students read through the notes. Elicit the type of information which is probably required – e.g. a time, a day, a phone number. Note that Part 2 tasks often have some of the information already completed.

2 📼 Note completion task.

Play the recording once only, and tell students to compare answers. If there is disagreement, play the recording once more.

TAPESCRIPT

Narrator: Thank you for calling Artsline, the telephone information service which gives details of the courses run at Weston Court, the Centre for the Creative Arts.

Weekend courses assemble on Friday evening and finish on Sunday afternoon. From Monday to Friday, day courses usually assemble at 9.15 a.m. and finish at 4.30 p.m.

A number of courses at the centre are part of a series which may last several weeks or months. You may book individual weekends at full cost or book as a series at a saving of up to £30 for the whole course. Detailed course information is available on request and will automatically be sent on enrolment. If you have any difficulty in choosing your course and require some personal advice, do not hesitate to call us on 745 99017 during normal office hours, Monday to Friday.

Accommodation for weekend courses is available in a study bedroom with private bathroom overlooking the lake at Weston Court. All meals (breakfast, lunch, afternoon tea and dinner) are included in the course fee.

To book a place on a course at Weston Court, please complete one booking form for each person and enclose a non-returnable deposit of £20 a course. You can pay by cheque or credit card. Acknowledgements will be sent for each booking together with a final payment slip giving the date by which the balance is due to be paid. We regret that we are unable to keep a place for you if we do not receive the full balance within seven days of the start of the course.

We reserve the right to cancel the course at any time if there is an inadequate enrolment. For reasons beyond our control, the content and timing of the courses may be changed.

Thank you for calling Artsline. To receive a brochure with details of all the courses available in the current session, please leave your name and address after the tone.

ANSWERS

(See underlined words in the tapescript.)

1 Friday evening   2 Sunday afternoon   3 a series
4 available on request   5 745 99017   6 study bedrooms
7 not returnable   8 7 days   9 content

ENGLISH IN USE 1 (page 59)

Part 1, Multiple choice cloze

This task continues the theme introduced in Speaking 1: Can creativity be trained?

1 Read for gist.

To ensure that students read the text to the end before attempting to fill in the gaps, set a time limit. Then discuss students' responses to the ideas as a class.

2 Multiple choice cloze.

Let students work in pairs to do the cloze exercise. Tell them to leave the ones they are not sure about and return to them when they have finished. Tell them to use their dictionary to check these. The Longman *Language Activator* is designed to help learners select the right word.

ANSWERS

1 A = to some extent, in a limited way (See *Activator* entry for PARTLY 1)
2 B The only alternative would be *belief*.
3 C
4 D
5 D
6 A
7 C = remember important facts you may need to know in future. (See *Activator* entry for REMEMBER 9)
8 A Another alternative would be *thinking*.
9 C
10 B = avoid (See *Activator* entry for AVOID 1)
11 A
12 D
13 B = deliberately forget sth (see *Activator* entry for FORGET 4)
14 D *set about* = start; *set off* and *set out* mean *begin a journey*, so D is the only option.
15 C

READING (page 60)

Part 3, Multiple choice questions

1 Introduction to the topic.

You can extend this exercise to novelists, painters or musicians. The aim is to get students thinking about the topic of the reading text.

2 Read for specific information.

The aim of this exercise is a) to encourage students to skim the text quickly b) to point out how the article is organised.

ANSWERS

1
Date
last year
1985
1983
1986
late 80s
1949
after school
1972
Currently

2

The article begins and ends in the present day. We would expect to see events related in chronological order in an entry in an encyclopaedia. The writer instead relates events in a way which will be interesting to the reader. The reader is most interested in Fenton now, so the writer begins and ends in the present day.

3 Multiple choice questions.

Remind students that the questions follow the order of the text. This task requires much closer reading than multiple matching tasks, as it involves understanding opinions and attitudes.

Tell them first to read each question and look for the answer in the article, highlighting the relevant part of the text. They can then look at the options and see which comes closest to their own answer.

ANSWERS

1 C It was not just what he read, it was how he read it. (lines 13–15)
2 D His agent negotiated a percentage . . . this must amount to a very large sum of money indeed. (lines 44–48)
3 B He's devoted to the outside world. (lines 65–66)
4 A "I wouldn't presume anything," Fenton answers briskly. (lines 88–89)
5 C Fenton had been doing monthly book reviews for him. (lines 112–114)
6 D If all you worked on was books, and you wanted to write them, I figured you'd end up constantly referring to your own reading. (lines 122–125)
7 B . . . it's hard to believe Fenton is going to stick around (lines 143–144)

4 Discussion: response to the text.

For question 1, tell students to find evidence in the text to support their answers.

LANGUAGE STUDY 1 (page 62)

Lexical cohesion

The exercises in this section are useful preparation for Paper 1, Part 2 (gapped text) and Paper 3, Part 6 (discourse cloze). You can use any Reading text to give similar practice.

1 Analysis.

The aim is to show how words similar in meaning are used to link ideas in a text.

ANSWERS

1 wealth, rich   3 poems, love lyrics
2 volume, book   4 WH Auden, the poet

5 Creativity

2 Analysis.
The aim is to show how lexical links connect paragraphs.

ANSWERS

1 The phrase *poets are meant to be* is an echo of *the way we . . . poets are meant to*. Paragraph 3 goes on to talk about how Fenton differs from the stereotypical image of a poet. He is very popular and very rich.
2 This refers to the money Fenton made as librettist for *Les Miserables*.
3 The word *devoted* in paragraph 4 is echoed with the words *this devotion* in paragraph 5.
4 Fans will not be disappointed with the poet's new collection of poems *Out of Danger*.
5 The writer of the article asked the question. The use of *presume* echoing the word *presumably* makes it clear that the question is being answered.
6 The writer mentions the East and repeats a phrase from one of Fenton's poems *Out of the East, it's a far cry*.

VOCABULARY (page 62)

Phrasal verbs with *off*

1 Practice.
These exercises introduce another way of working out the meaning of phrasal verbs, by looking at the meaning of the particle.

ANSWERS

1
1 broke   2 forks   3 sold   4 see   5 wore   6 stopped
7 put   8 sent   9 put   10 called

2
Off, as the particle of a phrasal verb, is likely to refer to separation/distance or to finishing/completion.

2 Sentence completion task.
Students complete the sentences in their own way, using appropriate phrasal verbs from Exercise 1.

ANSWERS

1 (I) put it off   3 put (me) off   5 stopped off (to see John)
2 see (. . .) off   4 sent off for it

▶▶ Extension activity

1 While students are doing Exercise 2, write the following words on the board. Then ask students to match them with an appropriate phrasal verb from the ten they have been studying.

a an engagement (to be married) (break off)
b the novelty (wear off = sth becomes boring)

c diplomatic relations (break off)
d the wedding (call off)
e the competition (see off = beat a competitor e.g. in a business situation: With their new sports model, they successfully saw off the competition.)
f a decision (put off)

2 Have students work in pairs to prepare a test for other students. Using dictionaries to help them if necessary, they should prepare a sentence completion or gap fill exercise to test any of the phrasal verbs in Exercise 1. Pairs then exchange their tests. See who gets them all right.

LANGUAGE STUDY 2 (page 63)

The items focussed on in this section help to prepare students for English in Use 2, the structural cloze, on **Students' Book** page 64. They are typical Paper 3 test items.

Refer students to the Notes on **Students' Book** page 203.

as/like, as if/as though

1 Presentation and practice.
You could tell students to do the gap fill exercise first, then check their answers by reading the information in the box.

ANSWERS

1 as   2 as   3 like   4 like   5 as if/though   6 as
7 Like   8 like

used to / be, get used to /use

2 Analysis.
The aim is to distinguish between the similar-looking forms – *used to*, *be/get used to* and *use* and clarify the semantic and grammatical differences.

POSSIBLE ANSWERS

1
a.   Auden would take Fenton out for lunch.
b.   Fenton made use of his award money to go to Vietnam.
c.   After a while I got accustomed to living in a big city.
d.   We are accustomed to getting up early.

2
a.   infinitive (to take)
b.   direct object (his award money)
c./d.   prepositional phrase (living, getting up)

3
a.   *used to* becomes *Did (he) use to . . .?*
b   *use* becomes *Did (he) use . . .?*
c./d.   *be/get used to* don't change: *Have you got used to . . .?*
        Are (you) used to . . .?

3 Practice.

This exercise focuses on the patterns that follow the three verbs in question.

ANSWERS

1 I'll never get used to *operating this machine*.
2 Have you got used to *being famous*?
3 Didn't you use to *work at the British Museum*?
4 He used a credit card to *buy the tickets*.
5 It might take a long time for you to get used to *working in such a busy office*.

suppose / be supposed to

4 Analysis.

ANSWER

1
a. think   b. You'll be coming by car I think / won't you?
c. considered   d. meant   e. meant   f. meant   g. think

2
suppose + *that* clause / *to* infinitive
be supposed to + infinitive

5 Practice.

ANSWERS

1 suppose   3 are supposed to   5 do you suppose
2 are supposed to   4 suppose   6 am supposed to

ENGLISH IN USE 2 (page 64)

Exam File: Part 2, Structural cloze

Introduce this task type by going through the **Exam File** with the class.

1 Read for gist.

Emphasise how it is important to read the text to the end before filling in the gaps. This will help students to understand the meaning and choose the right words. Set a time limit for the first reading, and ask some quick-fire comprehension questions, e.g.:
Where was Brian Patten born?
When did he leave school?
Why did he resign from his job on the local newspaper?
Why was money not a problem then? etc.

Having students retell the story like this will help them think of the missing words.

ANSWERS

The title refers to the day Brian Patten made his decision to become a poet.

2 Gap fill task.

Students work individually, then compare answers in pairs.

ANSWERS

1 at	6 off/out	11 used
2 as	7 much	12 no
3 with	8 were	13 if/though
4 had	9 that	14 that/the
5 them	10 to	15 being

SPEAKING 2 (page 65)

Part 3, Discuss and select; Part 4, Report decisions

1 Vocabulary.

The aim is to teach some vocabulary which will be useful for the task in Exercise 2.

Photo 1 shows *The Earth is an Angel*, a metal sculpture by Shirazeh Houshiary.
Photo 2 shows *Femme (Woman)*, a painting by Emile Claus (1849–1924).
Photo 3 shows *Bouquet of Flowers*, a painting by Gerard Cornelius (1680–1745).
Photo 4 shows *Helice*, an abstract painting by Robert Delaney (1885–1941).

2 Collaborative task: discuss and select.

1 Tell students to discuss the task for 3–4 minutes. Refer them to the **Language Bank**, and tell them to tick off the expressions they use during the discussion.

2 In Part 4 of the Speaking Test, both students report their decision/discussion to the examiner, who then asks questions and joins in the discussion. This can be simulated in class by putting two pairs together for this part, rather than treating it as a class discussion.

3 Extension of discussion.

These questions are typical of the more wide-ranging questions, moving away from the specific task, that the examiner might ask in Part 4. Students can continue in the same groups of four to do this exercise.

ENGLISH IN USE 3 (page 66)

Part 4, Word formation

1 Read for gist.

ANSWERS

Pachyderm refers to a thick-skinned animal such as an elephant or a rhinoceros. Picasso (1881–1973) was a famous Spanish painter. Kamala the elephant is being jokingly compared with Picasso.

2 Word formation task.

Tell students to pay special attention to negatives, prefixes and plurals. It is in these areas that mistakes are often made. Sometimes two changes have to be made to a word. Tell them to compare their answers with a partner before checking as a class.

ANSWERS

1 creation   5 enthusiastic
2 enrichment   6 artistic
3 activities   7 attractions
4 dexterity

3 Discussion: response to the text.
This can be done quickly as a class.

LISTENING 2 (page 66)

Part 1, Note completion

1 Pre-teach vocabulary.

2 Preparation.
Remind students that they should always read through the task before they hear the recording. Ask them to try to match the problems mentioned in Exercise 1 to players of the different types of instrument.

POSSIBLE ANSWERS

string instruments: violin, viola, cello, double bass, guitar
wind instruments: bassoon, oboe, clarinet, flute, saxophone, trumpet, trombone

3 🔊 Note completion task.
Play the recording. Tell the students not to worry if they miss something. They will hear the recording again.

TAPESCRIPT

Presenter: A recent report has highlighted the hazards of life as a professional musician. According to medical and musical experts, up to seventy per cent of musicians are affected by physical and psychological problems.

Musicians can progressively deafen themselves over the years because the volume at which music is played is greater than would be allowed in a factory. And it is loud enough to cause hearing loss. Muscle fatigue which affects the hands, forearms, neck and shoulders, is another major problem for players of all instruments, but players of string instruments who sit for hours with their instrument clamped between tilted chin and hunched shoulder, or wedged between the knees, are particularly prone to painful cramps. One trombonist has even commissioned a special instrument in order to counter elbow fatigue.

All these physical problems can be put down to poor training. Musicians pick up bad posture habits at an early age, and find it impossible to rectify these later. At least one expert claims that if mind and body are properly tuned to the task in hand, there shouldn't be any difficulties. There's an extra danger for players of wind instruments who may suffer from dermatitis, a painful skin disease. This is due to a mouthpiece made from a hardwood that can cause allergies.

But physical problems are only one aspect of the hazards musicians face. There are psychological complaints of which stage fright and acute anxiety are the commonest. The life of a musician has always been characterised by job insecurity, and this leads to depression and sleep disturbance. At the same time, heavier recording and touring workloads have increased the pressure under which musicians work. According to the survey, some seventy per cent of orchestral players are suffering from some sort of performance-related illness. And orchestras are now employing medical consultants to deal with musicians plagued by injury and worry.

This has to be good news. A professional sportsman's career is usually over at forty. But at that age a professional musician has hardly begun to explore his craft. Let's hope recognition of their problems does something to help them out.

ANSWERS

(See underlined words in the tapescript.)

1 deafness   6 dermatitis/skin disease
2 muscle fatigue   7 stage fright
3 (painful) cramps   8 (acute) anxiety
4 poor training   9 job insecurity
5 bad posture (habits)   10 medical consultants

Check students' answers by asking questions, e.g.:

What physical complaints are suffered by players of any instrument? What complaints are suffered by players of string instruments?
What is the cause? etc.

LANGUAGE STUDY 3 (page 67)

Present participle clauses

1 Presentation.
The aim is to familiarise students with participle clauses which can be used in the writing task. You could have students try Exercise 2 before going through the information in the box.

Refer students to the Notes on **Students' Book** pages 203–204.

2 Practice.
Students combine the sentences.

ANSWERS

1 The film is about five young men who are hanging around Los Angeles because they hope to become actors.
2 I didn't want to be late for the theatre so I took a taxi.
3 John sat in the park and read a book.
4 The story, which begins in the 1920s, is about a Chicago gangster.
5 The hero fails to convince the police that a crime has occurred so he looks for more evidence.

3 Practice.

There may be more than one correct way of combining the sentences.

SUGGESTED ANSWERS

3 + 4   At a time when classical music was opening out to a new public, Rattle came along, catching their imagination in a way no other British conductor of his generation has achieved.

5 + 6   He worked with various symphony orchestras before joining the CBSO as principal conductor.

8 + 9   Turning down offers from other orchestras at home and abroad, he concentrated instead on transforming the CBSO's standing and international reputation.

10 + 11   . . . he led the CBSO from the Victorian Town Hall to its ultramodern new concert hall in the Convention Centre, thus decisively expanding the classical music audience of the city.

12 + 13   Despite leaving his full time post with the CBSO in 1998, and handing over the reigns to his successor, Sakari Oramo, he returns regularly as guest conductor.

14 + 15   He also works with a number of other orchestras, dividing his time between Birmingham, Vienna and Berlin.

WRITING (page 68)

Exam File: Part 2, Review

1 Class/group discussion: introduction to the topic.

It is probably best to discuss these questions before going through the **Exam File**.

2 Analysis of a model.

The answers to questions 1–5 are the kind of things that need to be included when writing any film review. Questions 6 and 7 draw attention to the effect on the target reader of the style and register.

ANSWERS

1 The director is Ron Shelton and the film stars Kevin Costner, Don Johnson and René Russo.
2 Romantic comedy.
3 Ron 'Tin Cup' McAvoy.
4 The film is set in rural Texas. The story is about a former golfing champion who failed to achieve success in his profession because of his character. He falls in love with a newcomer to town, but she doesn't return his love. So he decides to win the US Open Championship in order to impress her and make her fall in love with him.
5 The reviewer is very positive about the film and thinks that the performances are excellent.
6 The style is semi-formal, although some informal words and phrases are used such as *never better, spot on*. It is reasonably objective in tone, with *I* being used only once at the end.

3 Topic vocabulary.

Elicit definitions or explanations of the words listed, e.g.:

thriller: an exciting film with lots of suspense
epic: usually set in Ancient Rome or Greece, or possibly the American West, over a long period of time, full of heroic deeds.
animated film: cartoons / computer graphics
director: the person who tells the actors what to do
star: the most important actor / actress
leading man: the most important male actor when there is a female star
supporting cast: the actors who are not stars
extra: an actor who does not speak, in crowd scenes, for example
stunt man: someone who does dangerous things instead of the actors
screenplay: the script
dialogue: what the actors say
soundtrack: the music
special effects: amazing scenes that could not happen in real life
box office success: a film that makes a lot of money
flop: a film that nobody goes to see

Students work in pairs or groups to answer the questions.

4 Vocabulary: adjectives.

ANSWERS

Positive: moving, sophisticated, atmospheric, entertaining, spectacular, stylish, funny, unsentimental
Negative: predictable, heavy-handed, clichéd, slow, over-hyped, disappointing, sentimental

5 Creativity

5 Vocabulary: intensifiers.

ANSWERS

very: can be used with all the adjectives in Exercise 4
except *spectacular*
absolutely: predictable, spectacular, spine-chilling
completely/entirely: predictable, unsentimental, over-hyped
totally: predictable, clichéd, unsentimental, spectacular,
over-hyped
utterly: predictable, clichéd, unsentimental
highly: moving, predictable, sophisticated, atmospheric,
entertaining, disappointing
hugely: entertaining, over-hyped, disappointing
quite (moderately): can be used with all adjectives listed
except *over-hyped* and *spectacular*

6 Pair/group discussion.

This exercise gives students the opportunity to use the
vocabulary presented so far and is good preparation for
the writing task.

7 Writing task.

Step 1 Task interpretation

ANSWERS

target reader: students
purpose: to help readers decide whether to see the
film or read the book
register: fairly informal and lively

Step 3 Layout and organisation

Students should not need more than four paragraphs, e.g.:
Introduction: Mention the director, genre and main
actors. Or start off with an assessment to catch the
reader's attention.
Paras 2/3: Describe the plot.
Para 4: Give an assessment and
recommendation./Summarise and repeat your
recommendation in a different way.

Step 4 Write

Students combine the sentences. Encourage them to
think of different possibilities.

POSSIBLE ANSWERS

1
1 The book is about Mark Fletcher, who is searching for
his elder brother, Stephen.
2 Although Stephen disappeared five years ago, Mark is
convinced that he is still alive.
3 Beginning his search in London, Mark bravely
confronts the many dangers and difficulties that lie in
his path.
4 When he finally finds his brother, Mark discovers the
bitter truth.

2

MODEL ANSWER

The Beast From the Deep
Directed by Matt Webb
Starring Fiona Hurley, Jason Knight

If you like spine-chilling, stomach-churning horror,
with lots of spectacular special effects, then this is the
film for you! But if you are just a tiny bit squeamish,
you'd better give this one a miss!

It's set on board a nuclear submarine on routine patrol
in the Antarctic Ocean and stars Fiona Hurley as
captain of an all-male crew. The submarine is attacked
by a gigantic 100-metre-long sea-monster, half shark,
half octopus, and it turns out that the monster is also a
captain – of an alien spacecraft that crashed into the
ice two million years ago. It's been re-activated by the
energy from the submarine's nuclear power plant,
which it wants to power its spacecraft for the journey
back to its own planet.

Yes, the story is utterly ridiculous, but the special
effects make up for it. The acting is pretty wooden and
the dialogue makes you laugh in the wrong places, but
with Fiona Hurley to look at, who cares? The plot is
quite predictable, too. The sea-monster naturally takes
a fancy to Fiona – we've seen this before, in 'King
Kong'. There's a scientific genius on board, played by
Jason Knight, whose brilliant idea saves the day, and
the world – and of course Fiona. After the violent,
explosive climax, there's not much of the monster left,
or of the Antarctic either.

So there you are – bad acting, ridiculous story, but a
great night out if you like that sort of thing. I loved
every minute of it!

52

Exam Practice 1

If these tasks are done under exam conditions, 45 minutes should be enough.

READING

Part 1, Multiple matching

ANSWERS		
1	D	I wasn't getting enough support at Glasgow.
2/3	B, D	It was an exhausting regime, especially with two hours driving each day. At Glasgow it took ages to get to the swimming pool.
4	C	Some people would get up really early and get their work done before play started. Others would . . .
5/6	B, D	The university has been very helpful and given me an extension to complete my degree. However, the university has been very supportive . . . my exams so I was allowed to take them in August.
7	A	I'll keep on running for at least another ten years.
8/9	A, D	. . .your head feels woozy and it feels wonderful to run it all off I particularly enjoyed my training when I was revising for exams – it was good to get away from all the stress of studying.
10/11	A, B	This still left plenty of time for socialising. – and even got a bit of social life too.
12/13	B, C	I was on tour in Argentina in the summer term I missed the whole of the second term when I was chosen to tour New Zealand . . .
14	D	I would have liked to have got a sports scholarship to extend my degree for another year but . . .

ENGLISH IN USE

Part 1, Multiple choice cloze

ANSWERS
1 A   2 D   3 B   4 C   5 B   6 D   7 A   8 D   9 C 10 A   11 B   12 D   13 A   14 C   15 C

ENGLISH IN USE

Part 2, Structural cloze

ANSWERS
16 had   17 rather   18 Now   19 so   20 with   21 that 22 most   23 her   24 towards   25 much   26 without 27 it   28 myself   29 used   30 what

6 Commitments

SPEAKING (page 74)

1 Talk about photographs.

Students work in pairs, following the format of Part 2 of Paper 5. Tell students to make use of the items in the **Language Bank**. Remind them that they are allowed to disagree with each other in Part 2 when each makes a brief comment on what their partner has said.

▶▶ *Alternative procedure*

Treat this as a class discussion.

Photo 1 shows a mother and her baby.
Photo 2 shows a goalkeeper stretching for the ball in a football match.
Photo 3 shows an Australian lifeguard with a surfboard.
Photo 4 shows a nurse helping an elderly lady with a zimmer frame.

2 Quiz.

Tell students to do the quiz individually, then discuss and justify their choices in pairs or groups.

ENGLISH IN USE (page 75)

Part 4, Word formation

1 Read for general understanding.

The aim of the pre-question is to ensure that students read the text straight through to get a general idea of what it's about, before they do the task.

2 Word formation task.

Remind students to pay special attention to plurals.

> **ANSWERS**
>
> 1 ourselves   3 loyalty   5 tendency   7 justice
> 2 activities   4 choices   6 economic

3 Group discussion: response to the text.

READING 1 (page 76)

Part 4, Multiple matching

1 Predict/skim for gist.

1 Do this as a class. Don't spend too long on it.

2 Remind students that by reading any sub-headings or captions and the first and last line of each paragraph, they will be able to get a good idea of the main points in the article.

> **POSSIBLE ANSWERS**
>
> **2**
> **A** David Battup took total responsibility for childcare when his wife left. This hasn't had any effect on his career.
> **B** George Beattie works nights so that he can take care of his children during the day. He passed up the opportunity of promotion.
> **C** Tom Spenser leaves all the childcare to his wife unless it is completely unavoidable. He focuses on his career.
> **D** Stephen Lowe puts his daughter in his company's nursery. His company have helped him to balance career and fatherhood.

2 Multiple matching task.

Remind students they should read all the questions first. In this task, the key words and phrases have been highlighted for them. Elicit alternative ways of expressing these ideas as a preparation for the multiple matching task.

> **ANSWERS**
>
> 1 B   2 D   3 A   4 C   5 A   6 D   7 C   8 B   9 C
> 10 A   11 B   12 C   13 D   14 B

3 Task analysis.

> **ANSWER**
>
> Question 1: physical indication
> Text: . . . I began having stomach pains (lines 54–55)
> Question 2: on-site care
> Text: my company's childcare information service . . . helped us make the decision to put our baby into their workplace nursery (lines 153–6)
> Question 3: help
> Text: gave me a lot of support (line 13)
> Question 4: react to him differently
> Text: . . . become more spontaneous (lines 102–103)
> Question 5/6: understanding
> Text: supportive (line 24)
>   sympathetic (line 165)
> Question 7: plays the major role
> Text: . . . would focus on the children (lines 109–110)
> Question 8: limits his chances to socialise
> Text: . . . you feel excluded by the conversations (lines 70–71)
> Question 9: worrying about work
> Text: . . . you can't get work out of your mind (lines 118–119)
> Question 10: made him more aware of the feelings of others
> Text: I have learnt to . . . empathise with other people (lines 29–30)

Question 11: sleep deprivation
Text: . . . manage on a maximum of five hours sleep per night
Question 12: not satisfied with
Text: . . . have some regrets (line 120)
Question 13: out of place
Text: I feel like a fish out of water (lines 141–142)
Question 14: advancement
Text: promotion (line 86)

4 Vocabulary search.

ANSWERS

1 hold down
2 come to terms with
3 a whole new ball game
4 chit chat
5 miss out on
6 stick to your guns
7 pile up
8 fish out of water
9 drop someone off
10 the odd (telephone call)

5 Group discussion: response to the text.

Have students appoint a group secretary to report the group's conclusions briefly to the class. This is good practice for Paper 5.

VOCABULARY (page 78)

Prepositions

This exercise could be set for homework. All these prepositions have occurred in the text.

ANSWERS

1 to 2 on 3 to 4 for 5 into 6 on 7 of 8 with

PRONUNCIATION (page 78)

Elision (disappearing sounds)

The practice in this section will help students with Listening 1.

1 Elision within words.

Some words have letters which are not pronounced when you are speaking at normal speed although they are pronounced if you speak very slowly. Elision does not refer to silent letters, such as *h* in *honest* which are never pronounced, no matter how slowly you speak.

Point out to students that elision is a process of sound simplification which makes words easier to say. In particular, elision reduces the number of sounds in

TAPESCRIPT

See Students' Book.

ANSWERS

1/2 t   3–5 d   6 i   7 first e   8 o

2 Optional elision within words.

Both pronunciations of these words can be commonly heard. Students will probably prefer the easier ones – with elision.

TAPESCRIPT

long form	short form
1 asked	/ɑːskt/
2 clothes	/kləʊz/
3 often	/ˈɒfən/
4 necessary	/ˈnecəsriy/
5 secretary	/ˈsekrətri/

ANSWERS

1 asked
2 clothes
3 often
4 necessary
5 secretary

3 Elision between words.

Explain that elision happens between words as well as within words. An important fact about elision is that it can make the past simple and the present simple sound the same: *they seem nice* sounds the same as *they seemed nice* and *I packed ten shirts* sounds the same as *I pack ten shirts*. This means that students should listen for time words that go with certain tenses, such as *ago*, or *every day*.

This phenomenon occurs in extracts 5–8.

TAPESCRIPT

See Students' Book.

LISTENING 1 (page 79)

Part 1, Note completion

1 Introduction to the topic.

Use the photographs to introduce the topic of the Listening, and pre-teach key concepts.

Photo 1 shows a nuclear family (mother, father, daughter and son) having breakfast.
Photo 2 shows three, possibly four, generations of a

6 Commitments

family having a meal outdoors in Tuscany, to illustrate the 'extended family'.

2 Pre-teach vocabulary.

ANSWERS

1 **dependent children:** usually under eighteen, rely on their parents for support
2 **lone parent:** either mother or father caring for the child(ren) on his/her own
3 **step-family, step-parents, step-children:** family members as a result of remarriage
4 **childminder:** a person who is paid to look after the child(ren) while the parents are at work
5 **carer:** anybody including parents and childminders who looks after the child(ren)

3 📼 Note completion task.

Tell students to read through the notes before playing the recording. Elicit predictions about what information is needed to complete the gaps.

Students may have trouble with Number 6 – this requires a word that is not in the recording.

TAPESCRIPT

Presenter: The latest survey of social trends makes interesting reading. The major changes relate to the family. There has been a big increase in <u>one-person households,</u> that is, the number of people living alone. These <u>now account for twenty-eight per cent of all households.</u> The growth of these households has been at the expense of the traditional two-parent and two-children household. <u>The proportion containing a married couple with dependent children has now fallen to twenty-five per cent.</u> The commonest type of household now consists of a married couple with no dependent children. <u>Lone parents with children account for seven per cent of all households.</u>

More women are staying single, with an increase from <u>eighteen per cent to twenty-six per cent.</u> Throughout Europe, marriage rates have fallen overall, and <u>the age at which people marry has increased.</u> Women tend to marry at an earlier age than men and live longer than them. <u>More and more women are tending to delay having children,</u> at least until they are in their thirties, or are deciding to remain childless.

<u>Divorce rates have also increased slightly in the last ten years.</u> For every two marriages, there is now one divorce. <u>Eight per cent of children now live in step-families.</u>

This brief, statistical statement of trends should alert us to the way in which the family is changing and developing. Alongside the nuclear family, traditionally two parents and two children, a new social pattern is developing, that of the extended network of step-parents, step-children and other relatives. In a successful step-family, a child can have, possibly, four committed adults to rely on, rather than two. New relationships are

forged with step-brothers and sisters and there may well be new grandparents. <u>In fact, the grandmother is often the most important figure in the extended family,</u> often acting as the major carer when mothers go out to work.

<u>It seems that families are infinitely adaptable and that many different types are possible.</u> They may change and reform but, hopefully, its members continue to love and support one another.

ANSWERS

(See underlined words in the tapescript.)

1 28%   2 25%   3 7%   4 26%   5 later
6 in their thirties   7 divorce (rates)   8 8%
9 grandmother   10 adaptable

4 Discussion: comprehension check.

The aim is a) to check students have fully understood the recording, by asking them to recap the main points and suggest why the changes have happened b) to prepare for the task in Writing 1 by supplying some useful language patterns.

5 Follow-up discussion.

WRITING 1 (page 80)

Exam File: Parts 1 and 2, Report writing

Before going through the **Exam File**, remind students that they may be required to write a report in the exam. Find out if any of the students has experience of report writing. Ask the class to suggest

a) what are the main reasons for writing a report.

b) what are the main features of reports in terms of register and layout.

Students then read the **Exam File** to compare.

Step 1 Task interpretation

ANSWERS

target reader: researchers belonging to an international organisation
purpose: to supply information as part of a survey they are carrying out

Step 2 Generating ideas
Check students understand what the task requires them to cover. They can work individually or in pairs for this step.

Step 3 Layout and organisation
Tell students to head their report quite simply: *Report on trends in family life.* They can sign and date the report at the end, but they should not use *Yours faithfully* as in a letter.

Step 4 Write

1 Students compare the opening paragraphs and decide which is more appropriate to the task.

ANSWER

Paragraph A is better because it introduces the points that will be discussed in the report very clearly and is written in a more formal style.

---

2 Emphasise that over-long, complex sentences should be avoided in a report, as they can make it difficult to read quickly.

MODEL ANSWER

Report on trends in family life
Introduction
The aim of this report is to describe changes in family life over the last twenty-five years or so and to discuss the possible reasons for these changes.

Past and present
Traditionally the family consists of a mother and father and dependent children. Nowadays, there are rarely more than two children, whereas in the 1950s a family with four children would have been considered quite small and in the early years of the twentieth century it was common for women to have at least ten children, although not all would have survived infancy. These changes are explained by more effective birth control and the expense of bringing up children in the modern world.

Current trends
In the last couple of decades, there has been an increase in the number of one-parent families, mainly women with dependent children. This is partly explained by the increasing divorce rate. The government is concerned about the number of fathers who have lost contact with their children and do not support them financially because this has serious implications for the social security budget. There is also a tendency for couples to live together and have children but not get married. Because of this, the rise in the number of illegitimate births may not imply an increase in the number of one-parent households.

Conclusion
The effect of these changes is that the number of households is increasing and there is a greater variety of family types. This has implications for housing provision since a greater number of fairly small families means that there are more households that require somewhere to live.

READING 2 (page 81)

Exam File: Part 2, Gapped text

Use the **Exam File** to introduce this reading task type. CAE students generally find this task very difficult, but reassure them that they will be given a lot of help, guidance and practice during the course. In this section, the reading text has only five gaps and five missing paragraphs, so that students should be able to cope without too much difficulty. Point out that the practice they have already done on grammatical and lexical cohesion in Units 4 and 5 will stand them in good stead.

1 Introduction to the topic.

2 Skim and summarise.

It is important that students read through the main or base text to the end before they look at the missing paragraphs. Tell them to highlight or jot down on a piece of paper the key events will help them to form a clear idea of the story, which will make identifying the order of the missing paragraphs easier.

Elicit the main points by asking questions:

Where did Amanda go to work as an *au pair*?
Why was she surprised when she first arrived at the family's home?
How did the parents treat the adopted baby?
How much experience did Amanda have of childcare?
Why was the relationship between Amanda and the mother bad?
Who did Amanda blame for the situation?
What did Amanda do finally?

SAMPLE SUMMARY

Amanda, 18 years old, goes to work as an *au pair* in Boston. She's surprised to find there's no baby to look after. An adopted baby arrives and is treated like a new toy. Though she has little childcare experience, Amanda is left in charge of the baby. The baby becomes attached to her, and the mother becomes jealous. Life is made very difficult for Amanda who blames herself. She finally leaves the family.

---

3 Reading task.

Direct students' attention to the clues in brackets, which have been provided to help them. Tell students to highlight words and phrases that help them decide where the missing paragraphs fit.

When checking answers as a class, ask students to justify their answers with reference to the parts they have highlighted.

ANSWERS

1 D (gives us information about the family in Boston)
2 B (mentions the baby, which is also mentioned in the next paragraph)
3 C (continues to give information about Amanda's childcare responsibilities)
4 E (contains a clear lexical link with *the car* in the next paragraph.)
5 A (describes the solution to the problem Amanda talks about in the preceding paragraph)

Notes on the text:

You might need to explain the following points, which are, however, essential to completion of the task.

they would wheel me and the baby out: a colloquial expression which implies that people are being manipulated
an adopted new-born baby was delivered to the house: this expression makes it sound like a parcel from a mail-order catalogue.
Jaguar: an expensive British car. British *au pair* girls are unlikely to come from poor families, although North American employers may have this false impression.

4 **Vocabulary search.**

ANSWERS

1 a little apprehensive
2 put her at her ease
3 the couple behaved as if they had a new toy
4 like psychological warfare
5 took the blame on herself
6 guilty / great sense of loss

5 **Vocabulary extension.**

These items are ones that can cause confusion. This exercise is useful preparation for the discussion in Exercise 6.

ANSWERS

1 to blame 2 the blame, fault 3 fault 4 blaming

6 **Group discussion: response to the text.**

LANGUAGE STUDY 1 (page 84)

Refer students to the Notes on **Students' Book** page 204 before confirming their answers to the questions.

Substitution

1 **Analysis and practice.**

Discuss with students any differences between English and their own language in regard to what elements of a sentence can be substituted.

ANSWERS

a. play a supportive role
b. go round to other people's houses for coffee
c. stuck to my guns
1 *one* = interpretation of a situation (noun phrase)
2 *so* = the couple's friends were very surprised too (clause)
   Note: The subject and verb are inverted after *so.*
3 *the same* = that it's important that I spend more time with the children (clause)
4 *done* = seen the film; *if not* = if he hasn't seen the film (clauses)
5 *so* = put my family before work (clause)

Omission

2 **Analysis and practice.**

Again, take the opportunity to compare what is possible in English with what is possible in the students' language(s).

ANSWERS

a. was
b. cars which
1 work (verb)
2 he is (noun + verb)
3 finished the report (clause)
4 have been held up (verb)
5 did not accept the invitation (clause)

LISTENING 2 (page 84)

Exam File: Part 3, Sentence completion

This is the first Part 3 sentence completion task students have done, although they did Part 1 sentence completion tasks in Units 1 and 2. The information in the **Exam File** explains the differences. Remind them also that Part 3 Listenings are around 4 minutes long.

1 **Introduction to the topic.**

Students can work in pairs or groups to answer the questions, which help to prepare them for what they are going to hear.

2 **Sentence completion task.**

Elicit students' predictions about the missing information before playing the recording.

TAPESCRIPT

Interviewer: Today we have the third in our series of programmes in which fathers and sons talk about the profession that they have both chosen to follow, and in later programmes there will be some mothers and daughters. In the studio with me are Martin Forester and his son Sebastian, both violinists. Let me start with you, Martin. What was Sebastian like as a child?

Martin: Well, I have to say that <u>he was a very serious, very studious child – rather different from what he is like now</u>, I must say! He was always keen on music although conversations in the house must have left him with no illusions about how tough the life of a professional musician is. Even when he was a teenager, he wasn't any trouble – he just kept on practising and studying. We always got on well, except that in his teens he would sometimes <u>go for days without talking – he has certainly changed in that respect too.</u>

Sebastian: <u>Yes, I'm afraid Dad gives me a harder time now than when I was younger.</u>

Interviewer: Oh, why is that?

Sebastian: I think it's because I make more money than him!

Martin: No, no, that's not it. I'm pleased he's been so successful, but it hasn't surprised me. He has always worked hard and he deserves his success. <u>It's just that I've always worked in a very traditional way, with classical orchestras and so on whereas Sebastian, although he can do what I do, has a different approach.</u>

Sebastian: Yeah, <u>Dad nearly went through the roof when I told him I was going to play with a rock group. He just hates pop music – it's strictly classical for him.</u>

Martin: That's right. <u>Although I did overreact a bit because I misunderstood what Sebastian was telling me.</u>

Sebastian: Yeah, Dad thought I was giving up classical music completely and becoming a permanent member of the group but in fact I was just playing for the group on one record on which they needed my style of music. Even for me it was a new thing to do, and I did have some doubts about it when their agent first approached me. But that record stayed in the charts for nine months and because of that, for the first time in my life, <u>I made serious amounts of money.</u>

Martin: <u>And also Sebastian's name became very widely known.</u> A lot of people go to his classical concerts because they heard him first on the pop record.

Sebastian: Yeah, for Dad that was the best thing about it. But the other good thing is that now I can pick and choose what I want to do because I've got a degree of financial security. I know it wasn't always like that for Dad.

Martin: When Sebastian was young I was often away on tour and sometimes the tours were overseas and could be quite long. I didn't like being away from home but that is how it was for a professional musician. The kind of work Sebastian does is different. He does a lot of recording, work for films and television, that sort of thing. <u>He can choose whether he wants to go on tour or not. I couldn't do that.</u>

Interviewer: I understand that you've had a big disagreement quite recently, haven't you?

Sebastian: Yes, but it wasn't really serious.

Martin: Well, I don't know about that! I was really shocked I couldn't believe what you'd done!

Interviewer: What did you do?

Sebastian: Well, you know how musicians at classical concerts are supposed to wear formal evening dress, you know, tails, white bow tie, and so on. <u>Well, I've always thought this was a bit silly, and it is not very comfortable either, so I just wore jeans and a tee-shirt when I played at a concert. Dad was horrified.</u>

Martin: Yes, I was and not just me! Quite a lot of people in the audience walked out and the leader of that orchestra has refused to let Sebastian play with them again. I think it is really important to maintain the traditional standards.

Sebastian: I know you do, Dad, but I don't and I don't need to worry about one orchestra not wanting to play with me. It makes no difference to me. I don't depend on them.

Interviewer: And wasn't there an incident involving press photographers?

Sebastian: Yes, but that may lead to a court case, so we can't really talk about it. My lawyers are handling it.

Martin: <u>It was another regrettable incident, although it does seem that it wasn't Sebastian's fault, not in my view, anyway.</u> He has a big public image, which I never did, so I feel at a loss to advise him on how to handle these matters. I've never really had to deal with the press at all. But, you know, although Sebastian is now 28, I sometimes think he is going through a delayed adolescence. I never thought someone who was so quiet and studious as a child and teenager would turn out like this.

Interviewer: So he has surprised you?

Martin: In that respect, yes. But I am not surprised that he is such an excellent violinist, one of the best in the world, I'm sure. I knew he would be even when he was very small.

Interviewer: Martin and Sebastian Forester, thank you very much.

ANSWERS

(See underlined words in the tapescript.)

1 serious/studious	6 misunderstanding
2 talkative	7 rich and famous
3 critical	8 freedom of choice
4 traditional/conventional	9 wore/was wearing
5 badly/strongly	10 not to blame

3 **Group discussion: response to the text.**

LANGUAGE STUDY 2 (page 85)
Making suggestions and recommendations

The structures in this section will be useful for the task in Writing 2, Students' Book pages 87–88.

Refer students to the Notes on **Students' Book** page 204.

1 Analysis: *suggest*.

Mistakes with *suggest* are very common in students' work.

In particular, warn students not to use the infinitive after *suggest*.

ANSWERS

Sentences 2 and 5 are not correct.
a) *suggest* something *to* someone but not *to* + infinitive
b) that, should
c) there is no *s* on the third person verb in 6 because it is a reduced version of *he should wait*
d) gerund, *that*-clause
e) yes

Giving advice

2 Analysis: *advise/advice*.

Mistakes with *advice* and to *advise* are also very common. Make sure students know the pronunciation difference between the verb and the noun.

Check the answers to Questions a) and b). Then tell students to work in pairs to answer Question c) which gives them the opportunity to apply the structures that have been focussed on.

Refer students to the Notes on **Students' Book** page 205.

ANSWERS

1 I advise you to go to university and get more qualifications.
2 Let me give you some good advice: don't become an actor!
4 I'd advise you to accept the offer.
a) *advise* + object + infinitive
Also possible are: *advise* + *that* + clause/*advise* (+ object) + *against* + gerund
b) *advice* with *c* = noun; *advise* with *s* = verb
Other similar pairs include: *practice/practise, licence/license, device/devise*

3 Practice.

Students complete the sentences in their own way.

Giving warnings

4 Practice.

The aim is to check students realise that *warn* is used for bad things, rather than *advise*.

Refer students to the Notes on **Students' Book** page 205.

ANSWERS

1 warning   5 warning
2 warning   6 warnings
3 warned   7 warning
4 warn   8 warning
Warn is for danger and other bad things. *Advise* can be used in both good and bad contexts.

Concession

5 Analysis and practice.

Point out to students that although *despite* and *in spite of* mean the same and are both followed by the same grammatical patterns, they must use one or the other. The common mistake made by students is to write or say *despite of*. This is the kind of mistake that may be tested in Paper 3, Part 3 (error correction).

Refer students to the Notes on **Students' Book** page 205.

ANSWERS

1
In spite of the fact that the course costs a lot, I'd advise you to apply for it.
In spite of / Despite the cost of the course, I'd advise you to apply for it.
2
1 In spite of the fact that you have failed your exams, I suggest you carry on with the course.
2 Even though your life is difficult at the moment, my advice is to be patient.
3 Despite the long journey to work, I'd advise you to accept the job.
4 In spite of the danger, I think you should take the risk.

6 Extension.

The aim is to show that the same idea can be expressed in a variety of ways.

POSSIBLE ANSWERS

1 However well-prepared you think you are, I warn you not to travel in that part of the desert.
2 Hitch-hiking may be an opportunity to travel around cheaply, but I advise against it because of the risks.
3 However many times you've travelled abroad, you can still get homesick.
4 No matter how tired you are, you should never fall asleep when you're travelling alone.

7 Group/pair discussion/role-play.

This is an opportunity for students to use in speech the patterns they have just practised in writing.

WRITING 2 (page 87)

Exam File: Part 1, Informal letter

Step 1 Task interpretation

Note that *Love* would probably not be used by a man. He would use *Best wishes* or *Cheers*.

ANSWERS

1
text type: informal letter
purpose: to offer advice to a friend
register: informal, chatty
begin/end: Dear Francesca . . . Love . . .

2
I've got lots of addresses / Mum and Dad have hit the roof / They go on and on / I know there won't be any problems / I can just get jobs / I bet you're envious / it will be the adventure of a lifetime

Step 2 Selecting and summarising

Let students work in pairs for this step.

Step 3 Layout and organisation

Point out that students don't necessarily have to follow the suggested plan. You could go through the Language Bank at this point.

Step 4 Write

MODEL ANSWER

Dear Francesca

It was lovely to hear from you, and this time you really had some interesting things to tell me. I can understand that your parents are worried about your travelling round the world but you will be pleased to hear that I think you have made the right decision. Now is a good time for you to travel, before you start studying at university.

However, I am not sure that you have thought carefully enough about what travelling involves. No doubt that is why you are asking me for advice! You imply in your letter that you are going to travel alone. Have you thought about travelling with someone else? Having a companion can make things a lot easier – and safer. Also, why not live, and work, in one country instead of keeping on the move all the time? Staying in one place means you can make friends and get to know a different language and culture much better and if you have a job, you will always have some money to live on. Your parents would be happier with that because they would know where to contact you. If you are constantly travelling, they won't know where you are. This is a possible compromise that you might consider.

Globetrotting is very exciting – I wish I were going with you! On the other hand, there are serious dangers. I have just heard from another friend who has been robbed of everything except the clothes he is wearing, just because he fell asleep on a long-distance coach journey. Keep in touch.

Best wishes

7 Home sweet home

SPEAKING 1 (page 89)

1 Talk about photographs.

Although not in precise exam format, this is useful practice for Part 2 of the Speaking Test.

Photo 1 was taken in the 1950s and shows a housewife wearing an apron. She is vacuuming with an old-fashioned upright vacuum cleaner.

Photo 2 is contemporary and shows a young man loading a dishwasher.

2 Pre-teach vocabulary.

The aim is to check understanding of vocabulary items which appear in the Reading text.

Notes:

skirting board: a narrow piece of wood which conceals the gap between the wall and floor in many homes in Britain.

hoover: the verb derives from the trade mark name of the company which manufactured them originally. It is more commonly used than *vacuum* in British English. All vacuum-cleaners can be called hoovers in British English, regardless of which company makes them.

3 Group/pair discussion.

Notes:

Quote 1 is intended to be provocative in a humorous way. It should not be taken entirely seriously.

one of the old school: a person with old-fashioned ideas

4 Continuation of discussion.

READING (page 90)

Part 1, Multiple matching

This is a difficult text in terms of vocabulary and it is important to prepare students carefully so that they get a good grasp of the main idea: from an early age women are made to feel housework is important, but men are not.

1 Skim for main ideas.

Tell students to read the text quickly and highlight parts of the text that help them to answer the questions. Set a time limit of 5 minutes to encourage them to skim.

ANSWERS

1 According to the article practically all this work is still being done by women. (lines 24–25)
2 They feel guilty if they don't do them. Students could have highlighted the following lines:
I buy all those plastic bottles to make myself feel better about not doing much housework. (lines 9–12)
So they sit there . . . silently reproaching me for not being able to remember when I last cleaned the bath. (lines 17–20)
But the skirting boards still make me feel anxious. (lines 68–69)
It could also be argued women also feel guilty if they do do housework:
A major reason I have a job outside the home is that I know that otherwise I'd spend all day wiping my skirting boards. (lines 63–66)
The older I get, . . . But I despise myself for it. (lines 97–100)
3 The importance of keeping up appearances and being respectable has been impressed upon them from an early age. (See lines 131–144.)

2 Pre-teach vocabulary.

Notes:

hob: the top of the cooker
U-bend: part of the pipe under a sink
chrome fixtures: taps, shower attachments made of chrome

ANSWERS

kitchens: hob, laminated surfaces, food processor
bathroom: U-bend
both: sink, chrome fixtures

3 Multiple matching task.

Tell students to read the questions and highlight key words. Check understanding by asking a few questions, such as:

1 What's the verb from *repetitive*? Why do housework chores have to be repeated? (mess up)
2 What manufacturers are being referred to? (of household cleaners). What claims do they make for their products?
3 What differences do you think are referred to here? (Women believe housework should not be important, but still feel guilty if they don't do it.)
4 What does *partner* mean? (It is now used very widely to refer to a husband or wife as well as an unmarried companion). Why would a women let her partner get away with not doing household tasks?

Emphasise that highlighting the names in the text is vital for this kind of task. It enables students to find information quickly.

ANSWERS

1	D	There's something very repetitive about performing a task only so that it can be messed up. (lines 80–83)
2	A	though the surfaces look pretty much the same to me. (lines 7–8)
3/4	A,G	Women may be company directors . . . and talk about equality but when it comes to housework, they just carry on getting out the Hoover. (lines 25–32) . . . and found that girls continue to do significantly more despite professed beliefs in sexual equality (lines 121–124)
5	B	I sometimes wonder if I encourage his incompetence because it makes me think he needs me. (lines 55–58)
6	C	A major reason I have a job outside the home is that otherwise I'd spend all day wiping my skirting boards. (lines 63–66)
7	H	Women were the guardians of this respectability, and their ability to keep the house smart was a key factor. (lines 137–140)
8/9	B,F	. . . he just wouldn't notice it was thick with grease and dust (lines 60–62) Men simply don't think . . . we don't even discuss it. (lines 107–112)
10	C	I employ a cleaner three time a week, so I can think it's her fault (lines 69–71)
11	F	it's a very personal, individual matter (lines 110–111)
12	E	. . . I find myself reverting to type and worrying about my home. But I despise myself for it. (lines 98–100)
13	E	feelings about social class confuse her attitude to housework (lines 84–86)
14/15	E,G	I grew up in a lower middle-class household where my mother cleaned and tidied up manically (lines 86–89) Professor Emler believes domestic attitudes are impressed on children very early. (lines 128–130)

4 **Group discussion.**

Encourage students to think about the way they themselves were brought up to regard household chores. You can widen the discussion to other differences in the upbringing of boys and girls.

5 **Vocabulary search.**

Students should highlight the phrases in the text. Note that this kind of practice is useful for Paper 3, Part 5 (register cloze), which tests understanding of register.

ANSWERS

1 pretty much the same
2 when it comes to
3 carry on
4 thick with grease and dust
5 messy
6 reverting to type
7 little impact
8 comes down to
9 can live with
10 as good as new

ENGLISH IN USE 1 (page 92)

Part 3, Error correction

1 **Revise spelling rules.**

Tell students to check their answers by referring to the Notes on **Students' Book** page 213.

1 Similar-looking words

ANSWERS

1 thorough 2 thought, through 3 Although
4 throughout 5 throughout

2 *i* before *e*

ANSWERS

The rule is *i* before *e* except after *c* when the sound is /iː/. The rule is based on sound and does not apply if *ie* has a different sound.

3 Doubling final consonants

ANSWERS

~~bake, leak, deal~~
We double final consonants when the last two letters of a word are a single vowel followed by a consonant.

4 Final *-e*

ANSWERS

We drop the final *-e* when the syllable to be added begins with a vowel.

5 Homophones

ANSWERS

1 wear 2 court 3 write 4 site

7 Home sweet home

6 Silent letters

ANSWERS

bombed / debt / castle / chemical
(Possible answers) chorus / character / comb / tomb /
wrestle

7 Suffixes

ANSWERS

A acceptance
B inventor

2 Practice: identify spelling errors.

ANSWERS

popped, neighbour, caught, guard, believe, screamed,
poisonous, making, thorough, there

3 Practice: identify punctuation errors.

ANSWERS

1 '. . . housework,' said Helen Butler. 'It's . . .'
2 'Is this Jane's bag?' 'No, it isn't, it's mine.'
3 its fur.
4 Mexican

4 Error correction task.

This task type includes both spelling and punctuation
errors in the same text. There is only one error per line.
Tell students it is important to read the whole text first as
with other Paper 3 tasks. The question provides a reason
for reading.

Draw students' attention to the three examples, which
show how to correct each type of error.

ANSWERS

1
The title is a pun on *bored* and *boa constrictor*.
2

1 ✓	6 menagerie" when	11 redundant
2 their	7 week, "The	12 supervisor
3 fascination	8 It's	13 accountant
4 ✓	9 ✓	14 company. A
5 collecting	10 ✓	15 Indian

VOCABULARY 1 (page 94)

Phrasal verbs with *up*

1 Analysis.

Students read the examples and match the phrasal verb
particles to the meanings given.

ANSWERS

1 pile up (A)
2 messed up (B – destruction)
3 grew up (A) / cleaned (up), tidied up (B – completion)

2 Practice.

1
Remind students that they may have to change the form
of the verb.
2
A useful hint is that where *up* acts as an intensifier, it is
often optional. For example, you can say 'They decided
to *sell* their business'. Adding *up* adds a greater sense of
finality, but is not essential to the meaning of the verb.

ANSWERS

1 and 2
1 do (A) (= improve)
2 step (A) (= increase)
3 turned (A) (= raise)
4 clear (B)
5 draw (B)
6 signed (B)
7 looking (A) (= improve)
8 keep (A)
9 sell (B)
10 back (B) (= support)

PRONUNCIATION (page 94)

Linking words up

1 Analysis.

There are four types of linking in spoken English:

1 Final consonant sounds + following vowels:
he's^always.
2 Linking /j/ sound between the last vowel sound of one
word and the first vowel sound of the next: my own car
= myyown car.
3 Linking final /r/ which is only pronounced when
followed by a vowel sound: her own home = herown
home.
4 Linking /w/ sound between the last vowel sound of
one word and the first vowel sound of the next: go in =
gowin.

You can also hear an intrusive /r/ sound, which is not in the spelling, in such phrases as: law and order (can sound like 'laura norder').

Students can improve their fluency and rhythm by linking words up in these ways, rather than pronouncing each word separately.

TAPESCRIPT

See Students' Book.

Weak forms

2  **Practice.**

Using weak forms will help students sound more natural in English.

TAPESCRIPT

See Students' Book.

3 🖾 **Practice.**

The aim is to alert students to the weak forms that they will hear in the recording. It is also an opportunity to pre-teach vocabulary items. Explain that the Listening is about the benefits of building houses underground. Check understanding before playing the recording.

TAPESCRIPT

See Students' Book.

ANSWERS

1 linking: secure^and
2 weak forms: for; people've; a
3 linking: are^energy^efficient
4 of; of
5 linking: better^insulation
6 linking: are^all; space^underground
  weak forms: of

LISTENING (page 95)

Part 1, Note completion

1 Introduction to the topic.

2 🖾 **Note completion task.**

Remind students of the word limit.

TAPESCRIPT

Presenter: Underground houses can be comfortable, secure and convenient but few people live below ground. There has long been a prejudice against it. For centuries, people have held a deep-rooted belief that living below ground is wet and unhealthy. Local planners seem to continue this attitude, which is unfortunate as such homes can have many benefits. And public interest in such houses is growing.

One benefit of underground houses is that they are virtually invisible on the landscape. This means that the houses fulfil the ecological need of preserving the landscape.

Another benefit is the fact that such houses are energy efficient. Earth is a dense material with a high thermal mass. This means that it requires a lot of energy to warm or cool it. But it is also a relatively poor conductor. This means that temperatures underground remain steady. This has big implications for the cost of heating an underground home. Compared with an average above-ground home, heating costs are reduced by seventy-five per cent. Those houses that do get constructed underground are usually lit by natural light coming through glass panels in the roof, which means that the houses are light and airy. In the country, glass roofs can provide astonishing views of wildlife, something most owners find really interesting and enjoyable.

In the city, there is increasing acceptance of the usefulness of building below ground. Urban planners now recognise that this type of building allows houses to be constructed much closer together. Estimates indicate that houses can be built at double the level of density of houses above ground. Despite the compactness, better insulation means that any problem of noise from the neighbours is virtually non-existent.

In the city, public buildings underground are necessary because of lack of space for development above. Parking areas, exhibition space, cinemas and libraries are all making profitable use of space underground and are a success with users. The traditional need for natural light is being overcome by producing a feeling of spaciousness through the use of mirrors and by using lighting that emits full-spectrum light, which is similar to natural light. All this leads to a reduction in the feelings of claustrophobia usually associated with being underground.

From the middle of the twenty-first century, we should expect more and more homes to be built underground.

ANSWERS

(See underlined words in the tapescript.)

1 prejudice	6 views of wildlife
2 wet (and) unhealthy	7 buildings in the city
3 seen	8 lack of space
4 75%	9 using mirrors
5 glass panels	

3 Comprehension check.

The aim is to check that students have understood the information in the recording by encouraging them to summarise the main points. The vocabulary items will help them.

4 Group discussion: response to the Listening.

Speaking 2 (page 95)

Part 3, Express priorities; Part 4, Report conclusions

1 Collaborative task.

The questions are designed to encourage students to discuss the themes suggested by the pictures, not simply what the pictures show. This is the difference between FCE and CAE.

Photo 1 shows the interior of a minimalist-style house, with bare floorboards. Two walls are glass and overlook the garden. There is very little furniture in the room and just one pot plant.

Photo 2 shows the exterior of a large old wooden house in the country. It is in poor condition and looks rather ramshackle, but full of character.

2 Report back.

To simulate exam conditions two pairs can form a group of four for this part of the task.

Language Study (page 96)

Talking about the future

Refer students to the Notes on **Students' Book** pages 205–206.

1 Analysis: future forms.

The aim is to check and revise students' understanding of the form and use of these tenses.

> **ANSWERS**
>
> **1** and **2**
> 1 Future Perfect
>   they will have finished (para 3); Kawabata will have designed (para 7)
>   = a point in the future when sth will be completed
> 2 Future Simple
>   everything will be glass (para 1); I'll get visitors (para 4);
>   it won't break (para 5); you won't be able to see (para 5);

> one wall will function (para 6); you'll be able to download (para 6)
> = a prediction
> I'll take it (para 2)
> = a spontaneous decision
> 3 Present Continuous with future reference
>   is having a house built (para 1)
>   = an existing personal arrangement
> 4 'going to' future
>   people are going to be amazed, I'm sure of that (para 4)
>   = certainty based on present evidence
> 5 Future Continuous
>   I'll be living (para 4); I'll be moving in straightaway
>   = a planned event in progress in the future
> 6 Present Simple with future reference
>   The builders arrive next Monday (para 3)
>   = a future event scheduled now
> **3**
> 1 possible
> 2 probable/possible

2 Practice.

Students can do this in pairs.

> **ANSWERS**
>
> **Group 1:** 1, 2, 6, 8, 9, 10
> **Group 2:** 3, 7
> **Group 3:** 4, 5, 11

Future time in subordinate clauses

3 Analysis: tenses in future time clauses.

The aim is to warn students against the common mistake of using *will* after temporal conjunctions.

> **ANSWERS**
>
> 1 Each clause has future reference.
> 2 a. present simple + future continuous
>   b. 'going to' future + present simple
>   c. future simple + present simple
>   d. future simple + present simple
>   e. future simple + present perfect
>   f. present perfect + future perfect
> 3 Because the verb in the main clause is a future form, it is unnecessary to use a future form in the subordinate clause. This is called redundancy.
> 4 It indicates that one action is completed before another.

4 Practice.

ANSWERS

1
1 I *will phone* you as soon as I *get* the results.
2 He *will not be* satisfied until he *gets* all his money back.
3 Once he *wins* the gold medal he *will retire*.
4 After you *pass/have passed* the test, you *will receive* a certificate.

Speculating about future trends

5 Practice: discussion.

The aim is for students to use in speech the future forms they have been practising.

6 Extension of the discussion.

This exercise could be set for homework.

WRITING 1 (page 98)

Part 2, Article

Begin by revising the features of an article. See **Exam File**, Unit 4, **Students' Book** page 54.

Step 1 Task interpretation

ANSWERS

text type:	article for a magazine
target readers:	students in various different countries
purpose:	to inform (and entertain)
register/tone:	semi-formal

Step 2 Generating ideas
Elicit the four areas students have to write about (location, design, labour-saving devices, home entertainment). Remind them that highlighting the key points in the question is a good idea. They can then tick them off when they check their work.

Let students brainstorm ideas in pairs. They can look back at earlier sections in the unit for ideas and useful vocabulary if they wish.

Step 3 Layout and organisation
Tell students they now need to select from the ideas they have generated, as they only have 250 words. They should choose the most interesting and important ideas.

Step 4 Write
Remind students that their first paragraph needs to be interesting enough to attract readers' attention and make them want to read on. (See Unit 4, **Students' Book** page 54.)

Remind them also that their article should not simply end abruptly once they have written 250 words! It is equally important to bring it to an effective close. They can do this for example by asking a question, or summarising the main point in a single sentence. (See model answer below.)

MODEL ANSWER

Homes of the future
Where will we live fifty years from now?
If present trends continue, more and more people will move out of big cities. Where will they go? Not to isolated, faraway places as you might think – even with the benefits of modern technology, there are still real disadvantages to living in very remote areas. The favoured destination seems to be small towns, which offer a more peaceful lifestyle and less pollution.

What will our houses look like?
On the outside, the homes of the future will probably look much the same as now. Impersonal, ultra-modern designs, however stylish, seem to have only minority appeal – most people prefer traditional designs with plenty of character. Current trends suggest that people will simply adapt existing houses by installing sophisticated modern equipment based on computer technology.

More help around the house . . .
Computer technology means that housework and cooking will become things of the past. Chores such as hoovering and even drawing the curtains will be computer controlled. You won't even need to be at home to do them! Just tap an instruction into your laptop and the dinner will be cooked when you arrive home!

. . . means more time to relax!
There will be plenty of things to do with all this leisure! Advanced forms of electronic entertainment will offer a huge choice of programmes, right in your own home. The Internet will give people access to books, works of art and all kinds of information. Cinemas, art galleries and museums may well disappear altogether!

What a great future to look forward to! And it may come sooner than you think!

ENGLISH IN USE 2 (page 98)

Exam File: Register cloze

Introduce this new task type by going through the **Exam File** with the class.

1 Preparation.

The aim is to show the way in which the same ideas can be expressed formally or informally, as preparation for the exam style task that follows.

ANSWERS
2 *gave up*
3 *get to*
4 *it going*
5 *turned up*
6 *get*
7 *the most*
8 *get in*

2 Register cloze task.

Tell students to follow the advice in the **Exam File** and read both texts all the way through before starting on the task. Elicit a summary and check comprehension of any new vocabulary before letting them do the gap fill. Let students work in pairs. Remind them of the two-word word limit. They should find alternatives for the italicised words in Text 1 to fill in the gaps in Text 2. (Note that this help is not provided in the exam.)

ANSWERS
1 two weeks
2 belongs to
3 look round / look at
4 terrible mess
5 locked / shut
6 woman
7 next door / nearby
8 let us
9 plates
10 dirty
11 complain / get upset
12 give him
13 end

VOCABULARY 2 (page 100)

This section is useful preparation for the task in Writing 2.

Still

1 Analysis and practice.

The aim is to revise the various uses of *still*.

ANSWERS
1
Still expresses irritation in sentences 1 and 5. In sentence 2, you could substitute *Oh well*. Sentence 3 could be paraphrased as *another five minutes*. In sentence 4, you could say *yet worse*.
2
1 He's *still* on the phone – I wish he'd get off!
2 My letter *still* hasn't arrived – I wonder what on earth has happened to it! I hope it hasn't got lost in the post!
3 Oh, no! The queue *still* hasn't got any shorter.

It's time

2 Practice.

Point out the mismatch between time and tense. The expression refers to present time.

ANSWERS
1 It's (high) time you learned.
2 It's (about) time he finished it.
3 It's (about) time she got a job.
4 It's (high) time you did.

WRITING 2 (page 100)

Part 2, Informal letter

You may need to explain that it is very common for young people in Britain to share flats, rather than living at home with their parents. Sharing helps to make rent and bills affordable.

Step 1 Task interpretation

ANSWERS	
text type:	letter
target reader:	friend
purpose:	to ask for advice
register/tone:	informal
begin/end:	Dear (first name) / Best wishes/Love

Step 2 Generating ideas

Let students work in pairs for this stage.

Step 3 Layout and organisation

Remind students that in a letter to a friend the first paragraph will usually contain some sort of greeting and one or two questions about the other person, perhaps an apology for not writing sooner. Elicit some ideas, e.g.:

How are things with you? I do hope you're well, and enjoying life.

How did you do in your driving test? / Have you been doing anything interesting lately?

(See also the model answer below.)

You can then move on to your own news in the second paragraph.

Step 4 Write

You could extend the activity in Exercise 1 and elicit or present further useful vocabulary. See the model answer below for some more useful expressions.

▶▶ *Extension activity*

Have students exchange their letters with a partner. Each student then writes a reply offering advice and suggestions based on the specific problems described in their partner's letter. You could read out the reply/replies that contain(s) the best advice.

MODEL ANSWER

Dear Fiona

I'm so sorry I haven't written for ages. You're probably wondering what's happened to me!

Well, I've got a problem and I need your advice. As you can see from my address, I've moved to a new flat. It's a really nice place, bright and airy, but the rent is quite expensive. So about three months ago, I invited Susanna to move in with me and share the bills – she's a friend of mine from college. And now I wish I hadn't!

She's so inconsiderate! The worst thing is that she plays music in her room at top volume. Sometimes it wakes me up at 7 in the morning! If I want some peace and quiet, I have to leave the flat. She <u>will</u> turn it down if I ask her to, but next time it's as loud as before. She just doesn't seem to get the message.

On top of that, she's extremely untidy and messy and she never cleans up after herself. Going into the kitchen after she's used it is <u>not</u> a nice expereience. I've dropped all kinds of hints but it hasn't done any good at all.

I really don't want a big confrontation, but I can't see any way of avoiding it. Things can't go on like this! I know you've had a lot of experience of dealings with difficult people. Have you got any suggestions? I need something tactful but effective. If you can help, I'll take you out for a slap-up meal.

Best wishes,
Johanna

8 Honesty, the best policy

SPEAKING (page 101)

1 Talk about photographs.

This is useful practice for Part 3 of the Speaking Test. Refer students to the **Language Bank**. Check they understand expressions such as *have no qualms about* (not be worried about).

Photo 1 shows a Neighbourhood Watch sign. Neighbourhood Watch is a scheme operated in many residential communities in the UK, in which people agree to watch for any suspicious activity near their neighbours' houses when they are away. It is supported by the police and insurance companies offer lower premiums for household insurance in such areas.

Photo 2 shows a door with a bunch of keys hanging from the lock.

Photo 3 shows a police car in a high street.

Photo 4 shows a book on karate, a method of self-defence.

2 Class/group discussion.

The aim here is to encourage students to move away from the content of the pictures towards discussing the theme more generally.

3 Extension of discussion.

The aim is to encourage students to express personal opinions, which they are free to do in the Speaking Test. The expressions *dial 999* and *turn a blind eye* appear in the Reading text that follows.

READING 1 (page 102)

Exam File: Multiple choice questions

Discuss the suggested method of approaching this task type. (See also **Exam File** Unit 3, **Students' Book** page 36.)

1 Skim for gist.

The aim is to encourage students to use the title and opening paragraphs to predict what is in the article.

2 Pre-teach vocabulary.

These colloquial expressions are commonly seen in newspaper and magazine articles. You could explain that the colloquial term *a grass* comes from the title of an old song called 'Whispering grass'.

ANSWERS

1 F   2 E   3 A   4 B   5 C   6 D

3 Multiple choice questions.

Point out to students that they need to find textual support for the option that they choose. Tell them to highlight the relevant parts of the text so they can justify their answers when you check the task.

ANSWERS

2   B   Sylvia couldn't believe what she was hearing. (lines 25–26)
3   D   Even though . . . Sylvia felt no remorse. (lines 62–64)
4   C   Sylvia looked like every other middle-aged housewife on the estate where she lived. (lines 84–87)
5   C   But those sorts of threats won't stop Sylvia informing. (lines 112–113)
6   B   if I can prevent my children growing up in a world of crime, then I'll do so. (lines 138–141)

Notes on the text:

Penny Black: a rare and valuable type of stamp, as well as a possible name, indicating Sylvia's great value to the police

I'll do your kneecaps in: shooting people through the kneecaps (from back to front) is a common punishment in terrorist and criminal gangs

in plain clothes: not in uniform (used about police and military personnel

4 Group discussion: response to the text.

Students can discuss these questions in groups of four. Encourage them to use vocabulary from the text.

LISTENING 1 (page 104)

Part 1, Note completion

1 Introduction to the topic.

The aim is to get students thinking about the topic of the Listening. You could pre-teach: *prospective husband, put sb under surveillance, vet* (v.) and *misdemeanour* during the discussion.

2 Pre-teach vocabulary: adjectives describing people.

3 🔲 Sentence completion task.

While checking answers, you can point out the use of the colloquial expressions *get cold feet, do something behind someone's back* (Question 8).

TAPESCRIPT

Presenter: Johnnie and Lina met on a train. He was charismatic, good-looking, debonair; she was bookish, conventional, reserved. It was an attraction of opposites; they fell in love, got married. Then Lina's dream became a nightmare. Who were Johnnie's mysterious business contacts? Was he after her money? Or was she losing her mind?

Yes, it's film director Alfred Hitchcock's paranoia classic, *Suspicion*. But it could also be a case for private investigator Caroline Hodge. Three years ago, <u>after watching a documentary about rich women in Florida she devised a special package for women who want to check out their prospective husbands.</u> It can cost less than a wedding hair-do: the result is a 'Pre-Marital Status Report'.

The woman supplies her fiancé's name, address and employment history. The investigator checks out <u>previous marriages, debts and name changes.</u> If checks reveal possible problems or if information cannot be found, <u>customers may want to opt for surveillance. The man will be followed, photographed and even befriended by an investigator.</u>

Caroline Hodge says she has overcome the traditional image of private detective agencies by <u>making sure that clients consult with female staff</u> (although surveillance is usually carried out by men). She says that she doesn't need to advertise, getting two or three major vetting jobs each month, and a handful of straightforward cases in which the man is found to be honest.

The appeal of the service is obvious. <u>Career girls stand to lose the home they have worked hard for, their savings, investments and treasured possessions. Of the men found to be less than honest, her experience shows that about ten per cent are cold and calculating.</u> The rest are looking for a good thing. They are weak and selfish.

Hodge says that she will turn some clients away. She will reassure someone who comes to them and has no grounds for suspicion. It's normal to get cold feet just before your wedding. <u>She also discourages parents from having reports done behind their daughters' backs.</u> The women who use the service are <u>typically aged between thirty and fifty</u>, with at least one divorce behind them. They have stressful jobs as, for example, accountants, directors, PAs, interpreters. Hodge explains that they are women who have put off getting married or involved because they have been on the career ladder. They've bought their own home and car and have money in the bank. Yet despite clear evidence of unsuitability, Caroline Hodge knows that some of her clients won't make the right choice. The older ones go ahead and marry them anyway. <u>But she never intervenes, just presents the facts.</u> She won't tell you not to get married and she can't guarantee that your marriage will work. But as she says, 'At the end of the day, if we can stop one lady from getting involved with a lout, it's great.'

ANSWERS

(See underlined words in the tapescript.)

1	a TV documentary	6	career girls
2	getting married	7	10%
3	and debts	8	parents
4	surveillance	9	30–50
5	female staff	10	the facts

4 **Discussion: response to the Listening text.**

VOCABULARY 1 (page 104)

Informal expressions with *be* + particle

1 **Presentation and practice.**

This section practises some more colloquial expressions which are all in common use. When you check answers, ask students to suggest contexts for each expression, e.g.: *They're off!* – a radio commentator at the start of a horse race.

ANSWERS

1 H (usually of competitors in a race) 2 G 3 D 4 K
5 A (a book) 6 I 7 L 8 J 9 B 10 E 11 C 12 F

Nouns formed from phrasal verbs

2 **Presentation and practice.**

Note: Most phrasal verb nouns have hyphens between the two parts, but it is possible to see some of them written without hyphens.

ANSWERS

2 The police received a tip-off . . .
3 We can't repair this car, it's a write-off.
4 There was a better turn-out than I expected.
5 Jack likes nothing better than a good work-out.
6 . . . we made a stop-over in Singapore.
7 It's a slip-up.
8 The play is a sell-out.

ENGLISH IN USE 1 (page 105)

Part 5, Register cloze

The incident described in the letter is a well-known confidence trick.

Tell students to underline the phrases in the first text that they have to express using different words in the second text. The gaps in text 2 follow the sequence of text 1. Remind students of the two-word maximum word limit.

ANSWERS

1
The writer mentions a car accident and a burglary.

2
1 company (the car park where I work)
2 delay (make a quick start)
3 disbelief / surprise (I couldn't believe it)
4 a collision / an accident (someone had smashed into it)
5 minor (wasn't too bad)
6 driven (would still go)
7 initial (at first)
8 false / incorrect (I was mistaken)
9 apology (saying sorry)
10 expensive / excellent / very good (for the best seats)
11 unobtainable / impossible to obtain (like gold dust)
12 returning (when we got back home)
13 advantage (made the most of)

LISTENING 2 (page 106)

Exam File: Note completion

Remind students that Part 3 Listening tasks have two or more speakers who interact with each other. The questions focus on opinions and attitudes rather than factual information.

1 Introduction to the topic.

Use this opportunity to pre-teach some vocabulary from the tapescript, e.g.:

tread a fine line (between truth and falsehood): keep a careful balance between two kinds of behaviour, one of which is probably wrong

send (out) mixed signals: give a misleading impression of what you really believe, by saying contradictory things

spill the beans: reveal information/secrets

white lie: a lie that isn't very serious

rite of passage: literally, a ceremony or ritual carried out in tribal societies to mark the transition to adulthood; metaphorically, adopting ways of behaviour that indicate the end of childhood and the beginning of adulthood

2 Note completion task.

Ensure students read through the task before you play the recording.

TAPESCRIPT

Jenny Lake: In today's society, we seem to accept a flexible attitude to telling the truth. Politicians, advertisers, marketing men all tread a very fine line between truth and falsehood. But things are different when it comes to the young. Children and teenagers are still taught that they should never tell a lie. I talked to Tom Philpot and Susanna Waller, both child psychologists, to try to get some insight into the type of problems created by our attitudes.

Tom Philpot: A major problem is the mixed signals we send children. If a four-year-old on the beach gives you a bucket of sand and says, 'Here's a cake I made just for you.' We probably say, 'Thank you,' and pretend to eat it. We probably even say how delicious it is. But when children get to twice that age, say they're eight or nine, and they come home from school and tell us they won a prize for writing the best story but then their teacher says they're doing very badly at writing, we tend to tell them off because we know they are lying.

Susanna Waller: Yes. Of course, in the first story, we think we are just participating in a fantasy created by the child, but when it comes to lying about school, we take it more seriously. The situation makes a difference, but the age of the child affects our reaction too. By the age of eight, we expect a child to have some understanding that the truth is required in serious matters.

Jenny Lake: So parents have to instil some understanding of what's appropriate when?

Tom Philpot: Yes, that's it. Most children lie at some stage in their lives, and it is something that parents find very difficult to accept and deal with. They often feel that they have failed to impose a moral standpoint. But they need to see moral development as an ongoing thing.

Jenny Lake: When do children know the difference between what is right and what is not?

Susanna Waller: It's usually around the age of three that a conscience starts to develop. But children go on for much longer playing fantasy games which involve a lack of reality.

Tom Philpot: But throughout childhood, there may be special reasons for telling a lie. Loyalty is a good example. Children may well lie to protect their friends. Protecting their friends can be more important than coming out with the truth. Especially if their friends would be likely to get into trouble as a result of them spilling the beans.

Jenny Lake: Yes, I think we can all imagine situations like that. But what can parents do to get the basic point across?

Tom Philpot: Children need to know that telling other people the truth is the basis of a good relationship. It's a good idea to explain why lying is counter-productive. Children can be told that if they become known as liars, people will not believe them even when they are being truthful, that people don't like being told lies. They need to learn that from an early age.

Susanna Waller: Though, as we said, parents are often not the best models. Sometimes they can give an appalling example to children. Parents don't hesitate to tell 'white lies', the price of civilised life they have been called, but teenagers particularly often regard such things as hypocritical, and can take a very literal interpretation of what is 'the truth'.

Jenny Lake: Is punishment a good thing when children lie? <u>Is this something psychologists would be in favour of?</u>

Susanna Waller: <u>Most definitely not.</u> Children who are punished a lot learn to lie to avoid punishment, rather than not doing the things which bring the punishment, so it often makes things worse. And as most lying stems from underlying causes, it is far more important that parents try to work out what is going on and deal with that.

Jenny Lake: What about teenagers?

Susanna Waller: Of course, at this time most young people want to be independent, and teenage lying can be seen as a bid for independence. The occasional lie about a minor issue isn't really a problem but if a <u>teenager is constantly telling lies, the parents should ask themselves why.</u>

Tom Philpot: <u>And one reason may be that the parents are being excessively strict.</u> Or maybe the teenager's friends are being allowed to do things which the parents object to for no reason. Through adolescence young people need to make more and more of their own decisions. At the same time there'll be necessary rules and restrictions, and adolescents need to know that their parents are firm about these for their own security.

Susanna Waller: Absolutely, lying to parents is almost a rite of passage. But most teenagers grow up to be as trustworthy and honest as their parents are. I'd advise seeking professional help if there is persistent or pathological lying. But if parents have established a dialogue and trust with their offspring, they should be able to work these problems out …

ANSWERS

(See underlined words in the tapescript.)

1 mixed signals
2 fantasy game
3 lies about school
4 a conscience
5 loyalty
6 telling the truth
7 white lies
8 punishing children
9 strictness

3 **Pair/group discussion: response to the Listening text.**

Encourage students to think of more situations where it might be acceptable to tell a lie.

LANGUAGE STUDY 1 (page 106)

Nominal clauses after thinking verbs

1 **Analysis and practice.**

Point out that nominal clauses don't require a question mark even if they are introduced by a question word.

Refer students to the Notes on **Students' Book** page 206 to check their answers.

ANSWERS

1
The introductory word can be omitted in c., when it introduces a statement, not an indirect question.

2
1 I don't believe that it's right to punish a child for lying.
2 I don't know whether/if I should always tell a friend the truth.
3 I don't understand why you never talk to me.
4 Did you know that 77% of women vacuum every 2–3 days?
5 Can you remember whether/if you locked the door behind you when you left the house?
6 I can't imagine how I could have forgotten our anniversary.

Nominal clauses in indirect speech

2 **Analysis: sequence of tenses.**

Refer students to the Notes on **Students' Book** pages 206–207 to check their answers.

3 **Practice: report statements.**

POSSIBLE ANSWERS

1 He assured me that he would never let me down.
2 She proudly announced to her parents that she had a new boyfriend.
3 He admitted to Mrs Smith-Brown that he had broken the Ming vase.
4 She complained that he never bought her flowers any more.
5 We concluded that he must have gone home.
6 He reminded Mary that it was her mother's birthday on Saturday.
7 He explained to the General that the battle was over and that they had won.

Other verb patterns after reporting verbs

4 **Presentation.**

Point out to students that using verbs other than *say* and *tell* may mean using different grammatical patterns and the tense changes associated with reported speech may not then apply.

Refer students to the Notes on **Students' Book** page 207 to check their answers.

5 Practice.

Encourage students to report the sense of the words and not to reproduce the enquire quotation.

POSSIBLE ANSWERS

1 She begged him to forgive her for forgetting his birthday and promised never to do it again.
2 He advised me to take a few days off as it would do me good.
3 Her friends insisted that she should visit them again soon.
4 She begged her friend not to tell anyone what she had just said.
5 He warned them against going climbing in such bad weather.
6 He denied being in the car and insisted that he was at home reading a book when the accident happened.

READING 2 (page 108)

Exam File: Part 2, Gapped text

1 Introduction to the topic.

If students have no experience of hitchhiking themselves, they may have heard stories about it or seen films and television programmes.

2 Read and summarise.

Remind students to read the base text to the end before looking at the missing paragraphs. This will help to establish the sequence of ideas in their minds and making a summary will confirm this. They are then well-prepared for the task.

SAMPLE SUMMARY

Writer picks up hitchhiker at *a service station*. Hitchhiker tells sad story about *having his rucksack stolen*. Writer takes him home to *her parents' house*. Takes him back to London *on Sunday or Monday and books him into a hotel*. Writer discovers that hitchhiker *is a con-man*.

Notes on the text:

High Commission: Australia has a High Commission and not an embassy in the UK because it is part of the British Commonwealth

Stonehenge: there are no prehistoric stone circles like Stonehenge in Australia – this should have been a clue that something was wrong

3 Identify missing paragraphs.

Encourage students to make use of the clues in italics, which focus on lexical links between paragraphs. Tell them to highlight other words and phrases that help them to decide where the missing paragraphs fit.

ANSWERS

1 D (*my passenger* links back to *picked up* in paragraph 1)
2 B (*the High Commission* is mentioned in the previous paragraph: *Thursday at the Australian High Commission was a blur . . .*)
3 A (*He told us about* picks up on the last sentence of the previous paragraph: . . . *talking more about himself.*)
4 E (here we confirm that the writer took David back to London on Sunday evening.)
5 C

4 Vocabulary search.

Encourage students to look at the context carefully but to use dictionaries if necessary.

POSSIBLE ANSWERS

1 looking thoroughly worn out and miserable
2 new to the country so unaware of potential hazards, an obvious target
3 in a friendly, good-natured way
4 a gullible and foolish person (colloquial)
5 someone with 'left-leaning' principles who is easily affected by feelings of pity or sympathy
6 annoyed and disappointed
7 unfriendly and rude

5 Text analysis: use of direct and indirect speech.

Discuss how a mixture of direct and indirect speech is used to add variety and interest to articles of this type.

Ask students to turn paragraph 3 into direct speech. This is an opportunity to go over again the pronoun changes required in reported speech.

Paragraphs A and B also contain an extended report of what David told the writer while they were in her car. Paragraph A in particular could be difficult for students to follow if they don't realise this.

6 Group discussion: response to the text.

VOCABULARY 2 (page 110)

Word formation

1 **Gap fill task.**

This is useful practice for Paper 3, Part 4. Encourage students to record vocabulary in this way, noting down all the variants of the base word.

> **ANSWERS**
>
> 1 mistrust (n.) 3 trusting   5 untrustworthy
> 2 trustworthy   4 trusted (adj.)

Abbreviations

2 **Vocabulary: abbreviations.**

The abbreviations in this exercise are all pronounced as individual letters. Compare this with *aka (also known as)*, which is now usually pronounced as if it were a single word.

Note: Abbreviations such as *sae* (stamped, addressed envelope) are written and pronounced 'an sae' because when said as abbreviations they begin with a vowel.

Ask students if they know any abbreviations.

> **ANSWERS**
>
> 1 identity card
> 2 knocked out
> 3 personal computer
> 4 as soon as possible
> 5 estimated time of arrival
> 6 cash on delivery

Expressions to do with honesty/dishonesty

3 **Vocabulary: idiomatic expressions.**

Let students work in pairs to think of paraphrases for the expressions.

> **ANSWERS**
>
> 1 What the politician was calling the truth could very easily be thought to be untrue.
> 2 give away information intentionally or unintentionally
> 3 someone who can't stop themselves from lying
> 4 admit it
> 5 completely untrue
> 6 made it obvious that he was guilty

WRITING (page 110)

> **Exam File: Parts 1 and 2, Report writing**

Review the features of a report with the class. See also **Exam File** Unit 6, **Students' Book** page 80.

Step 1 Task interpretation
Tell students to highlight key words in the task.

> **ANSWERS**
>
> Students are asked to:
>
> 1 describe safety and security problems from a student's point of view
> 2 suggest solutions to these problems
>
> Given that the target reader is the principal, and the purpose of the report is presumably to bring about improvements by advising the principal on what the problems are and suggesting solutions, the appropriate register will be neutral to formal and the appropriate tone will be serious and objective.

Step 2 Selecting and summarising
1 Students highlight key information in the reading input.

> **ANSWERS**
>
> | **Safety problems** | **Security problems** |
> |---|---|
> | litter everywhere | computer equipment |
> | coffee spilt on floor | stolen |
> | violent attacks on students | missing keys |
> | by thieves taking | identity cards not shown |
> | computer equipment | too many exits and |
> | | entrances |

2 Students should select from the suggestions in the input.

> **ANSWERS**
>
> **Recommendations**
> chain computers to desks
> employ security guards
> introduce a new system for keys
> replace stolen litter bins
> make ID cards compulsory
> forbid taking food and drink out of the cafeteria
> install video cameras

Step 3 Layout and organisation
Point out that the task is to write the report from the **students'** point of view, so the information should be organised in a way that shows what is most important to students. It is a good idea to be specific. For example, students could give an example of a serious accident caused by litter or spilt coffee.

Remind students that the format for the beginning/ending of letters is not appropriate for a report. They can head the report:

Report on safety and security in college.
They can sign it at the bottom, but without using a letter style formula such as *Yours sincerely.*

Step 4 Write
1 Students read the example conclusion and rewrite it in an appropriate, formal, register.

MODEL ANSWER

In conclusion, we must take urgent steps to combat crime in local neighbourhoods. I would strongly advise setting up a Neighbourhood Watch group which I am sure would discourage crime in the area.

---

2 Remind students that the **Language Bank** contains useful phrases that they can use in their report.

MODEL ANSWER

Report on safety and security in college
Introduction
This report looks at the problems of safety and security in the college as they affect students. It is based on recent events reported in the press, and complaints from the college caretaker.

Safety and security in the college
In recent months the college has suffered several break-ins and over 15 computers have been stolen. In a college where resources are scarce, this type of theft is very worrying. However, even more worrying is the fact that several students have been attacked and injured by the thieves. Many students are concerned about their safety, especially those who attend evening seminars.
Another cause for concern is the number of accidents caused by litter or spilt food and drink in corridors and study areas. In two cases, students had to be taken to hospital for emergency treatment.

Recommendations
The problems of litter, food and drink can be easily remedied. Imposing a fine would be an effective way to discourage littering. Another measure would be to forbid taking food and drink out of the cafeteria.
The problem of attacks on students deserves more serious consideration. To improve security, the college should make carrying student passes compulsory at all times. More security guards should be employed to make random checks at all entrances to the building. This would be an effective deterrent against thieves, and help to prevent further violence. As an additional security measure, you should also consider installing video cameras.
I urge the college to adopt the recommendations in this report as a matter of urgency.

LANGUAGE STUDY 2 (page 112)
Verbs with two objects

The aim of this section is to prepare students for the task in English in Use 2. The unnecessary use of prepositions is often tested in Paper 3, Part 3 (error correction).

Refer students to the Notes on **Students' Book** pages 207–208 to check their answers.

ANSWERS

1	for + IO	5	to + IO	9	impossible
2	to + IO	6	to + IO	10	for + IO
3	for + I	7	for + IO	11	impossible
4	impossible	8	for + IO	12	for + IO

ENGLISH IN USE 2 (page 112)

Exam File: Part 3, Error correction

1 Students should read to the end before starting to look for the errors. Elicit answers to the question before letting students do the error correction task.

2 Remind students that up to five lines may be correct in this task type.

ANSWERS

1 being (*prepared* is an adjective, not a verb here)
2 ✓
3 despite (to identify the unnecessary link word, you have to read lines two, three and four – this is why it is so important to read the whole text for understanding)
4 up (*break up* is a phrasal verb meaning something different – elicit possible contexts)
5 to (see Language Study 2 for an explanation of why this is wrong)
6 ✓
7 ✓
8 than (a comparative doesn't make sense)
9 it (the object of *point out* is the noun clause beginning that *she could . . .*; therefore it is unnecessary to have another object *it*)
10 about (*about* needs to be followed by a noun phrase)
11 ✓
12 myself (*I asked myself* but *he asked me*)
13 up (*make up = invent*)
14 ✓
15 the (wrong use of the definite article with a plural – see the Notes on **Students' Book** page 200)
16 a (*take part* is a fixed phrase with no indefinite article)

Making a living

SPEAKING 1 (page 113)

1 Talk about photographs.

This exercise practises some useful work-related vocabulary.

Photo 1 shows a car engine assembly line in Mexico. It illustrates shift work.
Photo 2 shows a woman working on a laptop computer in a home environment, illustrating teleworking.
Photo 3 shows a farmer with lambs. This illustrates seasonal work.
Photo 4 shows a man at a desk piled high with files and papers and best illustrates a 9–5 job.

2 Extension of discussion.

These questions require students to move beyond a description of what they see in the pictures and consider wider issues, as they are expected to do in Paper 5, Part 2.

READING (page 114)

Part 1, Multiple matching

1 Introduction to the topic.

This exercise activates students' ideas and vocabulary before they read the text.

2 Multiple matching task.

Point out to students that information about several people is not spread throughout one article as in Unit 1. Each person is described in one section of the text, as in Unit 2, so highlighting names in the text is not a useful technique here.

However, highlighting key words and phrases in the questions and similar expressions in the text is very useful. Tell students to do this, and discuss different ways in which the key ideas might be expressed in the texts, e.g.:

Question 2: Students might look for references to time. What would be irregular hours to start and finish work?
Question 3: What other words are there for *salesperson*?
Question 4: What other expressions mean the same as *be highly regarded*.

ANSWERS

1	B	Nigel Moon . . . always wanted to buy a windmill (lines 25–26)
2	A	It was 3 am . . . She had to be at the airport for 4.30 am (lines 1–3)
3	C	She regards herself first and foremost as a retailer (lines 48–49)

4	D	Young is a woodworking virtuoso. (lines 68–69)
5	A	I think that if you look well groomed, then you look as if you've got self-control and self-respect. (lines 11–13)
6	C	We don't have pay retainers and we don't have exclusive contracts with our artists so we rely on their loyalty to come back. (lines 56–57)
7	A	I usually run through all the questions that are going to be asked at the pre-flight briefing. (lines 13–15)
8	B	. . . sell Downfield and buy a more efficient mill (lines 43–44)
9	D	. . . traditional skills in Japan (lines 73–74), traditional Windsor chair (line 83)
10/11	B, C	. . . it is an exhausting, seven-day-a-week occupation. (line 39) She regularly works ten hours a day, seven days a week. (lines 48–49)
12	B	. . . he can be seen dashing frantically around the five floors. (lines 29–30)
13	C	She still needs to be in the gallery much of the time. (lines 64–65)
14	D	After learning the basic skills in Japan, Young went to England . . . (line 77)
15/16	B, D	. . . when it is running on the sails . . . the electric system helps to keep production going. (lines 33–35) . . . to simplify the traditional Windsor chair to fit modern requirements (lines 81–82)

3 Vocabulary.

Encourage students to use the context to help them work out the meaning of the words.

ANSWERS

1 A retainer is an amount of money paid to someone to ensure you keep his/her services in the future.
2 Artists get a fixed percentage of the price of the painting.
3 If you give a discount, you reduce the price.
4 The turnover is the total amount of money earned by a business.
5 If you commission someone to do something, e.g. write a report or make a work of art, you ask them formally to do it.

▶▶ *Extension activity*

You could extend this exercise and introduce other words and expressions related to the key word MONEY.

1 Ask students to explain the differences between the words in each of the following groups.

1 pension / income / welfare / allowance
2 sponsorship/ subsidy / investment
3 cash / change / currency
4 economic / economics / economical

Students can check their answers by looking at the entry MONEY in the Longman *Language Activator*.

2 Ask students to decide what these idioms to do with money mean, and when they might be used.

1 He's got money to burn.
2 Do you think I'm made of money?
3 Her family's rolling in it.

Tell them to check their answers by looking at the entry RICH in the Longman *Language Activator*.

Then discuss if there are any similar idioms in students' own language(s).

4 Read for inference/attitude.

An exercise of this type is useful practice for Paper 1, Part 3, which requires a detailed understanding of a text, including opinions and attitudes.

Tell students to read the section of the text in which each expression appears, and use the context to help them understand what is meant. When discussing the answers, you can also explain the following points.

Text A

pre-flight briefing: a meeting where the crew of an aircraft are given their instructions and any important information about the flight
stamp their authority on: this is metaphorical, deriving from the meaning of *stamp* = make a mark with a stamp

Text C

opening shows and bottles of wine: the two different meanings of *open* make this intentionally humorous

---

ANSWERS

1 The meetings can be very tense and difficult – it seems that some senior staff deliberately ask tricky questions. The air stewardess obviously doesn't look forward to them.
2 This remark indicates that she thinks her job is not glamorous at all, even though many people think it is.
3 This indicates that the job involves hard physical work, and Nigel feels he is no longer able to cope.
4 It isn't possible to control who comes into a shop, and some people may cause trouble or be difficult to deal with – the job is therefore harder than you may think.
5 He felt a conflict between making money and creating works of art. It seems that he decided money was less important.

---

5 Class/group discussion: response to the text.

Encourage students to use vocabulary from the text to justify their answers. This is a good opportunity to put to use what they have learned.

ENGLISH IN USE 1 (page 117)

Part 1, Multiple choice cloze

1 Introduction to the topic.

Students can work in pairs. As them to think about the jobs already mentioned in the unit, and list the ones they think they themselves could do.

2 Multiple choice cloze.

Remind students to read the whole text to the end first. Check their answer to the question before letting them do the multiple choice task.

ANSWERS

1 B (*reach or achieve your goal* = succeed in doing sth)
2 A (*leads* is the only word that can be followed by *to*)
3 C (the other words given cannot be used of a person, only of things)
4 D (*necessity* = sth that you need, not sth that is required of you; *obligation* = duty)
5 B (*a must* is a fixed phrase that means sth that you must have; *requirement* would also fit here, but it can't be used as English doesn't like repetition)
6 A (*the ticket to success/fame etc.* is an idiomatic expression)
7 C (as no one knows exactly how many types of occupation exist, *estimated* makes most sense here)
8 D (reduce the number or range of)
9 D (*play a part* is a collocation)
10 A (this is taken from the context of betting on the probability of a horse winning a race; other expressions are: *the odds are that . . .* = it's likely that; *the odds in favour of a victory by our team.*)
11 B *aptitudes* refers to abilities – this makes best sense in the context)
12 C (collocation)
13 A (collocation)
14 C (the use of *the* rules out option A; all the other words combine with *the* but only option C makes sense in the context)
15 B (collocation)

---

3 Group/pair discussion: response to the text.

Encourage students to use words and phrases from the text in their discussion.

POSSIBLE ANSWERS (QUESTION 4)

• accountant
• nurse
• sales executive/assistant

WRITING 1 (page 118)

Exam File: Part 1, Job application

Introduce the Writing lesson by discussing how people go about getting a job in the students' country: do they go to an agency, answer adverts in the jobs section of the paper, put adverts in the paper themselves?

Find out who has written a formal letter of application for a job. Discuss what a letter should contain (it should only deal with key points that are especially relevant to the requirements specified in the advert; more detailed information should be in an accompanying CV (resume) or application form).

Then go through the summary in the **Exam File**.

Step 1 Task interpretation

ANSWERS

Students have to produce two pieces of writing.

text types: letter applying for a job; note
target readers: letter: potential employer; note: friend
register/tone: letter: formal; note: informal

Step 2 Selecting and summarising

1 Students should make a list of the job requirements as mentioned in the advertisement and match their experience to each requirement. For this kind of writing, students do not have to be truthful about their experience and qualifications. They can invent any details they like.

2 Point out to students that the annotations on the advertisement indicate that they have to include some questions in their letter – this is part of the task, and they will lose marks if they don't include questions.

Step 3 Layout and organisation.

Note that there are two pieces of writing to do, with very different layouts. Encourage students use the suggested paragraph plan for their letter. It is always best to decide on the number of paragraphs and their content and then make notes.

Step 4 Write

Point out to students that both advertisements mention the name of the person to write to, so students should use that name in the salutation. The title *Ms* should be used instead of *Mrs* or *Miss* in cases of doubt. So students should write *Dear Ms Clairmont* if they apply for the job of Tour Leader, but *Dear Mrs Turner* if they apply for the other job.

Encourage students to make use of the **Language Bank** as a resource.

MODEL ANSWER

Letter

Dear Ms Clairmont
I am writing to apply for the post of tour leader with your company. At present, I am in the final year of an Economics course at Bologna University.

I am very interested in working as a tour leader as I believe that I have the qualities and experience necessary for the job. Firstly, I speak Italian and French fluently, as well as English. Secondly, as president of the university cycling club I am used to organising outings and events for large groups of people. Thirdly, I have already done some part-time work for a local travel agency during the holidays, so have some experience of planning travel schedules and arranging accommodation. In addition, as this is my final year at college, I would be available for work beyond the summer period.

I would appreciate it if you could send me more details. I would like to know when the job would begin, where the students are from and where the study tours are based. Would knowledge of a specific language be required? Could you also send me more information about the hours of work and salary?

I am available for interview from next week. I look forward to hearing from you.
Yours sincerely

Note

Dave,
Thanks for sending the ads! I decided to apply for the Study Tours job in the end – it sounded more interesting and I felt I had the right qualifications! I sent my application yesterday. I'll find out if I've got an interview next week. I'll let you know how I get on!
Best wishes

LISTENING 1 (page 120)

Part 3, Multiple choice questions

1 Introduction to the topic.

You could pre-teach some vocabulary from the tapescript during this stage, to prepare students for the task, e.g.: *camaraderie, cut-throat world, be out for oneself* (Question 2) *alert* (Question 4).

2 Multiple choice questions.

Get students to turn the stems into questions before playing the recording the first time. You could put them on the board and tell students to close their books and jot down brief answers during the first listening. Elicit:

1 What is Barbara doing at the moment?
2 What does she think about working practices now?

3 What kind of places does B. prefer to work?
4 When does she work best?
5 What has she had to accept?
6 When do offices run smoothly, in B.'s opinion?

Students open their books and compare their answers with the options in the exercise. Tell them to circle the best option. Play the recording a second time and let them check.

TAPESCRIPT

Presenter: These days, fewer and fewer people work in factories or outdoors, on the land, and the majority of school and college leavers today will find themselves working in an office. So is that something to look forward to or not? With me today, I have Mrs Barbara Mayor, who's going to tell us about her experience of office work. Barbara, can you begin by telling us what you do?

Barbara: Well, I'm not working at the present time and I haven't since before Christmas of last year. I've always been employed as a legal assistant. Unfortunately, my last office closed down, partly I think due to the economy. Things weren't going well and they just weren't making any money, so it was kind of a forced retirement in a sense, but one I've extremely enjoyed. I don't know what I'm going to do, whether I'll go back to it, or whether I'd really like to look for something else to do.

Presenter: One of the benefits of working in an office is the social aspect – you are working with a team of colleagues who often become your friends too. Have you found this? Can you tell us about your relations with colleagues?

Barbara: In the past, I've had various different jobs and just worked with wonderful people. In the last several years, though, the experiences haven't been good, and I don't think it's the offices so much as the times, people changing, people seem to be caught up more in their own worlds than they used to be. There used to be more camaraderie, people used to be more helpful and there were fewer barriers to break down. Now I find it's more of a cut-throat world, people are out for themselves, not just in the office but in everyday living – people seem a lot more isolated.

Presenter: So it seems office life is changing, and perhaps not for the better. What would you say is the most important factor that makes somewhere a pleasant place to work?

Barbara: Having camaraderie with the people that you work with, people working together as a team, not isolated people who are doing things for their own ego, wanting to outshine everybody else. I think you have to work as a team and have a goal. You know, the goal is to get the job done, or the project or whatever it is at the time.

Presenter: Most people think of the working day as being 9 to 5, but many companies have introduced flexible working hours, so employees have a certain amount of choice about when they start work and when they finish. This takes into account people's circumstances, like whether or not they have children, and the fact that everyone has a slightly different rhythm of work. So, Barbara, when do **you** think you work best?

Barbara: Well, I work best, I'm more alert first thing in the morning. In the evening I tend to slow down. I think I work best when I'm working with people who are prepared to work with you, not against you. People who don't have their own agenda.

Presenter: Yes, indeed. Now, these days many offices are open plan, aren't they, unlike in the past, when employees usually each had their own room. But of course, everyone still has their own desk or workstation. So, Barbara, how do you like to organise your workplace?

Barbara: I'm very organised. I have to have a place for everything and everything in its place. I can't work in confusion. I don't thrive under stress, which is very difficult in the legal profession because everything does tend to have a time limit on it, so you're constantly under this pressure of things having to be done in a certain time period, you know, and I like to keep very organised and know what things have to be done. … I feel if you take care of the little things, big things don't become a problem, and this is very often a problem in offices. They don't like to give you the time to take care of the small, mundane things that make an office run smoothly. They just want you to kind of get in and start working and sometimes you need to organise and see what's ahead, and look at the calendar for next week, and worry about what's coming up. And then I find things tend to look smooth, starting from kind of small up.

ANSWERS

(See underlined words in the tapescript.)

1 D   2 B   3 D   4 C   5 C   6 D

3 Group/class discussion: response to the Listening text.

VOCABULARY 1 (page 120)

Phrasal verbs with *down*

1 Analysis: meaning of *down*.

The aim is to show that the particles of phrasal verbs have some meaning. Knowledge of this can help students to work out the meaning of new phrasal verbs they encounter.

ANSWERS

1 A   2 C   3 B

---

2 **Practice.**

Let students work in pairs. Remind them to change the form of the main verb to fit the sentence.

ANSWERS

1
1 run   2 let   3 burnt   4 died   5 torn
2
1, 2, 4 = decrease (C)
3, 5 = destroy (B)

SPEAKING 2 (page 121)

Exam File: Part 3, Express and support your opinions; Part 4, Report conclusions

Introduce this Part 3 task by going through the **Exam File** with the class.

1 **Collaborative task: discuss and select.**

Allow students 3-4 minutes for the task. Remind them to use the **Language Bank** as a resource, and tick off expressions as they use them. You could do the activity as a class first, to give practice in using the expressions. It will allow you to model intonation if you join in the discussion yourself.

Picture 1 shows a social event, a party.
Picture 2 shows people white-water rafting on a survival training course – a popular activity which is believed to build the team spirit necessary for survival.
Picture 3 shows another social event – this time an evening at a bowling alley.
Picture 4 shows a one-day training seminar.

2 **Report back.**

To simulate exam conditions, two pairs can form a group of four. In the exam, 3-4 minutes are allowed for this general discussion.

ENGLISH IN USE 2 (page 122)

Part 6 Discourse cloze

1 **Introduction to the topic.**

The aim is to activate students' ideas on this topic and introduce vocabulary.

2 **Read for gist.**

Remind students that reading to the end will help them begin to understand the sequence of ideas, which is important for this task type. The answers to the questions form a summary of the main points of the text.

ANSWERS

People are suffering from overwork because the reduction of the workforce in many companies forces them to work up to 55 rather than 35 hours per week. This can lead to marital breakdown.

---

3 **Gap fill task.**

Emphasise that students must pay particular attention to meaning when selecting from the options given. Structurally, all the options will fit in any gap. Grammatical clues do not always help in this kind of exercise.

ANSWERS

1 D   2 E   3 F   4 A   5 G   6 C

---

4 **Group discussion.**

Students can discuss these issues in groups of four. Tell groups to write down three solutions to the problem of overwork. A group secretary can report the solutions to the rest of the class and the best solutions can then be selected.

LANGUAGE STUDY (page 123)

Writing complex sentences

One of the assessment criteria for Paper 2 is 'good range of structure', so it is important for students to use a variety of ways of combining ideas in writing. The work in this section pulls together and gives further practice in a range of patterns covered in earlier Language Study and Writing sections.

1 **Analysis and practice.**

1 There are three ways of combining sentences in English:

• co-ordination, using *and, or, but, so*
• subordination, using conjunctions such as *although, while, when* etc.
• adverbial links, using words such as *nevertheless, yet, meanwhile* etc.

Explain that co-ordination is a fairly loose means of combining ideas. The co-ordinating conjunction *and* adapts its meaning depending on the context, and basically expresses any positive link between two ideas. It is most common in spoken English, where emphasis can be created through stress and intonation.

9 Making a living

Refer students to the Notes on **Students' Book** page 208 to check their answers.

ANSWERS

1	time sequence	6	condition
2	addition	7	contrast
3	cause and effect	8	cause and effect
4	contrast	9	time sequence
5	cause and effect	10	addition

2 For stronger or more emphatic connections in written English, subordination and/or adverbial links should be used where appropriate rather than *and*. This exercise gives practice in combining ideas using these methods to make the meaning relationship clearer.

Make sure students understand the punctuation rules for subordinate clauses and adverbial links. Refer them to the section on Punctuation, Grammar Notes page 212. An adverbial link word such as *nevertheless, however, as a result* cannot follow a comma in the same way as a subordinating conjunction.

POSSIBLE ANSWERS

4 [Employers] just want you to start working *whereas* sometimes you need to organise and see what's ahead . . .

5 He worked flat out on the project for a year with the result that he had a nervous breakdown. / . . . and, as a result, he had a nervous breakdown.

6 If you take a two-week holiday away from it all, you'll feel a lot better.

7 Even though I've worked here for two years, I haven't had a raise. / I've worked here for two years, yet I (still) haven't had a raise.

8 When my boss praised me for my report, I felt very pleased.

9 As soon as he got home, / Immediately he got home, he started on the report.

3 Like the conjunction *and*, relative clauses and participle clauses are fairly vague, general-purpose ways of combining ideas. The meaning relationship often has to be inferred if there is no preposition or conjunction such as *after* or *despite*.

Refer students to Unit 5, **Students' Book** page 67 to review how participle clauses can be used.

POSSIBLE ANSWERS

5 *After working* flat out on the project for a year, he had a nervous breakdown. (present participle clause)

7 *Despite working* here for two years, I haven't had a raise. (present participle clause)

9 *On arriving home*, he started on the report right away. (present participle clause)

10 I'm currently on a work placement in a local company, *where* I'm being trained in office skills. (relative clause)

2 Improving sentences.

1 This exercise warns students against writing over-complicated sentences as doing so may lead to error. Sometimes it is best to write shorter, simpler sentences that students know are correct.

Go through the examples as a class.

ANSWERS

Example 1: How this sentence is best improved depends on the context. If it is a piece of spoken English, it would be best to split it into two sentences:
I have heard a lot about your company from one of your employees, who is a friend of mine. He told me that it is owned by a multi-national.
If the sentence is part of a letter of application, and the aim is to impress a potential employer with your knowledge of the company, then it should be rewritten to remove unnecessary information that will not interest the employer, e.g.:
I understand/believe that your company is owned by a multi-national / is part of a multi-national corporation.

Example 2: This sentence combines two ideas that are unrelated and therefore cannot sensibly be combined in a single sentence. Also, the punctuation is wrong: *in addition* is a sentence adverbial and requires either a full stop or semi-colon before it.
During vacations, I gained work experience in various companies. In addition, I speak German fluently.

2 Let students work in pairs to analyse what is wrong with the sentences and rewrite them.

ANSWERS

1 I am writing to apply for the job of tour leader (which was) advertised in yesterday's local paper. (Avoid wordiness.)

2 At present I am studying for a degree in Business Administration at Melchester University. (Avoid repetition: *at present* and *currently* mean the same thing.)

3 I am very interested in this job and believe that I have the abilities and experience needed. (Avoid unnecessary link words.)

4 As President of the cycling club in my college, I have a lot of experience in organising outings and leading groups of people. (*although* = wrong meaning)

5 I would appreciate it if you would send me more details about what the job involves, including hours of work and salary. (wrong use of *especially*)

PRONUNCIATION (page 124)

Weak forms

This section helps to prepare students for the task in Listening 2 by focusing on weak forms that might obstruct comprehension. It also introduces vocabulary from the Listening.

1 🔊 **Weak and strong *to*.**

The weak form of *to* is used in front of consonant sounds. The strong form is used in front of vowel sounds and when it is the last word in a sentence.

TAPESCRIPT
See Students' Book.

2 🔊 **Weak *and*.**

TAPESCRIPT
See Students' Book.

LISTENING 2 (page 124)

Part 2, Note completion

1 **Preparation.**

Give students time to predict the answers before they hear the recording. They should remember what *teleworking* is from Speaking 1.

2 🔊 **Note completion task.**

Remind students that in Part 2 of Paper 4, they only hear the recording once. The tapescript does however contain repetition, so that they will hear key ideas twice although expressed in different ways.

Check answers after playing the recording once only. If students are not sure of anything, play it again.

TAPESCRIPT

Presenter: Do you really want to work in an office? No? Well, you're certainly not alone. The traditional office has changed little in the last hundred years. Oh, yes, there have been changes in technology but the idea of an office with a desk for each person and a number of filing cabinets and a few potted plants to liven things up, seems the way things have always been.

Things are changing though, and for one good reason – cost. It's expensive to have an office building on a prime site in a modern city. The price of land in city centres is incredibly high. It costs a lot to keep the building clean and heated or air-conditioned, and there is general maintenance and repairs that have to be paid for. So more and more companies are turning to the 'virtual office'.

'What's that?' you may well ask. Well, on arriving at work, instead of going straight to your own desk, you check in, rather like checking into a hotel, and then you request a workstation. In effect, this is your desk for a certain time, and it won't be the same one every time. You are allocated a free desk for a fixed time, and you take your possessions out of a locker and carry them to the workstation you have been given. When you have finished, you take your possessions back to the locker and the desk is ready for the next lucky worker.

Not surprisingly, companies and their accountants love the idea. Accountants know that they are saving a lot of money by spending less on office equipment, heating and lighting. Employees are much less enthusiastic. You've lost your space, so the office is even more impersonal. You can't leave anything lying around. If you're in the office at peak times, you can even find yourself without a desk and working standing up.

Another form of working – teleworking – is more popular with staff because, for one thing, they don't have to travel to work. It's also a way for the company to economise because staff work from home, providing their own office, light, heat and shelter. They keep in touch with the office and clients by computer, fax and telephone. Usually the company will provide this equipment and pay for the necessary connections to its own computer. Many workers enjoy the flexibility they have over how they organise the working day, and the chance to escape from daily commuting, but some feel isolated without the chance for a chat around the coffee machine.

So there it is – losing your own desk, companies saving more money, more people staying at home. We'll have to see how long the traditional office lasts in the light of these new developments

3 Group discusion.

Students can discuss these questions in groups of four. Tell them to appoint a group secretary who should list the pros and cons of the virtual office. The secretaries then report back to the whole class.

VOCABULARY 2 (page 125)

Idiomatic expressions to do with work

Students use the expressions listed to make a short comment that matches the meaning of each sentence.

▶▶ Extension activity

To practise the expressions, ask students to think of people and situations in their own lives where they could use the expressions. Prompt them by asking questions, e.g.:

Can you think of someone you know (without mentioning names!) who doesn't do a stroke of work? Have you said anything to this person? Has this affected their performance in exams for example?

How can colleagues best deal with someone who doesn't pull their weight in the team?

Get students to collect more expressions using the Longman *Language Activator* and write their own examples for the expressions they like. See the entries:

WORK HARD (beaver away, work your fingers to the bone etc.)

LAZY (lazybones, layabout etc.)

WRITING 2 (page 125)

Part 2, Article

Revise the features of an article. Refer students to **Exam File**, Unit 4, **Students' Book** page 54 if necessary. Key features are:

- register and tone appropriate to target readers
- interesting title and first paragraph to attract readers' attention
- a different main idea in each paragraph
- sub-headings to show what the main points are – optional
- varied and interesting language
- effective closing paragraph – a sentence summary of the main idea, a question

Step 1 Task interpretation

Step 2 Generating ideas

Encourage students to add as many ideas as possible to the ones in the **Students' Book** even if some are not used. They can choose the best when they plan their paragraphs. Let them work in pairs for this stage. Encourage them to look for useful vocabulary in previous sections of the unit.

Step 3 Layout and organisation

Point out that the title of the article has been given in the task. Remind students that they can base any headings on the points listed in the task. This will ensure they do cover all the task requirements.

Step 4 Write

Remind students to try to make their opening paragraph as interesting as possible, and to round the article off rather than finishing abruptly.

MODEL ANSWER

9–5 in the 21st century
Changes in the workplace
Working life in my country has changed considerably over the last few years. One trend that is sure to continue is the large increase in the number of 'teleworkers' – people who work from home. More and more of us are likely to decide that the stress of the daily rush hour just isn't worth it, and choose to set up an office in our own homes.

The benefits of teleworking
One obvious benefit of working at home is the flexibility it provides. People will be able to work at the time of day when they are most productive, for example in the evenings. Parents will be able to organise their working hours according to their children's needs. Another benefit will be a reduction in traffic, so that our environment will be cleaner and healthier.

Are there any drawbacks?
Unfortunately, not every job is suited to teleworking. Some jobs will still require staff to be in the office every day. In addition, not everyone will find working at home ideal. Some people may lack self-discipline and motivation while others will miss the constant contact with other workers. Video phones and Internet communication are a poor substitute for face-to-face communication. And there will no longer be the opportunity to have a chat with friends during coffee breaks!

   Nevertheless, working at home will undoubtedly become an increasingly important feature of working life. And despite certain disadvantages, I feel it will have a positive effect on the quality of people's work and lifestyle as well as on the environment.

10 Just deserts

SPEAKING 1 (page 126)

This section introduces the theme of the unit and leads into the Listening task.

1 Talk about photographs.

Though not in precise exam format, this is useful practice for Part 2 of the Speaking Test. The questions guide students to briefly describe the photographs, then to discuss issues related to the content. The ideas provided are ones that students could talk about in an exam situation.

Photo 1 shows a car being broken into. The lock is being picked with a piece of wire.
Photo 2 shows a boy shoplifting.
Photo 3 shows graffiti.

2 Collaborative task: discuss and select.

This activity can be done in pairs or groups. Refer students to the **Language Bank** and check they understand all the expressions.

LISTENING 1 (page 127)

Part 1, Note completion

1 [cassette] Note completion task.

Give students plenty of time to predict possible answers or types of answer. They can do this in pairs.

TAPESCRIPT

Presenter: It's a worrying phenomenon when people talk of persistent young offenders – <u>young people under the age of eighteen</u> who have been involved in repeated crime. More than ninety per cent of such offenders are boys – girls account for only about ten per cent of the figures. It has been estimated that approximately sixty per cent of boys from highly-disadvantaged backgrounds will eventually end up with a criminal record, usually for vandalism, theft and drug abuse. <u>This means that some forty per cent of boys from such backgrounds do not offend.</u> Why not? Are there any special factors that protect against crime? This has been the subject of a major research project that has been in progress for forty years. Here are some of the latest findings.

The backgrounds of offenders and non-offenders reveal surprising differences, indicating that it is not social disadvantage alone that leads to crime. The overwhelming risk factors for delinquent behaviour by boys relate to <u>their fathers' behaviour. Unsurprisingly, employment, or rather unemployment, is a key factor. A poor work record combined with alcoholism are the really</u>

<u>crucial indicators.</u> If the father has these two characteristics, he is likely to be an offender and so are his sons. Forty per cent of the sons of fathers who regularly commit crimes are persistent offenders themselves.

What about the factors that were found among the non-offenders? Here, the factors that tended to protect against a life of crime, even in families with a high level of disadvantage, were as follows: doing well at school, <u>having the opportunity for social activities such as joining a youth club</u>, living in a home where the parents worked together as a couple and where there was good communication, intimacy, affection and minimal quarrelling. These three factors were associated with less offending. Predictably, the attitude of the mother was found to be of the utmost importance. <u>Even if circumstances were bad, in the homes of non-offenders, the mother was in control and able to deal with difficult situations.</u>

Some of the findings of the study were less predictable. <u>For instance, offending became more common as families got bigger, and even in large families, the first- and second-born were less likely to offend.</u> The study also found that <u>offenders have suffered three times as many accidents in the home in early life as non-offenders had.</u> In homes where accidents were very frequent, this seems to be either because of negligence or lack of foresight. Firm management, and the ability to reason with children were protective factors, and mental strength was far more important than social disadvantage. <u>But when it came to toys, there seemed to be no effect on behaviour</u>, whether toys were present or absent.

ANSWERS

(See underlined words in the tapescript.)

1 18
2 40% (of boys)
3 (poor work)/employment record / unemployment
4 alcoholism
5 a youth club
6 difficult situations
7 first/second
8 first/second
9 accidents
10 toys

2 Discussion: comprehension check.

The aim is to check students have fully understood the Listening by asking them to think about and comment on the issues raised.

3 Group activity.

Students work in groups of four. A group secretary should note their recommendations and report back to the class.

VOCABULARY 1 (page 127)
Words to do with crime

1

This part checks students' knowledge of the basic vocabulary for this topic area. Students write numbers in the boxes to indicate the correct sequence of events.

2

Students can use the same numbers as in 1, once they have checked the answers.

ANSWERS

1	commit a crime	(criminal)
4	release someone on bail	(judge)
3	charge someone (with)	(police)
5	stand trial	(defendant/suspect)
2	arrest someone (for)	(police)
8	pass sentence (on)/sentence someone (to 6 months)	(judge)
6	deliver/return a verdict	(jury)
9	serve time/a prison sentence	(criminal)
10	release someone (from prison)	(prison authorities)
7	convict someone (of)	(judge/jury)

READING 1 (page 128)
Part 3, Multiple choice questions

1 **Introduction to the topic.**

2 **Skim for gist.**

The questions help students to locate the most essential information quickly. Make sure students have understood the meaning of *stalking* as it is the most significant word in the text.

You may need to explain the following words and expressions when checking answers:

unrequited lover: someone whose love is not returned
over-zealous: excessively enthusiastic
a sorry business: a depressing activity

ANSWERS

1
1 *the obsessed:* this refers to the fans who stalk famous people
2 *stalking:* a crime in which a person follows someone and harasses them in various ways over a period of time; literally, the word is used to describe animals stalking their prey

2
1 people in the entertainment industry, celebrities
2 they suffer from loneliness and despair; they find it difficult to form real relationships with others

3 **Multiple choice questions.**

Encourage students to read the stems first, turn them into questions and look for the answers in the text, before they read the options. Tell them to highlight the relevant parts of the text.

They should then read the options and compare with their own answers. Remind them that they must have textual support for the option that they choose.

Get them to justify their answers when you check the task.

ANSWERS

1 C . . . to ask for protection from an obsessive fan (lines 3–4)
2 A . . . if America's crime trends are anything to go by, Parliament may soon be forced to follow that country's lead in making it a punishable crime. (lines 17–22)
3 C . . . the loss of a major movie star can cost a company millions (lines 42–44)
4 C . . . an unrelenting tale of loneliness and despair (lines 67–69)
5 A . . . those who invent completely artificial relationships . . . The last category of stalker, usually known as the celebrity stalker, is the most difficult to track. (lines 88–95)
6 B Just when we've seen the most abnormal and bizarre, something else comes along to beat it. (lines 158–161)

4 **Vocabulary: meaning and register.**

Understanding the contrast between colloquial and neutral is relevant to Paper 3, Part 5 (register cloze). Students can do this exercise in pairs.

ANSWERS

1 up to now
2 if . . . is an indication (colloquial)
3 introduce
4 invented, developed (the first to do this)
5 frighten, make frightened
6 upsetting, depressing (colloquial)
7 understand something (colloquial)
8 prevent something bad happening

5 **Class/group discussion.**

For Question 1, students could describe films as well as real-life situations. Encourage them to use words and phrases from the text.

LANGUAGE STUDY (page 130)

The passive

1 Analysis: form and meaning.

1 The focus here is on form. Students should highlight both the past participle and the auxiliaries, taking care when they are separated by other words.

Refer students to the Notes on **Students' Book** page 209 to check their answers.

> ### ANSWERS
>
> a. may soon be forced
> b. have not been properly protected
> c. have been identified
> d. may be received
> e. have been sent
> f. being mentioned
> g. was convicted
> h. to be promoted
> i. not to have been selected
> j. It was felt
>
> 1 The passive is formed by using the correct form of *be* + the past participle of the main verb.
> 2 after a modal verb in the present = *be*
> after a modal verb in the past = *have been*
> after a verb taking the infinitive = *to be*
> after a verb taking a gerund = *being*
> after an adjective = *to have been*

2 The focus here is on meaning. Point out to students that the sentences cannot necessarily be made active, or at least not in a way that sounds convincing. This is why the passive was used in the first place!

> ### ANSWERS
>
> a. *Crime trends in Britain* may soon force parliament to follow that country's lead . . . (agent is obvious from the context, and the use of the passive avoids repetition of *crime trends*.)
> b. There is also the threat of lawsuits from actors who feel that *their company* has not properly protected them. (agent obvious)
> c. *ISM* (International Security Management) have identified three basic types of stalker: those who . . . (use of the passive makes new information the topic of the sentence for greater emphasis)
> d. *Members of a celebrity's entourage* may receive letters or phone calls instead of the celebrities themselves. (use of the passive places emphasis on the agent to point up the contrast between members of the entourage and the celebrities themselves)
> e. *They* should have sent the youngsters who did that to jail. (to avoid using informal *they* when the precise identity of the agent is not known)

> f. I don't remember *anyone* mentioning his name at the trial. (use of the passive avoids vague pronouns)
> g. *The jury* convicted Robert Bardo of murder. (agent is obvious)
> h. John had expected that *his boss* would promote him soon. (use of the passive makes the statement more impersonal)
> i. He felt disappointed that *they* didn't select him for the job. (to avoid use of vague *they* or make the statement more impersonal)
> j. *The company/His boss* felt that he had not yet acquired enough experience. (use of the passive makes the statement more impersonal)

! *make, see* and *let*

> ### ANSWERS
>
> 1 The infinitive **without** *to* is used after *make* and *see* in the active. The infinitive **with** *to* is used in the passive.
> 2 *Let* is not used in the passive, but must be replaced by *allowed to*.

2 Practice.

Students rewrite the sentences in the passive.

> ### ANSWERS
>
> 1 Be careful! You might have been run over! (agent not necessary)
> 2 Sally really wanted to be noticed by the director.
> 3 I don't like being followed around by the police.
> 4 I'd like to be offered the opportunity to travel round the world. (agent not necessary)
> 5 I am thrilled to have been paid this honour by our country's President.
> 6 Why weren't you all allowed to go home early from school today? (agent not necessary)
> 7 A child can't be made to do something he/she doesn't want to. (agent not necessary)

3 Presentation and practice: impersonal constructions.

Students rewrite the sentences following the patterns supplied.

> ### ANSWERS
>
> 1 It is alleged that movie starlet Angie Carter has been under the care of a psychiatrist recently. / Movie starlet Angie Carter is believed to have been . . .
> 2 It is believed that she's been feeling depressed about gaining weight. / She is believed to have been feeling depressed . . .
> 3 It is rumoured that her husband has been seeing other young ladies. / Her husband is rumoured to have been seeing . . .

4 In addition, it is reported that she is getting very difficult to work with on the set. / In addition, she is reported to have been getting very difficult to work with . . .

5 It is feared that her contract may be terminated. (This is the only option.)

Reduced relative clauses

4 **Analysis: identify reduced relatives.**

Make it clear to students that the sentences are perfectly correct as they are. It is not necessary to add a relative. The point of the exercise is simply to be able to identify reduced relative clauses.

Point out that reduced relative clauses can be both defining and non-defining. The presence or absence of commas makes this clear.

Refer students to the Notes on **Students' Book** page 209 to check their answers.

ANSWERS

1
a. which/that are
b. who is
2
1 A young man, **who had been** arrested on suspicion of murder, appeared in court today.
2 The evidence **which/that was** presented in court . . .
3 I wouldn't like to live in a house **which/that was** haunted by a murdered woman.
4 The house, **which was** occupied by the Vince family for generations, now stands . . .
5 . . . the men **who were** involved were never caught.

5 **Practice.**

Point out to students that reduced relative clauses can improve the style of their writing by making sentences flow smoothly, so it is to their advantage to be able to use them. Students should write the sentences out in full, paying attention to punctuation. Refer them to the previous exercise if they are not sure whether to use commas or not.

ANSWERS

1 Mr Manners, found guilty on all charges by the jury, faces life imprisonment.
2 The painting, although widely regarded as a fake, still sold for £2 million.
3 All the cars damaged in the accident were impounded by the police.
4 Mr Marks, wrongfully arrested by the police, is seeking compensation. / Wrongfully arrested, Mr Marks is seeking compensation from the police.
5 The passengers, rescued from the blaze by firefighters, were taken to hospital.

VOCABULARY 2 (page 131)
Collocation

This section consolidates some of the vocabulary that has occurred in the texts so far. It also shows how participles are not only used as verbs but also as adjectives.

1 **Participial adjectives.**

Students have to add two words to each sentence. Point out that they must change the verb form from the infinitive to a participle.

ANSWERS

1 spoiled/spoilt child
2 stolen goods
3 sworn enemies
4 helping hand
5 driven man
6 rampaging mob
7 hidden catch
8 breaking glass

2 **Word formation.**

This is in preparation for Exercise 3. Encourage students to use dictionaries if necessary to help them.

ANSWERS

1 crime / criminal / incrimination / incriminating / incriminatory
2 offence / offender / offensive
3 obsession / obsessive
4 accusation / (the) accused / accusing
5 deterrence / deterrent (n. and adj.)

3 **Gap fill task.**

Students complete the sentences after they have checked the answers to Exercise 2.

ANSWERS

1 incriminating
2 offensive
3 criminal
4 deterring, offenders
5 accused, obsessed
6 criminal

ENGLISH IN USE 1 (page 132)
Part 2, Structural cloze

You can remind the students how to tackle this task type by referring to **Exam File**, Unit 5 **Students' Book** page 64.

10 Just deserts

1 Read for gist.

You may like to give students some background information about the British jury system before they read the text.

Check comprehension of the text before letting students do the gap filling task.

Background information:

In Britain, a jury consists of 12 people over the age of 18. Jurors are ordinary people who have been selected at random to serve on a jury. In Britain if you are called for jury service, you must go. Refusing to serve on a jury is against the law, although exceptions can be made in certain cases. The jury's task is to decide if the accused is guilty or not guilty. The verdict may be unanimous or by a majority of at least 10–2. The judge decides what the sentence should be. Minor crimes are not dealt with by a jury but by up to three magistrates who hear the evidence and decide the punishment. Members of a jury, therefore, may hear details of very serious crimes.

2 Gap fill task.

ANSWERS

1 ago	6 anyone	11 could
2 what	7 be	12 it
3 since	8 no	13 dare
4 or	9 through	14 for
5 up	10 because	15 behind

LISTENING 2 (page 132)

Exam File: Part 3, Sentence completion

Go through the **Exam File** with the class.

1 Introduction to the topic.

Encourage students to bring up anything they know or have heard about identity parades, for example in TV programmes or films.

Use this opportunity to check comprehension of words from the tapescript, such as: *witness*, *alibi*, *assault/attack*

2 🖭 Sentence completion task.

Allow students time to read the questions and predict the answers before they listen. When there are three speakers on a tape, students should pay careful attention to the use of names.

TAPESCRIPT

Matthew Tennison: Detective series on television would never be the same again without identity parades. You know, the victim of an attack looks at the line of people and picks out the person who committed the crime. But psychologists have begun to question just how accurate such identifications are, and their comments may mean that the days of the identity parade are numbered. Anna Hill has been investigating the topic for a television programme. Anna, what do you see as the problem?

Anna Hill: You know, when people are made to stand in a line just for someone to look them over, it's as though everyone there is guilty. It's as if just standing there to be judged makes everyone appear less than one hundred per cent honest. Their faces may be blank, but the person making the identification could see criminal tendencies in any of them, however innocent and honest they may be in real life.

Matthew Tennison: Professor Manners, I think you have had personal experience of this.

Professor Manners: Yes, indeed, I have, and most disturbing it was. As you know, I've been a critic of identity parades for some time and I'd been on television expressing my point of view in my usual forceful way. Well, a few days later I was picked up by the police and forced to line up in an identity parade. To be perfectly honest, I thought they were just trying to get their own back at me for the views I'd expressed so strongly. But no. Apparently, there'd been a case of assault and they wanted to see if the victim could help in pointing out the attacker. The witness came into the room, looked at all of us lined up there and chose me. I knew then that things were serious.

Matthew Tennison: But you had an alibi?

Professor Manners: I most certainly did. At the very moment the assault took place, I was appearing on national television making my case against identity parades.

Matthew Tennison: So why had the woman identified you?

Professor Manners: Well, that's one of the most interesting points about identity parades. The witness is supposed to pick the face that fits their memories of the crime, but those memories are not as reliable as we might think. In this case, when the attack took place the TV had been on in the woman's flat and what she remembered was my face from the TV screen, not the face of the attacker.

Matthew Tennison: Scary.

Professor Manners: Certainly, especially when you consider that in most countries eyewitness evidence of identification is enough to get people convicted and sent to prison.

Matthew Tennison: Anna, you've been visiting police training centres in this country. What's been happening there?

Anna Hill: Well, the police realise how difficult it is for people to provide accurate descriptions. I took part in a typical police training session. They showed me and other trainees a video. There was a man with short, spiky hair and a leather jacket and he snatched a handbag from a middle-aged woman. Afterwards, we were all asked how old the man was. I had no doubt. I was sure he was in his thirties. <u>In fact, he was in his fifties.</u> My memories of other people in leather jackets and with spiky hair had affected the way I remember him. I simply assumed he must be <u>in his thirties</u>.

Matthew Tennison: So what are the police doing, now that they're aware of this tendency?

Anna Hill: <u>They're developing new interviewing procedures.</u> They want witnesses to be able to focus their minds and recall details accurately. They can't do this unless they are relaxed, and it helps if they are allowed to build up the whole context of the day rather than just zooming straight in on the incident. This new technique is called the 'cognitive interview'.

Matthew Tennison: Well, that sounds like an improvement.

Anna Hill: Yes, for interviews I think we'd all agree that it is. But it still doesn't address one of the main problems of the identity parade itself. You know, <u>witnesses are under huge pressure to make an identification.</u> With all those faces ranged towards you, it feels almost inevitable that one of those faces must be guilty. And so the witnesses feel that they are letting people down if they don't pick someone out.

Professor Manners: In the United States, some states are abandoning the traditional line-up for that very reason.

Matthew Tennison: So what are they putting in its place?

Professor Manners: They are using what they call 'sequential identification'. <u>This is a procedure where the witness examines one face at a time.</u> This enables the witness to focus more effectively on each face. And two studies have shown that using a sequential line-up almost halves the rate of false identification, without reducing the number of correct identifications.

Matthew Tennison: Well, it does look as though identity parades need changing, and if some of these ideas are put into practice, then they will be changed for the better. We'll be seeing some changes in TV scripts though.

ANSWERS

(See underlined words in the tapescript.)
 1 appears/looks/seems innocent
 2 criticise
 3 assault/attack
 4 an alibi/evidence
 5 witnesses' memories
 6 age
 7 appearance/clothes/hairstyle
 8 improved
 9 make an identification
 10 one face

---

3 **Comprehension check.**

To check students have understood the main ideas, ask:

What were the main criticisms of identity parades?

What reasons did the speakers give for their criticisms?

How are police procedures changing?

Did the speakers feel the changes will be effective?

What do the students think? Should identity parades be abolished altogether? What would take their place?

The text in the next exercise shows what terrible consequences inaccurate identification can have.

ENGLISH IN USE 2 (page 133)

Part 4, Word formation

1 **Preparation.**

ANSWERS

The crime was robbery. Alfred Beck was sent to prison, but the real criminal was John Smith.

2 **Word formation task.**

ANSWERS

1	innocence	5	accusation
2	notorious	6	confidently
3	imprisonment	7	resemblance
4	angrily	8	broken

READING 2 (page 134)

Part 2, Gapped text

1 **Introduction to the topic.**

The article in this section is not a narrative like the ones students met in Units 6 and 8, but an argumentative text. To do the task successfully, students need to understand the main ideas and follow the logical development of the argument. The two statements given in this exercise summarise the main issues raised by the article. By thinking of ideas to support their own opinions, students will be better prepared to follow the ideas in the article.

2 **Pre-teach vocabulary.**

These words are needed to do the gapped text task. Encourage students to use the context to work out the meanings before looking at the paraphrases/definitions given (A–I).

ANSWERS

1 H 2 F 3 E 4 G 5 C 6 B 7 I 8 D 9 A

3 **Read for the main ideas.**

Tell students to read the base text only and try to answer the questions. Set a time limit. Check their answers before letting them move on.

ANSWERS

1 The participants are the father of a murdered teenager and the teenager who murdered his son. The TV debate is about whether a murderer has the right to a grant to fund a degree course; the article links the TV debate to the wider issue of how prisoners should be treated in order to control crime.

2 The father is against giving grants for the education of prisoners.
The murderer points out he can't get an education without a grant.
The writer is in favour of providing prisoners with education, citing the zero recidivism rate of prisoners who complete their college education, and arguing that the best way to control crime is to help criminals not to commit crimes again.

4 **Identify missing paragraphs.**

Students should make use of the clues in italics, and highlight any other words that help them to decide where the missing paragraphs fit. When checking the task, get them to justify their answers with reference to the parts they have highlighted.

ANSWERS

1 C (lexical links with first paragraph – a father/his son)
2 F (lexical links – a convict/his prison term)
3 A (lexical links with next paragraph – furious/ passionate speeches)
4 D (lexical links with next paragraph – luxury holiday camp/three meals a day)
5 E (links between two ideas in last sentence of E and *We cannot have it both ways*)

5 **Response to the text.**

Students can compare the ideas and issues raised in the article with their own ideas in Exercise 1.

Take a straw poll to find out if anyone's views have changed after reading the article.

ANSWERS

- **In favour of harsh treatment:**
  Why should those who commit crimes be helped to study and to achieve when their victims cannot?
  Criminals should be made to pay for what they have done.
- **In favour of education and training:**
  Education gives prisoners the tools with which to build a useful life.
  Prison should aim to rehabilitate criminals by equipping prisoners with the skills to build a useful life when they are released.

6 **Text analysis: style and register.**

Analysis of this sort raises points that students will find useful when they write articles themselves for Paper 2.

POSSIBLE ANSWERS

His points made sense. (main text)
Now they are simply scary. (main text)
Something has to change. (main text)
We cannot have it both ways. (main text)
Where's the fairness, where's the justice? (para C)
There can be a middle ground. (para D)
Using a mixture of short sentences and longer ones adds variety and interest to an article for the general reader. Short sentences, and the occasional use of fragments, can be used to create a dramatic effect.
The register is semi-formal – the writer uses short and long sentences, direct and indirect speech, rhetorical questions *(Where was the fairness?)* etc.
The use of personal pronouns, and references to the writer's own feelings make the tone personal rather than purely objective. At the same time the writer clearly considers the subject matter serious not frivolous.

SPEAKING 2 (page 136)

Exam File: Part 3, Debate; Part 4, Summarise conclusions

Use the information in the **Exam File** to introduce this new task type.

The photo illustrates a harsh prison environment. It shows a chain gang wearing prison clothing. They are digging in a quarry. A guard armed with a shotgun is overseeing their work.

You could discuss the photo before or after students have done the Speaking task.

1 **Collaborative task: pair discussion.**

The extracts in this exercise continue the theme of Reading 2. Remind students to use the **Language Bank** as a resource.

2 **Report back.**

This reporting back stage can be done in groups of four to simulate Part 4 of the Speaking Test.

3 **Text analysis: style and register.**

The aim is to show how the passive tends to be used in formal, written English. The re-writing task can be set for homework, and gives students further practice in using passive forms in context. Refer students to Language Study, **Students' Book** pages 130–131.

ANSWER

Extract A sounds more like spoken English.

WRITING (page 137)

Part 2, Article

Step 1 Task interpretation

Remind students to highlight key words in the writing task so they can be sure they have covered all the necessary points in their answer.

ANSWERS

text type:	article for a magazine
points to include:	details of typical teenage crimes with reasons why they are committed / pros and cons of different punishments
target readers:	expert judges/general readers
register/tone:	neutral

Step 2 Generating ideas

Students should list as many ideas as possible even if some are not used. There are plenty of ideas in earlier parts of the unit – too many to use in a 250-word article. Encourage students to think of anything else they have recently read or seen on this topic as well.

Step 3 Layout and organisation

Students organise their notes according to the suggested plan.

Remind them that an article must have a title – which is given in the task description – and may have sub-headings too.

Step 4 Write

Encourage students to make use of the **Language Banks** as a resource. This article will have quite a lot of specialised vocabulary.

MODEL ANSWER

How should society deal with young offenders?
The rise in the number of young offenders in today's society is increasingly worrying. This article looks at the causes of criminal behaviour among young people and considers the best ways of dealing with it.

Why do young people become offenders? Petty crime is often the result of boredom. Teenagers hanging around the streets often commit acts of vandalism because they have nowhere to go and nothing else to do. There are two solutions to this type of crime. Firstly, affordable leisure facilities and youth clubs should be provided. Secondly, a period of community service would encourage a sense of responsibility towards the environment.

Solutions to more serious crimes such as theft are less easy to find. Offending teenagers usually come from disadvantaged backgrounds, and often a family member has a criminal record. A period on probation would be one solution, or imposing a fine on the parents.

In the case of violent crimes, such as assault and even murder, it can be argued that the young offender should be sentenced to imprisonment. However, statistics show that on leaving prison, young offenders are more likely to commit crime than before they arrived. Counselling, accompanied by time in a detention centre, could re-educate and reform.

To sum up, I believe that in order to deal effectively with young offenders, the causes of the crime must be considered as well as the crime itself. Young offenders are far from hardened criminals, so the emphasis ought to be on reform rather than simply punishment.

Exam Practice 2

Note that the numbers in the **Exam Practice** sections follow on, as in the exam itself.

READING

Part 2, Gapped text

ANSWERS
15 D (semantic links: *to lose them/I returned*)
16 C (lexical links with next paragraph: *caught up with them/confronted them*)
17 E (pronoun links: *one of them/they had dropped* lexical links: *my girlfriend's bag/the bag*)
18 F (parallel phrases: *Do I feel brave?/Do I feel proud?*)
19 B (repeated words: *A man returned/ The man they arrested*)
20 A (pronoun link: *That response* – refers to preceding paragraph)

ENGLISH IN USE

Part 3, Error correction

ANSWERS		
31 it	37 ✓	42 be
32 of	38 ✓	43 bit
33 by	39 so	44 that
34 if	40 the	45 to
35 ✓	41 for	46 ✓
36 them		

ENGLISH IN USE

Part 4, Word formation

ANSWERS		
47 individuality	52 rebellion	57 industrial
48 guilty	53 admirable	58 compensation
49 surprisingly	54 birth	59 unreasonable
50 embarrassment	55 refusal	60 regardless
51 Unfortunately	56 unfairly	61 employees

A sense of belonging

SPEAKING 1 (page 142)

1 Talk about photographs.

This is useful practice for Part 2 of the Speaking Test. Encourage students to use their imaginations to speculate about the day-to-day life of people in the different types of environment. They should then give their personal reaction to the photos by saying which lifestyle they would prefer and why.

Remind students to make use of the **Language Bank**.

Photo 1 shows a man and a woman talking in front of a pavement café in Greenwich Village, New York. He is wearing a white vest, long shorts and flip-flop sandals. She is wearing a white T-shirt and black trousers.

Photo 2 shows a cricket match on an English village green in front of a pub. The players are wearing cricket whites.

Photo 3 shows a countryside scene in rural Ireland. The sea, fields, stone walls and a cottage are visible. There are no people to be seen, but it should be easy to speculate about the life of the person who lives in the isolated cottage.

Photo 4 shows a group of people who are protesting about the fact that some very old trees are about to be cut down. People are cooking on an open fire and eating in front of makeshift tents. A man is wearing a red tie-dyed shirt and jeans and a little boy is wearing a checked shirt.

2 Extension of discussion.

In this part, the discussion moves away from the photos towards more general topics. This is relevant to Part 4 of the Speaking Test. It is also useful preparation for reading the texts in the following sections.

ENGLISH IN USE 1 (page 143)

Part 3, Error correction

1 Read for general understanding.

Students read the text and answer the questions to get a general idea of its content before looking for the errors.

Notes on the text:

The £10 passage scheme is no longer available.

Rabbits were introduced to Australia. They have no predators in Australia and multiplied at an alarming rate until the disease myxamatosis was introduced in an effort to reduce their numbers.

ANSWERS

1 Perth in Western Australia.
2 sick cattle; thousands of rabbits eating the grass
3 They overcame their difficulties through hard work and determination.
4 The 'dream' was a prosperous life in Australia. The people who 'sold' the dream were the British and Australian authorities who encouraged British families to go and start a new life out there by offering them subsidised travel.

2 Vocabulary: idiomatic expressions.

ANSWERS

1 in very bad condition, about to die
2 make a success of something through hard work
3 in spite of great difficulties

3 Error correction task.

Remind students that up to five lines may be correct, and that extra words must be wrong and not just unnecessary.

ANSWERS

1	at	(the preposition *at* must be followed by a noun phrase)
2	was	(*sigh* cannot be made passive as it is an intransitive verb)
3	by	(*by then nineteen* would be possible but not the other way round)
4	✓	
5	been	(not a passive)
6	✓	
7	of	(*worst* is an adjective modifying *nightmare* and must directly precede the noun)
8	✓	
9	also	(this again is in the wrong position – *and also the grass* would be allowable)
10	the	(see Grammar Notes **Students' Book** page 200 for use of definite articles)
11	✓	
12	having	(incorrect structure: the expression is *leave sth for sth else* (n.))
13	such	(*such* would need to be followed by *that* + noun clause)
14	all	(*everything* would be the right word)
15	more	(either *more than* or *over* – a mixture of two expressions here)
16	ourselves	(*do well* or *do **oneself** proud* – another mix-up)

11 A sense of belonging

READING 1 (page 144)

Part 1, Multiple matching

1 Skim for gist.

1 Remind students that headlines and sub-headings often sum up the key ideas of an article. Here the sub-heading in bold print – which is printed for visual impact in the middle of the text – sums up the entire article. This is a common feature of magazine articles.

ANSWERS

Wagon-trains and the *wild west* are associated with the cowboys and settlers of North America. It makes those people moving sound like pioneers taking part in something exciting and adventurous. This is in deliberate contrast to the reference to *welfare*. Unlike the pioneers of the American Wild West, these families are being supported by state payments.

---

2 Remind students to read the first and last paragraphs and the first and last sentences of the other paragraphs when they skim – this is usually where the most important information is located.

ANSWERS

1 a chance to live in the country (first para); city-dwellers hope to get a house and a job (lines 42–46/104–6); there is a lot of crime in the cities (lines 86–87); a better chance for their children (last para)
2 rural communities are rejuvenated (sub-heading) – more young people moving in; more children means jobs for local teachers (lines 122–124)
3 families, especially children benefit from growing up in the countryside away from problems of city life; moving gives them new hope and courage (last para)

---

2 Multiple matching task.

1 Remind students that when the text is continuous, not divided into sections, underlining the names given will enable them to locate rapidly the parts of the text where they are likely to find the answers to the questions.

Check answers before students do the Reading task.

ANSWERS

Jim Connolly – sculptor who grew up in the west, founder of Rural Resettlement
Paul Murphy – former Dublin bus driver working for Rural Resettlement
Rebecca Boland – 9-year-old daughter of Antony
Noeleen Boland – wife of Antony
Mary Roche – principal of local school

---

2 Students should highlight the parts of the text where they find the answers. Get them to justify their answers by referring to the evidence they have highlighted.

Notes on the text:

Yep: a variant of *yes* (not used by well-educated adults)
Gaelic football: this is a type of football played in Ireland, different from soccer, rugby etc.

IR £2,000: the Irish pound is called the *punt* and is not the same currency as the pound sterling

---

ANSWERS

1 A Antony's mother told him he was mad to be leaving Dublin. (lines 67–68)
2 B . . . Jim Connolly. A sculptor . . . what Connolly did was start up Rural Resettlement . . . (lines 5–14)
3 C Paul Murphy, a former Dublin bus driver, has become Connolly's second-in-command (lines 30–32)
4 D Rebecca Boland is already beginning to sound like a country girl from Clare (lines 47–49)
5 C Local people's worries . . . Paul Murphy's standard response . . . (lines 113–118)
6 F Now she has been made principal and another teacher . . . . has been taken on. (lines 129–132)
7 A Anthony hopes to find work as a farm labourer. (lines 112–113)
8 B Connolly looked round his village one day thinking something was missing and then realised . . . the people had gone. So . . . (lines 9–13)
9 C Paul Murphy's history of Loop Head . . . (lines 139–140)
10 E Noeleen said they had to go back to Dublin. She would not risk their children's lives again. (lines 82–85)
11 B Connolly went on Irish radio . . . . I'll help you find a house and a plot of land . . . (lines 22–25)
12 A Antony remembers a Ford Fiesta . . . 'Yep,' said my son, 'fab.' What worried me was that he would start doing the same thing when he got older . . . (lines 91–100)
13 C He has written a film script about his family's odyssey . . . (lines 144–145)
14 F Mary Roche watched the numbers at her school dwindle . . . Without the arrival of the settlement children, she would have lost her job. (lines 124–129)
15 A . . . his shoulders made broad and muscular by digging the land. (lines 71–73)

---

3 Group/class discussion: response to the text.
Students can discuss these questions in groups of four, with a group secretary taking notes. Follow up with a class report back session.

4 Vocabulary: phrasal verbs.
Make this into a competition, to see how many students can remember the phrasal verbs without looking back at the text.

ANSWERS

1	started up	5	bring up
2	fell through	6	taken on
3	make the numbers up	7	strike out
4	looks out on		

ANSWERS

1 <u>goob</u> bonus
2 <u>tem</u> million
3 <u>teng</u> cats.
4 <u>them</u> made
5 <u>ing</u> case

► ► *Extension activity*

Students work in groups. They select up to five expressions or collocations from the text, and write a paraphrase or synonym for each. They can use dictionaries for this stage.

They then take turns to test each other. One student from each group reads out a definition and the rest of the class tries to guess the word.

PRONUNCIATION (page 146)

Assimilation

1 🔊 **Assimilation after /d/ and /n/.**
Assimilation affects certain consonant sounds, especially /d/ and /n/. The quality of sound changes when they are followed by other consonants such as /b/ and /p/ or /k/ and /g/. This means that 'good boy' can sound like 'goob boy'; 'can be' may sound like 'cam be' and 'can go' may sound like 'cang go'.

Understanding that assimilation occurs and can make words sound different from what might be expected will help students with listening comprehension tasks. They don't have to practise assimilation in their own speech. It is the inevitable physiological result of speaking at a certain speed but does not happen in slow speech. Something similar happens in most languages and it is not really something you can deliberately choose to do or not do.

TAPESCRIPT

See Students' Book.

2 🔊 **Assimilation after *can*.**

TAPESCRIPT

See Students' Book.

ANSWERS

1 'can be' sounds like 'cam be'
2 'can come' sounds like 'cang come'
In both cases, *can* is unstressed.

3 **Practice.**
Tell students not to worry if they find this difficult to do. It is mainly a listening skill.

LISTENING (page 146)
Part 3, Multiple choice questions

1 **Introduction to the topic.**
Explain the difference between gypsies or Romanies, who have always travelled from place to place, and New Age travellers. The latter are not gypsies, but have deliberately decided to opt out of mainstream society, and live a life which they feel is more meaningful and closer to nature. New Age travellers are usually viewed with dislike and suspicion, just as gypsies have always been.

You can also explain that in England almost all land is privately-owned. This makes it extremely difficult to follow a travelling life style because there is almost nowhere that you can legally stop and camp.

2 🔊 **Multiple choice questions**
Encourage students to follow the advice in the **Exam File** in Unit 4, **Students' Book** page 52. They should read the questions only before listening the first time, and note down their own answers while listening. (See also Teacher's Book Unit 9, page 79.) Before the second listening, they read the options, compare their answers, then listen to check.

When going through the answers, you can explain the meaning of the following extract from the tapescript:
We live in a beautiful old trailer pulled by a big old (and legal) truck: It is commonly supposed that the vehicles of New Age travellers are uninsured and do not have road tax discs and certificates of roadworthiness. Nicola is indicating that her truck does have all these things.

TAPESCRIPT

Interviewer: . . . Do you find that you get different reactions from different people in the community?

Nicola: Yeah. I am described as a lot of things by different people. <u>To the police I am a 'New Age traveller'</u>, to the local authorities I am a 'camper' or 'hippy'.

Interviewer: And is this how you regard yourself?

Nicola: What I really am is the mother of three young children whom I wash, clean, feed and teach from 7.30 a.m. until 8.30 p.m. daily.

Interviewer: And where do you call home?

Nicola: We live in a beautiful old trailer pulled by a big old (and legal) truck. Before that my husband Richard and I rented a place in Birmingham, but we left there four years ago hoping to find somewhere more satisfying to live. What we wanted was a place where we wouldn't be afraid of walking in the streets, where we wouldn't have to worry about our children inhaling heavily-polluted air every time we let them out to play. We felt something was wrong, something was missing, so we went out searching for that missing something.

Interviewer: And has it been worth it?

Nicola: Yes, to our delight and surprise we found many beautiful uncultivated pieces of 'wasteland'. And many little places which had been forgotten about.

Interviewer: And were you and the family alone?

Nicola: Oh, no, not at all. In these places we found many like-minded people – there were ex-nurses, engineers, carpenters, financial consultants, social workers there was even a vicar. They were living in converted trucks, buses, horse boxes, trailers and, you know, wagons pulled by horses. All were seeking a different way of life – a better way of life away from the madness of modern living.

Interviewer: What's it like entering a travellers' camp?

Nicola: Anyone entering a travellers' camp for the first time must be prepared for the culture shock. It's a bit like I imagine it would be stepping back into the sixteenth century, yet seeing people working with twentieth century tools. The people will be wearing colourful, old clothes and often have windswept hair and dirty faces. There will be a fire heating a large iron kettle – someone cooking, someone singing, a mother quietly nursing her baby, children playing loudly and perhaps the sound of someone playing a whistle or violin. You will find a close community who look after one another, working with others to survive.

Interviewer: Sounds idyllic.

Nicola: Maybe, but life this way is hard. Each day we need wood for warmth and cooking, and sometimes we have to walk far to find dead wood which we'll them carry home, saw and axe into suitable pieces. Then there is the water to fetch and the washing to do. These are our daily chores which have to be done. In warm weather, these activities can be a pleasure since you get to see the land around you and watch it change through the seasons. But the winters are not so kind to us – I've been through more than one I'd like to forget, I can tell you. But that is when you really appreciate being amongst a community. You have to pull together. Everyone has a part and you're all equal.

Interviewer: Do you have to watch out for intruders?

Nicola: No strangers can come amongst us without being heard by the horses or the dogs or the geese. They will be watched, scrutinised and sometimes turned away.

But they might also be led to the fire and given food to eat and something to drink. We are always suspicious of the police, of the council and locals with shotguns. We have been hurt many times. So sometimes we hide. If we are seen, we'll be moved and every time we move, well, we have problems.

Interviewer: So what is the compensation for you?

Nicola: Well, I believe our way is one of the most environmentally acceptable ways to live today. Staying only briefly in places, we use the land only a little, and the land will soon right itself when we are gone. We make use of dead wood in the locality which makes room for new trees and plants to grow and we often plant trees ourselves. We use water sparingly. We collect and recycle other people's rubbish. You should never be able to tell where responsible travellers have lived.

Nomadism is a valid way of life yet we, like this planet, are in danger of extinction. Surely this is wrong?

ANSWERS

(See underlined words in the tapescript.)

1 C   2 D   3 D   4 A   5 C   6 A   7 B

LANGUAGE STUDY (page 147)

Cleft sentences: *wh-* type

1 Analysis.

Introduce the topic by pointing out that in speech we can use stress to emphasise the most important information in a sentence without changing the grammatical structure in any way. But we can also use certain grammatical structures to highlight important information. The passive is one grammatical way of highlighting information (see Unit 10). Cleft sentences are another way. Explain that *cleft* means *divided* or *split*.

The cleft sentence construction in this section emphasises one element by splitting the sentence up and inserting a relative clause beginning with a question word. The inserted words are in italics in the examples.

ANSWERS

1
1 Chicken curries from his favourite take-away *are what* Antony Boland misses.
2 A place where we wouldn't be afraid of walking in the streets *was what* we wanted.
3 The mother of three young children *is what* I really am.

2
The verb is emphasised.
The auxiliary verb *do* is used in the *wh-* clause as a substitute for the main verb.

2 Practice: sentence transformation.

Explain that cleft sentences usually have a contrastive function. They relate back to something that has been previously stated. This is why pairs of sentences are given in these exercises. Students rewrite the second sentence, which contrasts in some way with the idea in the first. Clues are given to help them.

When you check answers, practise the correct intonation. The words in bold in the answers below are stressed and spoken at a higher pitch.

ANSWERS

1 What **no one** looks forward to, though, are the long, cold winters.
2 But what **particularly** impresses them is the friendliness of the people.
3 But what they've **forgotten** to send us is the train timetable we asked for. / But what they've forgotten to do is send us . . .
4 What you really **mustn't** miss is the medieval castle.
5 What you **didn't** warn us about was the terrible roads.
6 What I **thought** we might do is book a Mediterranean cruise.

3 Practice: complete dialogues.

Students work in pairs and take turns to ask and answer the questions in their own way. Give further practice in intonation.

POSSIBLE ANSWERS

1 . . . dinner for two at a really good restaurant.
2 . . . to get a job in Canada.
3 . . . this college?
   . . . is the self study facilities.
4 . . . counselling for young offenders?
   . . . counselling.
   . . . long prison sentences!
5 . . . your problems at work.
   . . . that I've decided to resign.

Cleft sentences: *It + be*

4 Analysis.

Explain that this is another grammatical method which achieves the same aim.

5 Practice.

Students rewrite the second sentence in each pair. Model and practise the intonation. The words in bold are stressed and have rising intonation.

ANSWERS

1 It was her **teacher** who first spotted her potential as a runner.
2 It is the friendliness of the **people** that you will remember for the rest of your life.
3 It was **John** who introduced me to the place.
4 It is the surrounding **countryside** and the good **ski slopes** that attract people to this area.
5 It wasn't until the early **1980s** that many high-tech companies moved here.
6 It is because I love working with **animals** that I accepted it.

ENGLISH IN USE 2 (page 148)

Part 3, Error correction

Spelling and punctuation

The spelling exercises prepare students for the Error correction task on page 149.

1 Analysis: spelling rules.

Refer students to the Notes on **Students's Book** pages 212–213 to check their own answers.

ANSWERS

1 Plural forms
monkeys / journeys / odysseys
varieties / libraries / centuries / companies / cities
When -*y* follows a consonant it changes to -*ies* in the plural.
2 Adding -*ing*
studying, paying, saying, crying
lying, dying
No change after a final -*y*; final -*ie* changes to -*y*.
3 Suffixes
happiness, easily, beautiful, prettier, glorious
y changes to *i*.
4 Past participles
paid, said, laid

2 Practice.

Students complete the sentences using the words they have just practised spelling.

ANSWERS
1 studying, studies
2 paid, companies
3 copies, copied
4 dying, died

3 Read for general understanding.

Students should read to the end of the text to get a general idea of the content.

4 **Error correction task.**
Remind students that between three and five lines may be correct.

5 **Group discussion: response to the text.**
Students discuss these questions in groups of four. Encourage them to respond to specific points in the article, and to use vocabulary from the text.

Follow up with a brief whole class report back stage.

READING 2 (page 150)

Part 2, Gapped text

1 **Introduction to the topic.**

2 **Read for the main events.**
Students read the base text only. The questions focus attention on the key events of the narrative.

3 **Identify missing paragraphs.**
Remind students to highlight key words. Names are particularly important in this text.

Notes on the text:
bunny jumps: jumping up and down like a rabbit
cream bun fetcher: this means that she went and got

refreshments for her fellow-workers, something a junior employee would be asked to do
blows away the cobwebs: makes her feel refreshed

VOCABULARY (page 151)

Describing places: creating atmosphere

1 This helps to prepare students for the writing task ahead.

Expressions to do with living somewhere

2 Students complete the sentences.

WRITING (page 152)

(page 152)

Exam File: Part 2, Tourist brochure

Introduce this task type by going through the **Exam File** with the class.

1 Analyse a model: content and style.

ANSWERS

1 location, history, elegant atmosphere
2 places of interest, entertainment, sports facilities, eating out, shopping
3 the general visitor

2 Analyse a model: vocabulary.

ANSWERS

beautiful stretches of countryside, leisurely, relax, peaceful country atmosphere, elegant shops, richly varied, wide range of entertainment, excellent choice of restaurants

3 Writing task.

Students read the writing task and follow the steps to writing.

Step 1 Task interpretation

Remind students to highlight key words in the task.

ANSWERS

target readers:	student visitors from different countries
register/tone:	semi-formal, friendly
points to include:	must include background information, recommendations, practical information

Step 2 Generating ideas

Students should use the three essential content areas mentioned in the task as headings for their notes. They should include items of particular interest to the target reader.

Step 3 Layout and organisation

A brochure leaflet should have a title and subheadings. It should not be one continuous piece of prose, as this would make it difficult for readers to find the information they want quickly.

Step 4 Write

Tell students to present the information in a clear and straightforward way. Long, complicated sentences should be avoided in this kind of writing.

MODEL ANSWER

Welcome to Chester
Anyone visiting Chester for the first time will immediately be struck by its well-preserved Roman walls and medieval buildings. Built on the banks of the river Dee, this Roman city has much to offer the visitor.

Places of interest
If you want to find out about the history of Chester and its inhabitants, the Grosvenor Museum has a fine collection of Roman antiquities. The museum is open from 9 a.m. to 5 p.m. daily and with a student pass costs £5.50 to get in.

Sport and leisure
Northgate Arena is the biggest leisure centre in the North of England, offering a wide variety of sporting activities. So if you'd like to put in some extra training, or even just go for a sauna, Northgate is the place for you. The centre is open from 9 a.m. to 9 p.m., Mondays to Saturdays.

Shopping
The High Street precinct offers a wide variety of shops to suit every taste. Whether it's souvenirs for the family, or a new pair of trainers, you'll find what you're looking for here. If you're feeling tired after your shopping spree, visit the impressive Grosvenor Hotel. They do an excellent English High Tea for a reasonable price.

Night life
In the evenings there's a wide range of things to do. If you've had a hard day training, you could while away an hour or two at the Odeon cinema. For those of you who'd rather do something livelier, there's the newly refurbished McGowan's bar on Frith street. Live local bands play here from Monday to Friday.

SPEAKING 2 (page 154)

(page 154)

Part 3, Select and plan; Part 4, Report decisions

1 Collaborative task.

Make sure students understand that they must talk about the topic, not just what they see in the pictures. The pictures are simply prompts to start them thinking.

Refer students to the **Language Bank**.

Photo 1 shows a child wearing a colourful costume at London's famous Notting Hill Carnival, which takes place every August.
Photo 2 shows women Morris dancing in a village street. Morris dancing is a traditional form of dancing. It is performed by teams (sides) of dancers, wearing special costumes, often with bells on their legs.

11 A sense of belonging

Photo 3 shows a craftsman weaving a basket at a craft fair.

2 Report back.
This can be done in groups of four to simulate Part 4 of the Speaking Test.

3 Extension of the discussion.
These are typical of the more extended questions that the examiner will ask in Part 4.

4 Optional writing task: leaflet.
Students may enjoy writing and designing a leaflet to advertise their own event. They should follow the same guidelines as for the tourist brochure leaflet.

ENGLISH IN USE 3 (page 155)

Part 5, Register cloze

1 Preparation.
Students read the advertising brochure and answer the questions.

Ask students what they think of the idea of time ownership. Can they think of any drawbacks?

ANSWERS

1 A *time ownership home* is a property that you buy a share in, giving you the right to spend a certain amount of time there each year.

Additional information

Once you have bought your share, you do not have to pay any more money, except for service charges, and you can rent out the week to others, or sell your remaining years on the contract.

2 people who are quite wealthy

3 spacious terrace, supremely spacious living room, inviting, adorned with, elegant oak unit, exclusive . . . appliances, irresistible opulence, elegance, indulgence, sheer pleasure, superb attention to detail, lavished, exceptional

2 Register transfer task.
Students should underline the phrases in the brochure that they have to express using different words in the letter. The gaps in text 2 follow the sequence of text 1. Remind students of the two-word maximum word limit.

ANSWERS

1 cheaper	6 large	11 most people
2 for ever	7 sit down	12 your choice
3 children	8 see it	13 reasonable
4 view	9 missing	
5 calm	10 comfortable	

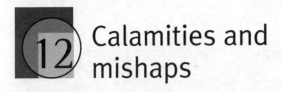

Calamities and mishaps

Pronunciation note: Check that students know *mishap* is pronounced *mis + hap*. There is no *sh* sound. The word derives from *happen*, that is, happen in a bad way.

SPEAKING (page 156)

1 Talk about visual prompts.

This is useful practice for Part 2 of the Speaking Test. The questions prompt students to speculate and hypothesise about what may/might/must have happened, as well as to suggest what the people in the pictures could or should have done to avoid getting into these situations. The **Language Bank** contains useful words and phrases.

Picture 1 shows a pickpocket stealing traveller's cheques from the back pocket of one of two tourists. Big Ben is visible in the background, so the tourists must be visiting London.

Picture 2 shows a man and woman looking horrified to find their tent has been trampled by a cow.

Picture 3 shows a man and woman next to their car, which must have broken down or run out of petrol, leaving them stranded in the middle of the country.

Picture 4 shows two people clinging to a small boat, which has capsized. The palm tree on the shore suggests a Caribbean island, so perhaps a hurricane is blowing up.

2 Collaborative task.

Students decide how to get out of one of the pictured situations. This collaborative activity is useful practice for Part 3 of the Speaking Test.

LISTENING 1 (page 157)

Part 4, Multiple matching

1 🖳 Multiple matching: Task One.

This is the first multiple matching listening task presented in exact exam format. Students should answer questions 1–5 on the first listening. Explain that the phrase *as you hear them* means *in the order that you hear them*.

They should write the letter that applies to the first speaker on the dotted line next to 1, and so on.

Give them time to read the questions and highlight key words before playing the recording.

You could check answers to Task One immediately, or continue with Task Two before checking, as in the exam.

Note on the text: (Speaker 1)
At 5.45 a.m. on January 17, 1995, there was a major earthquake in and around the city of Kobe in Japan.

TAPESCRIPT

Speaker 1: Well, <u>I woke around quarter to six</u> because the room started shaking, and I thought it was a nightmare at first, but it stopped and *I went to my mum's room to ask her what to do.* It was the top room and there was a view of the rest of Kobe, and I had a look outside and there were lots of fires everywhere, and you could hear fire engines and it was very scary. After the earthquake, our water supply was cut off and our electricity too. But there was a spring near us so we usually got water from there – we heated it up with gas cylinders to get hot water to wash in, but we didn't have much food. Water came back on after a few weeks, and our gas took a bit longer, I think about six weeks or something like that.

Speaker 2: I got my bag stolen once, with all my money and credit cards. I was out with some friends, it was actually pretty late at night, and <u>I put my bag down at my feet, and when I looked it wasn't there any more. I don't know what happened.</u> I called my mother and said, 'This is the phone call you hoped you weren't going to get, but here it is. Cancel all my credit cards.' And that was that until the next day, *when I went to the consulate and applied for a new passport.* And then on my way back to my hotel, I saw a policeman holding some travellers cheques that looked like mine, and they were. They were arresting a girl. She had my passport and my travellers cheques, so I got my passport back eventually, later on that day.

Speaker 3: Not last weekend but the weekend before, I was down in <u>Oxford Street</u> to buy a CD. I was just walking along the street and I was about to get on a bus – <u>the traffic is very heavy there</u>, so the bus was moving very slowly – and anyway, this young man was about to step off the bus. I think he was in a hurry and he jumped, and he got his heel caught in some lady's bag because it was very crowded, and he went flying over the railing and landed headfirst in one of the rubbish bins. *And everyone around laughed. It was quite funny, I thought.*

Speaker 4: Well, my story is not so much one specific event but a dreadful situation I got myself into, a really bad financial situation, and I had to get help, psychological as well as practical. A few years ago, <u>I was feeling really down</u> when my boyfriend and I split up, and like many people at that time I was being offered credit almost every time I went into a shop – there didn't seem to be any difficulty about getting shops to give you a credit account. So I just shopped and shopped, and it became a sort of compensation for everything else that was lacking in my life. Of course, it was wonderful at first, just buying anything I fancied. But the debts got bigger and bigger, and I found them harder and harder to pay. Well, to cut a long story short, *a friend advised me to get help* from a debt-counsellor, and things have got better, and I'm gradually paying off my debts, but, for a time things were really rough indeed.

Speaker 5: One day we wanted to get to a place and we had to go <u>along the stony beach</u>, and there was some mud beside the beach, and my sister was sort of walking across the mud and she slipped and then . . . um . . . Dad said like, this is how you walk across the mud, and then he sank into the mud and, well, I shouted to Mum, and Mum came along and tried to dig him out, and then she got stuck, and then they were both stuck, and then my sister got stuck as well. *So I had to run around and collect sticks and stuff to get them out,* and eventually we got them out, but Mum lost a pair of tights, and Dad lost some socks, and we lost one boot in the mud.

ANSWERS

(See underlined words in the tapescript.)

1 F 2 D 3 H 4 B 5 A

2 🔲 **Multiple matching: Task Two.**
Students answer the remaining questions on the second listening.

ANSWERS

(See italicised words in the tapescript.)

6 C 7 H 8 F 9 E 10 B

3 **Class/group discussion: response to the Listening text.**
This exercise checks comprehension, activates vocabulary from the text, and allows students to react to the content.

Ask: What happened? What did the speaker do?

Write useful vocabulary on the board. You can do this while monitoring groups if this is done as a group activity.

ENGLISH IN USE 1 (page 157)

Part 4, Word formation

1 **Read for general understanding.**
The questions ensure that students read the whole text before answering the questions.

Note:

tots: colloquial word for small children (under about seven), probably a short form of *toddler*.

2 **Word formation task.**
When checking answers, point out the difference between *tasty* (= sth that tastes good) and *tasteful* (= in good taste, stylish), which are often confused.

ANSWERS

1 hungry	5	unlucky
2 rescuers	6	malnutrition
3 wilderness	7	injuries
4 tasty	8	recovery

3 **Extension activity.**
Students can work in groups of four.

READING 1 (page 158)

Part 3, Multiple choice questions

1 **Read for gist.**
The aim is to introduce some key vocabulary from the text and ensure that students read to the end to get the general idea before they tackle the questions.

ANSWERS

1

1   *alms:* (old-fashioned) money given to the poor; synonym: *aid*
    pauper: very poor person; synonym: *the poor*
    hobo: tramp, homeless person; synonym: *pauper in rags*
    pose as someone: pretend to be someone
2   *this* – an experiment the writer carried out
3   The writer begged for money, first dressed as a homeless person and then as a business man.
4   He wanted to find out whether people's responses would differ according to the appearance of the beggar.

2 **Guess meaning from context.**
These items are ones students need to understand to answer the multiple choice questions.

ANSWERS

1 E   2 C   3 G   4 D   5 A   6 H   7 B   8 F

3 **Multiple choice questions.**
Remind students that they must find textual support for the option that they choose.

Get them to justify their answers with reference to the text when you check the task.

ANSWERS

1 C   I am not sure about the ethics of this – its basic method is deceit (lines 1–3)
2 D   They would pay on collection. . . . the woman made me pay there and then . . . (lines 30–34)
3 C   The shame of it made me start out with the wrong phrase, inviting an answer in the negative. (lines 51–54)

4 B A delicate, curly-haired man in his forties . . . (line 85–86); A man who looked like a builder . . . (lines 99–100)

5 A I had arrived there, stupidly, I explained, without any money . . . and I needed a ticket . . . (lines 110–111)

6 D They are prepared, on the whole, to give to a stranger . . . that readiness to give is not related to the need. . . . The only substantial difference between them is in what they look like. (lines 143–154)

4 Vocabulary: metaphorical use of language.

This section deals with examples of metaphorical language in the text. Let students work in pairs.

ANSWERS

dug: suggests a deeper more thorough search. *Put their hands in their pockets* suggests pulling out the first coin available rather than searching for a coin to give.
sift: means to separate fine grains of flour from lumps. Here it means *a painstaking search for the right person*.
mould: something used to give a shape to liquids that harden to the shape of the mould. Here it means *a similar background, attitude*. The same formative influences have shaped their character and outlook.

5 Discussion: response to the text.

Encourage students to use words and phrases from the text and refer to their own experiences.

LISTENING 2 (page 160)

Part 1, Sentence completion

1 Pre-teach vocabulary: phrasal verbs.

Students complete the sentences with the appropriate particle. Check comprehension.

ANSWERS

1 up   2 by   3 off   4 up   5 out of   6 out   7 with

2 🎧 Sentence completion task.

Give students time to read the questions and make predictions. Point out the word limit.

TAPESCRIPT

Narrator: Well, I came back from work that day and I was in a tearing hurry because I had to change into a black suit to go to a funeral, and I'd got my brother and his family coming to stay that night. I had to go straight from the funeral to pick them up at the airport, and I was anxious to clear the car out so that I'd got plenty of space for them. So I was doing that, and I knew that I

was going to need my handbag with me, so I left it on the passenger seat of the car parked outside my house. It was a beautiful day and I'd left the window open, and by the time I'd got myself organised and rushed out to the car, I looked on the passenger seat and there was nothing there, and I thought, 'Oh I've left my bag inside the house', and I rushed around every single room looking for it, but I really knew where I'd left it, and that someone had obviously just been passing by and had stolen it. And of course at that particular moment, as I said, I was late for the funeral, and that's the one thing you can't be late for. I didn't have any means of contacting the police, or anybody else for that matter, because my mobile phone which, of course, I could have used from the car, was inside the handbag.

So I rushed off in a great sense of panic. I got back home about seven o'clock, and then I reported the loss of my cheque card and credit card. I was just about to go down to the village to report the matter to the police when I thought, 'Well, I'll just pick up the messages on the answerphone', and there was this girl who said, 'I've found your address in a diary, and I've found lots of things that seem to belong to you when I was walking my dog, and I saw all these things in a bush.' And in fact she lived maybe three or four hundred yards away, and I was absolutely amazed and extremely pleased. I rang her up and told her who I was and she said, 'I've got all these things in a plastic bag. Do come and pick them up.'

And then I went to the police station and I tipped all this stuff all out of the plastic bag onto the counter in the police station and worked out by a process of elimination what was missing. I mean, my bag is very large. It had been completely scattered over this bush, my wallet, driving licence, all that kind of thing.

Anyway, inevitably, the cash was missing, just over £150. The mobile phone was missing and the spare battery. But my cheque book and card were there, and my credit card too. Quite extraordinary. Well, except that points to it having been children, who didn't know what to do, or who weren't old enough to be able to cope with trying to get money out of a machine or trying to pass a cheque off, or something like that. So I mean that was good news, but of course I'd lost a lot of money, although my diary was the thing I was most concerned about, so I was extremely relieved to get that, but I was a bit disappointed because the actual handbag itself was still missing.

So I phoned up this girl again and asked her where she'd found all these things. We met there and had another look to find if by any chance there was anything she'd missed. Rather than looking on the ground and in these bushes just at the side of the path where she'd been walking her dog, we looked up, and the handbag itself was hanging on the branch of a tree – so that came back as well.

ANSWERS

(See underlined words in the tapescript.)

1 attend/go to a funeral
2 collect/pick up her brother
3 to close the window
4 in the house
5 mobile phone
6 the answerphone / her answerphone messages
7 walking her dog
8 process of elimination
9 children
10 her diary

3 **Discussion: comprehension check.**

LANGUAGE STUDY 1 (page 160)

Uses of *get*

1 **Presentation.**

The examples in the exercise include lexical uses of *get*, as well as the causative use. Students can do the exercise orally in pairs.

Refer students to the Notes on **Students' Book** page 210 to check their answers.

ANSWERS

1
3 My bag was stolen once.
4 This is the phone call you hoped you'd never *receive*.
5 . . . caught his heel in some lady's bag . . .
6 . . . a dreadful situation I *became* involved in . . .
7 . . . any difficulty in *persuading* shops to give you a credit account.
8 A friend advised me to *seek/find* help.
9 Things have *improved*.
10 . . . and then mum *became* stuck in the mud
11 My brother was coming to stay that night . . .
12 . . . by the time I'd organised myself . . .
2
get + object + infinitive = sentence 7
get + object + past participle = sentences 3, 5, 12
sentence 7   = A
sentence 12   = B
sentences 3, 5 = C

2 **Practice.**
Students rewrite the sentences.

ANSWERS

1 I've got the plumber coming round to mend the boiler.
2 By the time I'd got ready the race had already started.
3 We're getting a building firm to build an extension for us.

4 Make sure you get here on time.
5 I got the right answer.
6 I must get this report finished by tomorrow.
7 It was my fault I'd got into debt.
8 Getting John to come with me was quite easy.
9 Things are getting worse and worse.

Linking ideas: condition

3 **Presentation: conjunctions expressing condition.**

POSSIBLE ANSWERS

1 *If you can't* prove that you took all the necessary precautions, the insurance company won't pay compensation.
2 *Unless* you can prove that you took all the necessary precautions, the insurance company won't pay compensation.
3 The insurance company will pay compensation *on condition that* you can prove you took all the necessary precautions.
4 *As long as* you can prove you took all the necessary precautions, the insurance company will pay compensation.
5 The insurance company will pay compensation *provided/providing that* you can prove you took all necessary precautions.
6 The insurance company will *only* pay compensation *if* you can prove you took all the necessary precautions.
Sentences 3 and 5 are more formal.

4 **Practice.**
Students write sentences. There can be more than one answer for each sentence.

POSSIBLE ANSWERS

1 You can only get a refund if you have your receipt. / You can't get a refund unless you have a receipt.
2 You can borrow my car on condition that / as long as / providing that you return it this evening.
3 Unless you wear a shirt and tie you cannot enter the club. / You can only enter the club if you are wearing . . .
4 You can take part in the cycle race as long as you wear a helmet.

5 **Personalisation.**
You can do this exercise orally. Make sure students use the link words from Exercise 3.

Linking expressions in spoken English

6 **Identify phrases.**
This is best done orally in pairs or groups. Students highlight/label the expressions from the tapescripts.

ANSWERS

- begin a story – *Well* (sentences 1, 5, 6)
  add a point – *and* (sentences 7, 9)
- change topic – *Anyway* (sentence 11)
- emphasise or reinforce a point – *actually* (sentence 3), *of course* (sentence 7), *for that matter* (sentence 8), *in fact* (sentence 9),
- signal the end of (that part of) the story – *that was that* (sentence 4), *to cut a long story short* (sentence 5)
- give an explanation – *I mean* (sentence 10)
- avoid being precise – *something like that* (sentence 2)
- introduce a repeated point – *as I said* (sentence 7)

7 Group activity.

Groups of four will be suitable. Encourage students to use appropriate language to show interest, and encourage the story teller to continue and give more detail. See **Language Bank**, Unit 1, **Students' Book** page 17. Other questions and comments could include:

What did you do next? How did you feel? That must have been (very frightening) etc.

READING 2 (page 162)

Part 2, Gapped text

1 Introduction to the topic.

2 Pre-teach vocabulary.

1 Get students to point to the parts of the body listed.

2 Students should be able to explain the function of the parts of the bicycle.

POSSIBLE ANSWERS

handlebars: the part of the bike which you hold onto with your hands and use to steer
pedals: the part of the bike you push round with your feet in order to make it move
saddle: the part of the bike you sit on
gears: a component which allows you to change speed

3 Read for the main ideas.

Make sure students read the base text to the end, as this is a useful strategy. Set a time limit and use the question to check their grasp of the main point.

Vocabulary note:

makes no bones about (last paragraph): has no hesitation or reservations

ANSWER

Cycling has been declared a health hazard because of the number of injuries suffered by mountain bikers.

4 Identify missing paragraphs.

Go through the type of clues listed with the class.

ANSWERS

1 D (this explains the question raised in the first paragraph; lexical links: *doctors/American doctors*)
2 F (this gives examples of injuries mentioned in the preceding paragraph)
3 A (lexical links: *beginners/advanced riders*)
4 B (lexical links: *fitness/get fit*, plus pronoun link: *He/Dr Kronisch*)
5 G (contains advice for novice/beginners which is continued in next paragraph)
6 E (pronoun link: *helmets/recommending them*)

5 Language study: substitution and ellipsis.

This is an opportunity to reinforce a language point that has already been studied in Unit 6. Make sure that students realise that the sentences are correct as they stand.

ANSWERS

1
1 jogging was never particularly good for you
2 healthy
2
1 But if cycling your way to health was ever an alternative, it may not be *an alternative* now.
2 Ron Phiffer has some advice for beginners to get a full medical if *they* are in doubt about *their* fitness.

6 Vocabulary search.

This exercise focuses on topic related vocabulary and encourages students to respond to the issues in the text. The vocabulary will be useful for the next activity.

ANSWERS

1
a) *joggers:* knee and calf injuries, back problems
b) *cyclists:* injury to wrists and collar bones, fractures, lacerations, shoulder injuries, knee and calf damage, back pain, saddle sores

7 Group activity.

Groups of four will be suitable. This activity gives students an opportunity to use words and phrases from the text.

ENGLISH IN USE 2 (page 164)

Part 1, Multiple choice cloze

1 **Pre-teach vocabulary.**
This vocabulary for parts of a boat occurs in the text. Have students point to the items visible in the photo of the racing yacht that illustrates the text.

Vocabulary notes:
deck: outside top level of a ship that you can walk on
hull: main part (frame) of a ship
stern: back part of a ship
bow: front part of a ship
mast: tall pole on which sails are hung

2 **Read for general understanding.**
Remind students that they should always read through to the end before making their choices. Elicit answers to the questions. Get students to tell you the main events – what activities the writer is involved in. Retelling the story can help them to think of the missing words.

Let students work individually on the multiple choice task, then check their answers in pairs, using a dictionary.

ANSWERS		
1 A	6 A	11 D
2 D	7 B	12 B
3 D	8 A	13 B
4 B	9 C	14 C
5 D	10 D	15 D

3 **Discussion: response to the text.**
This can be done quickly as a class.

LANGUAGE STUDY 2 (page 165)

Emphasising parts of a sentence: inversion

1 **Analysis and practice: inversion after time and place adverbials.**
Refer students to the Notes on **Students' Book** pages 210–211 to check their answers.

ANSWERS

1
The verb comes before the subject. The writer has done this for dramatic effect.
2
1 Suddenly up came this man and demanded to see our passports.
2 Off rushed the boy clutching the letter.
3 On the pavement lay a £20 note.
4 Here comes our train.
5 Not to be overlooked is the matter of money.
6 Equally important is the question of how to convince people.

2 **Analysis and practice: inversion after *hardly/no sooner than*.**

ANSWERS

1
b. uses the phrase *just as* which gives a sense of immediacy.
2
1 Hardly had the football match begun when it began to rain. / No sooner had the football match begun than it began to rain.
2 Hardly had we sat down when there was a knock on the door. / No sooner had we sat down than there was a knock on the door.
3 Hardly had I picked up the phone to call him when he walked in the door. / No sooner had I picked up the phone to call him than he walked in the door.
4 Hardly had the aircraft landed when it took off again. / No sooner had the aircraft landed than it took off again.

3 **Analysis: inversion after other negative adverbials.**

ANSWERS

If there is no auxiliary verb you have to insert *do*.

4 **Practice.**
Students rewrite the sentences with inversion.

ANSWERS

1 Not since I was a child have I had such a wonderful holiday.
2 Never in my life have I felt so frightened.
3 Seldom do you come across such a promising first novel.
4 Not until later did we hear that our team had won an award for bravery.
5 Only from sailing do you get that kind of thrill.
6 Not only did the thief steal my wallet, he stole my jacket as well!
7 Not only were we not allowed to stay up late on week nights, we weren't allowed to watch TV either.

5 **Analysis and practice: inversion in conditional sentences.**
Emphasise that this structure is very formal.

ANSWERS

1 Were we to accept their demands, we would be setting a dangerous precedent.
2 Had the government acted properly, the disaster would not have occurred.
3 Should you require assistance, phone this emergency number.

WRITING (page 166)

Part 1, Report writing

Review the features of a report with the class. See **Exam File**, Unit 6, **Students' Book** page 80, and Unit 8, **Students' Book** page 110. Remind students that the format for the beginning/ending of letters is not appropriate for a report.

Step 1 Task interpretation

Remind students to highlight key words in the task.

ANSWERS

target readers:	college Principal
register/tone:	neutral/formal
points to include:	must include information about the trip, advice for the future, including a recommendation; this is a combination of an information report and a recommendation report

Step 2 Selecting and summarising

Students should highlight key points in the input material – there are no annotations to help them. There are two key areas to make notes under – information and advice. Encourage students to include specific details of their own to make the report more convincing.

Step 3 Layout and organisation

Students can use the headings supplied to organise their notes from Step 2.

Step 4 Write

Point out to students that neither piece of input material is in an appropriate style. They must use the information but in a different style.

Refer them to the **Language Bank**.

MODEL ANSWER

Report on sailing course at Herrington Adventure Centre
I recently supervised a group of students on a one-week sailing course offered by Herrington Adventure Centre. The aim of this report is to describe the Centre and comment on the suitability of the course for future students.

What the Centre offers
The Centre offers students the chance to develop their skills in their chosen outdoor activity. As well as taking advantage of the excellent facilities for specialist activities, residents at the Centre can make use of the well-equipped gymnasium. Equally importantly, courses aim to develop students' ability to deal with difficult circumstances. Students will find themselves in situations where they have to take decisions and come up with practical solutions.

Advice for future participants
What participants must consider is whether their level of experience and fitness is sufficient. The course is not for beginners.

Once on the course, safety is an important consideration. No matter how experienced participants may feel, they must not attempt an activity without first consulting a supervisor. An incident on this year's sailing course could have had tragic consequences without the speedy intervention of the emergency services.

Finally, the course is full board, with accommodation in single-sex dormitories, but participants should bring their own sleeping bags for camping trips and appropriate clothing.

Recommendation
Despite the unfortunate incident this year, I have no hesitation in recommending the Herrington Adventure Centre. It offers the chance for students to develop their ability in outdoor activities, as well as the opportunity to develop character and social skills. Provided basic safety precautions are followed, the course should be an enjoyable and rewarding experience.

ENGLISH IN USE 3 (page 168)

Part 2, Structural cloze

1 Introduction to the topic.
Students can work in pairs or groups to discuss the statements. Take a poll of how many are for or against each statement and write the results on the board.

2 Read for general understanding.
Students compare the ideas in the text with their own ideas in Exercise 1, then summarise the main points.

Note:
Outward Bound®: this is an organisation that provides the type of activities listed.

3 Gap fill task.
Let students work in pairs.

ANSWERS

1	more	6	If	11	was
2	to	7	have	12	out
3	twice	8	used	13	which
4	does	9	through/by	14	such
5	for	10	be	15	in

4 Discussion: response to the text.
Encourage students to use words and phrases from the text in their discussion.

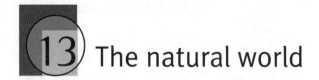

13 The natural world

SPEAKING 1 (page 169)

1 Talk about photographs.

Check that students understand such words as *thrive, be extinct*. Go through the **Language Bank** and check understanding of words for animal behaviour.

Photo 1 shows a pigeon drinking from a fountain. Pigeons are found in large numbers in urban areas. They are scavengers and eat more or less anything.

Photo 2 shows a fox. Foxes are found in Europe and North America, living in woodland, open countryside and increasingly in urban areas. They hunt at night. Urbanised foxes will scavenge from dustbins.

Photo 3 shows the golden eagle, which is found in Northern and Southern Europe. It breeds in mountainous areas, pine forests and on sea cliffs. Eagles require large amounts of space as they are birds of prey, and are not easily seen. They are rare but only some species are endangered – such as the American eagle, due to loss of habitat.

Photo 4 show a grey wolf. Grey wolves used to be the most widespread mammal apart from man outside the tropics. They are now restricted to some forests in Eastern Europe, mountainous regions of Southern Europe and the Middle East, and wild areas of North America and Asia. This decline is due to persecution and habitat destruction. Wolves will only survive if man maintains suitable areas as refuges.

Photo 5 shows a hedgehog. These animals are found in Europe, Africa and India, but not in the Americas. They are nocturnal. European hedgehogs like woodland but are increasingly found in parks and gardens. They used to be persecuted by farmers who wrongly believed they stole milk and eggs. They are not in danger of extinction, though thousands are killed yearly on the roads.

Photo 6 shows two badger cubs. Most badgers are nocturnal, though they may be seen in the early morning, especially in urban areas. Although the European badger lives in woodland and grassland, it is becoming increasingly urbanised, like the fox and hedgehog. It used to be hunted for its fur, but is now a protected species in Britain.

2 Extension of discussion.

This question extends the discussion away from the pictures.

3 Collaborative task: ranking.

The skills practised in this section are useful for Part 3 of the Speaking Test.

READING 1 (page 170)

Part 2, Gapped text

1 Introduction to the topic.

2 Reading task: gapped text.

Encourage students to follow the steps already practised in previous gapped text tasks. Remind them to look for grammatical and lexical links between paragraphs. They should highlight these, and refer to them to justify their answers during the checking stage.

Notes on the text:

tabby cat: the most common type of domestic cat found in Britain, with grey striped fur

scaffolding: this is more typically seen on the outside of buildings which are being constructed or repaired

ice ages: this means that the wildcat existed at the same time as the mammoth, which has been extinct for thousands of years

gamekeeper: a person employed on a large estate to protect the animals (game) which are going to be hunted by the owner(s) of the estate

brook: a small stream

ANSWERS

1 B (lexical and pronoun links with preceding paragraph: *Michael Richards/he, scaffolding tower/hiding place*)
2 E (lexical links: *on film/footage/filmmaker*)
3 G (lexical links: *amazing stuff/excited scientists too*)
4 A (lexical links with preceding and following paragraphs: *last century/over the centuries/last century*)
5 D (lexical link with preceding paragraph: *not as sweet as they look/they are wild*)
6 F (lexical and pronoun links with preceding paragraph: *they leave mum/Mum feeds them*)

VOCABULARY 1 (page 171)

Idiomatic expressions

1 Work on register is useful for Paper 2 and Paper 3.

ANSWERS

1
1 *pay off:* be successful
2 *strike lucky:* suddenly have good luck
3 *amazing stuff: stuff* is used here to refer to the insight into the wildcat's way of life provided by the film shot by Michael Richards
4 *along with:* together with
5 *for sure:* for certain, with any certainty
6 *cutie:* a sweet, adorable creature

2

1 The verb *pay off* is intransitive in this context. Other possible subjects of the verb include: *a plan*, *a risk*. e.g.: *He took a risk, but it paid off.*
In the transitive sense, you can *pay off a debt*, *pay someone off* i.e. give them money for what they have done.

2 There are many senses of *strike*, e.g.
HIT: strike a person, strike a match
FIND: strike gold/oil; strike it rich
AGREE: strike a bargain
Students can find these expressions in the Longman *Language Activator*.

Choosing the best word

2 **Near synonyms:** *pull.*

This exercise, like the next one, focuses on near synonyms. It is useful practice for Paper 3, Part 1 (multiple choice cloze).

ANSWERS

1
Haul has been used because it suggests something very heavy and difficult to handle.
2
1 towed   2 drawn   3 plucked   4 wrenched   5 tugged

3 **Near synonyms:** *look.*

Point out that not all the gaps require a verb form. You can discuss collocations such as *catch a glimpse*, *take a peep*, and words that have the same form as verbs and nouns, e.g. *view*.

ANSWERS

1
peer: look very carefully; suggests there is some difficulty in seeing sth
stare: look intently (with concentration).
catch a glimpse: a brief sighting; anything that is prey moves quickly and wouldn't be seen for long, hence *glimpse*
2
1 gazed   2 blinked   3 peep   4 winked   5 view

LISTENING 1 (page 172)

Part 2, Note completion

1 **Introduction to the topic: quiz.**

This section introduces some of the vocabulary students will hear in the Listening text. Let them work in pairs and guess the answers. Check their answers before the Listening, to see who in the class knows most about coral reefs!

ANSWERS

1 A   2 A   3 B   4 B   5 A

2 🔊 **Note completion task.**

Give students time to read through the notes before you play the recording.

TAPESCRIPT

Presenter: Human beings cause destruction wherever they go. The latest casualty is in the sea, where coral reefs are currently facing the most serious threat yet from tourism and the use of reefs for recreation.

Reefs grow extremely slowly and are produced by millions of tiny animals called stony-coral polyps. Aided by algae that live inside them, these animals produce from their bodies the limestone that forms the structure of the reefs. Since these creatures are so small, it takes a long time for the reef to increase in size.

It's in the ecosystems of the coral reefs that we find the greatest biodiversity on our planet, rivalled only by that of the rainforests. Coral reefs may appear strong but they are not. In fact, they are extremely fragile systems, vulnerable to damage from natural causes such as disease, and from harm inflicted by humans. Snorkelling, scuba-diving and reef walking, a new sport in which tourists walk along the reef wearing a helmet with an air-line going up to a boat, now play a major role in the destruction of reefs, as does the growing trade in reef curios.

Better teaching techniques and equipment have made snorkelling and scuba-diving more popular. But thoughtless divers can directly damage the reef in various ways: accidentally breaking the coral by collision, or by holding, standing or kneeling on the coral. Just touching the coral can damage the mucus that protects it from infection, increasing susceptibility to disease.

Reef walking is a major problem. When people walk across reefs, they stir up large concentrations of sediment, spoiling the appearance of the coral and reducing the growth rate. The trade in reef curios, especially pieces of coral and shells, is causing changes to the way reefs function. Rare marine species are particularly vulnerable, and their disappearance alters the complex food chains of the reef. The loss of any marine organisms, dead or alive, upsets the complex nutrient cycles so important to marine life.

So what's being done about these problems? International organisations have been set up to increase public awareness of reefs, reduce the impact of the curio trade and undertake reef conservation projects. However, the greatest impetus must come at a local level from those governments and commercial enterprises, those companies in the tourist industry whose livelihoods depend on their reefs remaining a tourist attraction, not a dead heap of rubble.

ANSWERS

(See underlined words in the tapescript.)

1 growth
2 damage
3 reef walking
4 trade
5 touching the coral
6 (complex) food chains
7 public awareness
8 tourism

3 **Group discussion: comprehension check.**
Students work in groups. A group secretary should note down their recommendations for the class report back stage. They should use their notes from the Listening exercise, which summarise the main problems that need to be dealt with.

SPEAKING 2 (page 172)

You might like to have students work in groups of three or four for all parts of this activity, with one student playing the role of the Interlocutor and introducing the tasks. (See **Teacher's Book** page 11 for a sample script used by the interlocutor.) If a fourth student plays the part of the Assessor, his/her role will be to listen and evaluate only. You should time each stage.

Part 2, Describe, comment and hypothesise

1 **Talk about photographs: individual long turn.**
1 This is the individual long turn (1 minute per candidate).

Photo 1 shows a couple sitting by a campfire on an African safari. This area appears almost untouched by man and there are no signs at all of it being developed for tourism.

Photo 2 shows a beach in Portugal. White houses and hotels can be seen on the cliffs and blue boats for hire are lined up on the beach. Although the setting is still beautiful, the area has obviously been developed for tourism.

2 In this part, each candidate has a chance to comment on what has been said. They have approximately half a minute each.

Part 3, Discuss and plan; Part 4, Report decisions

2 **Collaborative task.**
Students should try to reach a conclusion in the time given. Remind them to make use of the **Language Bank**.

3 **Report decisions.**
The examiner asks candidates to explain briefly what they have decided to do (about 1 minute).

4 **Extension of the discussion.**
In this final part of the Test, the examiner asks questions to extend the topic.

READING 2 (page 174)

Part 3, Multiple choice questions

1 **Introduction to the topic.**
Students should answer on the basis of their own knowledge and experience, as well as on the basis of what they have done in this unit so far.

2 **Scan and skim.**
These questions encourage students to get a general understanding of the text before tackling the multiple choice questions. Encourage them to use the sub-headings to help decide where the information they need will be, e.g. the answer to Question 5 will be found in the section **Winners and losers**.

ANSWERS

1 The title refers to wild animals now commonly found in urban areas. It is a play on the metaphorical use of *animal* to describe people who behave badly.
2 pigeon, fox, falcon, hedgehog, rock dove, spider, bat, starling, reptile, frog, human flea, cat flea, carpet beetle
3 **Group 1:** animals that lived in an area before it became part of the town; **Group 2:** animals that have moved into towns deliberately (for food, shelter).
4 The second group of animals have been most successful in adapting to the environment.
5 Large bats, reptiles, the human flea have not adapted well to urban living.

3 **Multiple choice questions.**
Encourage students to highlight the words in the text that they think give them the answer.

ANSWERS

1 D The former are generally native species . . . tend to be on the decline . . . . (lines 19–24)
2 B Pigeons truly epitomise town life . . . low biodiversity, high biomass. (line 42–51)
3 B From a wildlife point of view, a city is a city. . . . A foreign, city-dwelling species . . . has a good chance of finding a habitat similar to its home territory. (lines 56–69)
4 C The fox favours the appetising dustbins and compost heaps . . . (lines 88–89)
5 B Reptiles are doing badly in towns because derelict ground is disappearing. (lines 122–124)

4 Vocabulary: guess meaning from context.

1 Students can use their dictionaries if necessary to check their guesses.

2 Tell students to choose five words they think they will be able to use in speaking or writing and add them to their vocabulary books. They should note them down with example sentences.

You can extend this into an activity similar to the one suggested in Unit 11, Reading 1, **Teacher's Book** page 97. Students test each other on the meaning of the words they have selected.

ANSWERS

1
1 tamed by humans and used/reared by them for work or food
2 *High biomass* means that large numbers of a particular species are present.
3 unusual animals from warmer climates
4 visit regularly or live in
5 rest or sleep (used for birds and bats)
6 colloquial word for insects, often used when talking to children

5 Analysis of the text: style.

It is important that students can recognise humour and irony, which are so typical of many newspaper and magazine feature articles in English. They should not accept everything they read at face value! This article approaches a serious topic in a humorous and ironic way, as the extracts make clear.

ANSWERS

1 *hit the streets* makes the pigeons sound like gangsters; *sole food* is a pun on *soul food* – the traditional food of the American South (compare *soul music*)
2 *hot air* is used to mean the air in hot countries and the excessive talking about nothing of politicians

6 Extension activity.

This can be set as a homework task for research. Students can be asked to write a short report or prepare a class presentation.

VOCABULARY 2 (page 176)

Words to do with animal behaviour

1 Choose the right word.

Make sure students realise that the gaps may require different forms: a verb, a noun or a participial adjective.

ANSWERS

1 roam	5 crawling	9 trotting
2 roost	6 spins, flying	10 hop
3 wheel, roost	7 perch	
4 swoop	8 slither	

More animal expressions

2 Metaphorical uses.

All these metaphors are in common use. Remind students to pay attention to correct verb form.

Can students think of any more animal verbs or idioms in English? e.g.:

chicken: chicken out of sth

cat: like a cat on hot bricks

Ask them to compare these metaphorical uses with their own language. Are there similarities?

ANSWERS

1 badgering	3 rabbiting	5 dogged	7 wolfed
2 foxed	4 fishing	6 ducked	

LANGUAGE STUDY (page 176)

Present and perfect participle clauses

This section recycles and extends the work already done on participle clauses in Units 5 and 10.

Refer students to the Notes on **Students' Book** page 211 to check their answers.

1 Analysis.

Students should highlight the participle clauses in the examples.

After going through the questions, ask them to think of alternative ways of expressing the ideas without using participle clauses, but using adverbial clauses etc. instead.

1 Question 1 prepares students for the error correction work in Exercise 2.

2 Question 2 focuses on the meaning implied by each clause type.

ANSWERS

a. same	d. same	g. different
b. different	e. different	h. same
c. same	f. same	

• event close in time to action in main clause: examples a, d, f
• event that finished well before the action in the main clause: examples c, e
• participle clauses b, e, g, h give a reason for action in main clause

2 Practice: error correction.
Students can do this exercise in pairs. Get them to justify their answers during the class check.

ANSWERS

1 Having read and enjoyed the book, I lent it to a friend. (A perfect participle is required to indicate the sequence of actions: I finished the book before I lent it to my friend.)
2 Being hungry, I ate twice as much as usual at lunch. (The perfect participle wrongly implies that I was hungry before but not any longer; the present participle gives the reason why I ate twice as much.)
3 The wildcat being an elusive creature, Michael Richards had to be very patient when filming it. (Each clause has a different subject, so the subject of the participle clause must be stated and cannot be omitted.)
4 Having been persecuted for hundreds of years, the wildcat now has legal protection. (Again, each clause has a different subject; as we don't know the subject of the participle clause, we need to use a passive.)
5 By touching the coral reef, people can damage the mucus which protects it. (The subject *people* is required in the main clause, as this is the implied subject of the participle clause.)
6 Central heating having been introduced into our homes, they now provide a good breeding ground for exotic insects. (The current sentence implies that our homes have introduced central heating, not us!)

3 Practice: sentence combining.
The individual sentences form a connected story. Encourage students to combine the sentences so they read well as continuous text.

After checking answers, ask students what equipment Jack was carrying (photographic equipment or a gun?).

ANSWERS

1 Parking his car in the lay-by, Jack set off across the fields. (*Having parked his car* would be possible too, but is unnecessary as the two events are close in time.)
2 Having walked the path many times before, he didn't need to consult a map. (reason)
3 Reaching his destination, he unpacked his bag. (actions close in time)
4 Having settled himself comfortably, he scanned the horizon for sight of his prey. (actions close in time: present participle also possible, but use perfect participle for variety)
5 By late afternoon he decided to go back, having waited for six hours without success. (reason)
6 Hearing a sudden noise, he spun round and saw a magnificent stag close by. (almost simultaneous actions)
7 Having packed his equipment away, he was unable to shoot. (reason)

! Spelling reminder
Knowing the spelling rules for doubling letters is important when forming participles. Refer students to the Notes on **Students' Book** page 213.

Past participle clauses

4 Analysis.
Students should highlight the participle clauses.

ANSWERS

a. . . . missing since last night . . .
b. Trapped by high winds . . . too terrified to move . . . until found by
c. Exhausted by their ordeal . . . suffering from exposure
d. Their job finished, . . .

c. As the youngsters were exhausted by their ordeal and were also suffering from exposure, they have been taken to hospital.
d. Now that their job has finished, the rescuers are enjoying a well-deserved pint in the pub!

5 Practice: improve a story.
This could be set for homework.

Point out that although most of the sentences in the story can be combined using participle clauses, in practice it is not very good style to over-use a particular sentence pattern.

ANSWER

Having lost her compass, Sarah didn't know which way to go. Looking up into the night sky, she searched for the Pole star to find out which way north was. Tired out after walking all day, she decided to stop for a short rest. After a few minutes she felt better and picking up her rucksack, she set off again. Not having expected to get lost, she had not taken much food but despite feeling hungry, she kept on going. After walking for two hours, she saw the lights of the youth hostel. Feeling very relieved, she quickened her pace.

6 Extension activity: recount an anecdote.
This could be done in groups or set for homework as a written task.

LISTENING 2 (page 178)

Exam File: Part 4, Multiple choice

Point out to students that this is the alternative to the multiple matching task which they have practised before for Part 4. There are still five speakers but the task is to answer three-option multiple choice questions. Point out that they should use a different listening strategy from that suggested for four-option multiple choice questions.

1 🔊 **Listen for gist.**

These questions check that students have understood the basic themes. Note that in the exam, students should tackle the multiple choice questions on the first listening.

TAPESCRIPT

Speaker 1: It was one of my worst experiences on a mountain, I can tell you. I'd tried to climb it three times before and failed. <u>This time I'd made it to the top</u> but I knew <u>I'd taken too long to get there</u>. The sun was setting and I'd have to descend in the dark. That's really scary. There's no hope of being rescued, not at that height. You would have more chance of being rescued from the moon. <u>I couldn't stay there</u> – the temperature goes down below 40 degrees. <u>I knew I had to get down myself – and fast</u>. I kept thinking of Jill, my wife, and our son.

Speaker 2: We approached the mountain during the night, a twelve-hour walk it was, in the dark, to get into the best position to start climbing. We started the climb after breakfast and <u>reached the summit</u> in the early afternoon, as <u>we had planned</u>. What really surprised me was the noise. The wind reaches speeds of up to 150 kilometres per hour – it was like an express train but much worse, really icy cold. So much for the peace and tranquility of the mountains! <u>We were tired even before we began the climb. When we got down we just collapsed into our tents.</u>

Speaker 3: We got there by hiring a pilot to fly us in and land on a lake. We walked a bit and found a place to camp. It was a fantastic place but very hot – we got <u>sunburnt</u> quite badly. We were hoping to see bears, <u>but also a little bit worried because they can be dangerous,</u> and we were on our own, and we had no gun and no radio. Actually, we only saw a beaver and a moose. <u>We probably should have taken a radio so that we could call for help if necessary, but we were carrying so much stuff, all we needed for two weeks, including a lot of food.</u> The only food we could find there were berries we picked from bushes. Of course, it is a good place to hunt but . . .

Speaker 4: At the end of the first day, we put up our tents near a small stream and then went for a swim in it. It was icy cold but very refreshing. It was a perfect place to camp – fresh water, firewood, some berries on nearby bushes which tasted very sweet. <u>The sky was so clear – I didn't realise it was possible to see so many stars.</u> I just lay in the grass and looked at them. Things got worse after that. In the next few days, we were soaked to the skin, <u>frozen</u> and then <u>roasted</u> by the sun. <u>We gave up the idea of visiting the caves we wanted to see.</u> We'll try again next year.

Speaker 5: Not a lot of people know this but <u>you can easily take</u> your bicycle on an aircraft. <u>You just pack it</u> properly and it travels as a piece of luggage – not hand luggage of course. When you reach your destination, <u>you just unpack it</u> and you have your own transport. I've been all over Africa and Asia on my bike. <u>You can go</u>

where you like at your own speed and no one is surprised. Of course, <u>you need</u> a strongly-built bike and you have to be ready to carry out minor repairs – <u>you need</u> to take a few spare parts with you. And sun-cream, <u>you need</u> plenty of that and a hat. You are really <u>exposed to</u> the sun on a bike and it can be dangerous.

ANSWERS

camping: texts 3 and 4
climbing: texts 1 and 2
cycling: text 5

2 🔊 **Listening task.**

Give students time to read the questions before listening.

ANSWERS

(See underlined words in the tapescript.)

1 C	5 B	9 C
2 A	6 C	10 A
3 A	7 B	
4 A	8 A	

3 **Discussion: response to the Listening text.**

WRITING 1 (page 178)

Part 1, Leaflet and note

Step 1 Task interpretation
Remind students to highlight key words in the task description.

ANSWERS

Students have to produce two pieces of writing.

text types: leaflet and informal note
target readers: leaflet: young students who are taking part in a walking trip; note: secretary of youth group
purpose: leaflet: to inform and give advice; note: to confirm action taken

Step 2 Selecting and summarising
There is more information in the input material than can be used in the leaflet and note, so selecting what is relevant to the target readers is vital. Students should highlight key items in the two texts.

Step 3 Layout and organisation
For the leaflet, students organise the key information under headings appropriate for the task. They can use the ones suggested or their own ideas.

Refer students to the model brochure in Unit 11, **Students' Book** pages 152–153 if necessary.

Step 4 Write

The style of the leaflet should be simple and straightforward. Long and complicated sentences are not appropriate.

Refer students to the **Language Bank**.

MODEL ANSWER

Information Leaflet

Handy Hints for Walkers
Where will we be walking?
In the PEAK DISTRICT, one of the most beautiful national parks in England.

What should I wear?
Bring plenty of warm clothing!

DO WEAR:

- a windproof layer to wear on top.
- polyester and acrylic fabrics – they don't retain water!
- a good hat to prevent heat escaping through your head.
- 2 pairs of gloves. Bring along spares – the ones you're wearing may get wet!
- a strong pair of walking boots.
- a thick pair of socks.

DON'T WEAR:

- wool, down and cotton layers, such as T-shirts. They may feel warm when you're dry, but if you get them wet, you'll rapidly lose body heat.

What if I get cold?
1 For every walking trip make sure you take:
- supplies of carbohydrate.
- a flask of hot liquid.
These will keep you warm, awake and maintain your energy levels.
2 If you feel your body temperature dropping:
- conserve body heat. Dig a hole in the snow and lie in it. This will shield you from icy winds.
- wrap up your hands and feet well. This will help stop frostbite.

Don't forget to follow these tips and enjoy your trip!

Note

Liza,

Just a quick note to let you know I've finished the leaflet for the trip (enclosed!). I've included advice about what students should wear, as well as what to do if they get cold. Have a look through and let me know if I've missed anything out!

Thanks

ENGLISH IN USE 1 (page 180)

Part 6, Discourse cloze

1 **Read for general understanding.**

The aim of this section is to ensure students read the text to the end before completing the gaps. This is the strategy they should adopt in the exam.

ANSWERS

1 A dormant volcano has not erupted for some time but still show signs of volcanic activity; an extinct volcano is no longer active and an active volcano may explode at any time.
2 Huge holes are created and dust and ash is thrown up into the atmosphere.
3 Explosions can cause changes in the global climate.

2 **Discourse cloze task.**

Since all the options begin with the same grammatical pattern, students must make their choices according to the meaning.

ANSWERS

1 E 2 I 3 A 4 H 5 D 6 B

14 Human behaviour

SPEAKING 1 (page 181)

The quiz in this section will lead to the kind of negotiated discussion typical of Part 3 of the Speaking Test. The answers are a matter of individual choice.

READING (page 182)

Part 4, Multiple matching

1 Skim for gist.

The titles will present quite a challenge! Accept any ideas on what each article is about, but don't give the answers. Let students skim the texts to match the titles and texts. Then ask for a brief summary of the main points of each text.

You may prefer to do Exercise 3 at this point.

> **ANSWERS**
>
> **Text A** Restaurant shells out for oyster surfeit
> **Text B** Call me mother
> **Text C** The dockyard thief
> **Text D** Totally fobbed off

2 Multiple matching task.

Remind students to read the questions and highlight key words to help them identify the information they are looking for.

You could give them a time limit, and find out how many students have managed to complete the task within the time.

Notes on the texts:
Text A
small claims court: Britain, like the USA, has courts which deal with disputes over small amounts of money (less than £1,000). In these courts there is one judge and you can represent yourself without a using a lawyer

Text C
coppers, bobby: slang words for *policeman*
PC: short for *police constable.*

Text D
stuck slap-bang in the middle: precisely in the middle
Friday night drag: very slow progress in the Friday evening rush hour
Aussie: short for Australian
knackered old banger: very old car in poor condition (very colloquial)
a medallion man: (derogatory) a man wearing a medallion round his neck and with his shirt open almost to the waist

swanky new motor: same as *flash new Ferrari* (not complimentary)
jalopy: an old-fashioned word for an old-fashioned car
klaxon: an old-fashioned word for horn
chariot: contrasts with jalopy, suggesting something more aggressive
cranked her up: started the car by using a starting handle to turn the engine, not the ignition key
cruised off into the sunset: cowboys in American films traditionally ride off into the sunset; this indicates a happy ending

> **ANSWERS**
>
> 1 B It includes the charge for the lady's meal
> 2 D . . . quadrupled his aggressive behaviour . . .
> 3 A Arguing that "all-you-can-eat" should mean exactly that . . .
> 4 C . . . and found fifty-seven stolen wheelbarrows stacked inside.
> 5 A . . . and another customer was complaining.
> 6 B She said that her daughter would pay.
> 7 D To make matters worse, it was the height of the sweltering Aussie summer.
> 8 C . . . the puzzled coppers continued with the inspection every night for weeks.
> 9 /10 A/B "The man had piled up the oysters like a pyramid," said Ken Albrecht, the manager
>   . . . they called over the manager, demanding to have the total explained.
> 11 A Mr Wald left the court with a $125 award.
> 12 D . . . stalled as the traffic lurched forward.
> 13 B . . . you look so like my daughter . . . I do miss her terribly . . .
> 14 A . . . Arguing that "all-you-can-eat" should mean exactly that . . .
> 15 D . . . his colourful vocabulary.
> 16 A He countered by studying etiquette books . . . The judge failed to swallow the argument.
> 17 D . . . one enterprising bobby then followed the docker home . . .

3 Vocabulary: metaphor.

> **ANSWERS**
>
> 1 *Oysters* are a shell fish that have to be taken out of their shell to be eaten; *shell out* means having to spend lots of money. The restaurant owner had to pay a fine when he took his customer to court for eating too many oysters.
> 2 A *fob* is part of a key-ring – the ornament attached to it. If *you fob someone off, you try to stop them complaining with excuses.* In the anecdote, the driver of the old car takes Mr Macho's keys out of his ignition and throws them away to put an end to his aggressive behaviour.

VOCABULARY 1 (page 184)

Adding drama and colour

Go through the introduction with the class.

1 Using precise and colourful words.

ANSWERS

1
1 *downed:* suggests he ate very quickly without pausing for breath
2 *polished off:* suggests that he finished six dozen oysters rapidly and with ease
3 *guzzling:* suggests greed and over-indulgence
2
1 made her way to the table (with difficulty)
2 tottered (the implication is she walked unsteadily)
3 demanding (implies they were angry)
4 revealed (emphasises their complete ignorance of what had happened)

2 Avoiding repetition.

ANSWERS

1 elderly lady, old dear, mum, the lady
2 friend of mine, the bloke, shifty docker, suspect
3 dock police, coppers (colloquial), bobby (colloquial), PC
4 **car that stalled:** classic automobile, knackered old banger, jalopy, chariot, wagon
   its driver: unlucky driver, stranded motorist
   the driver of the Ferrari: medallion man, Mr Macho
   the Ferrari: flash new Ferrari, swanky new motor, open-top mean machine
5 **walking:** strolled up to, sauntered up to, strolled between, ambled back. All of these words suggest that the driver was calm and in control.

3 Using metaphor.

ANSWERS

1
To *swallow* an argument means to accept it, an appropriate expression in a case about food.
2
1 *crawl* means to move slowly on your hands and knees, the implication is that the progress of the cars on the highway was very slow.
2 When material frays, threads gradually become loose; if your temper frays, this suggests you are getting angrier and angrier.

4 Using euphemism.

ANSWERS

1 *put an animal down:* have it killed
2 *I'm washing my hair:* a traditional polite excuse not to go out with a man
3 *downsize:* make staff redundant
4 *It's time . . .:* We are firing you.

5 Emphatic devices.

ANSWERS

1 highly
2 very /
  does
3 far
4 himself
5 ever
6 on earth
7 very

6 Practice: rewrite an anecdote.

MODEL ANSWER

This story is absolutely true. It's about a man who bought a really expensive engagement ring for his girlfriend, who he was madly in love with. It cost him more than £6,000. One warm, summer evening he went round to his girlfriend's house and said, 'Are you ready to go out, my love? It's a very special evening tonight.'

'Is it?' she said. 'What's so special about it?' 'It's my birthday, of course!' said the man, who was extremely annoyed that she had forgotten such an important day.

He got much more annoyed when he noticed that she wasn't even wearing his ring. Completely losing his temper, he found her jewellery box and grabbed the ring out of it. Seething with anger, he jumped into his car and drove at top speed to the sea, where he stood on a high cliff and hurled the ring into the sea, 50 metres below.

By this time, the woman had called the police and her boyfriend was arrested on the cliff top, still furious. Police divers spent hours searching for the ring in the deep water below the cliff, but all to no avail.

The girlfriend insisted on charging the man with theft and a few months later he appeared in court. When it was revealed in court that he was still paying the shop for the ring, at £200 per month, the judge took pity on him and let him off. He left the court a free, but wiser and sadder, man.

SPEAKING 2 (page 185)

See Unit 13, **Teacher's Book** page 112, for a suggested procedure for the Speaking activity, to simulate exam conditions.

Part 2, Describe, comment and hypothesise

1 **Talk about photographs: individual long turn.**

Remind students that in exam conditions, each candidate has one minute to describe their photo(s) and half a minute to comment on what their partner has said.

Photo 1 shows rubbish which has been dumped in a stream and on the bank.

Photo 2 shows exhaust fumes coming from a car in a busy high street.

Part 3, Suggest solutions to a problem; Part 4, Report conclusions

2 **Collaborative task.**

This part of the Test takes 3–4 minutes.

Refer students to the useful expressions in the **Language Bank**. It gives examples of quite emphatic language that students can use in the task.

3 **Report back.**

In exam conditions candidates have about a minute to summarise their discussion before the examiner widens the discussion by asking some general questions relating to the topic.

LISTENING 1 (page 186)

Part 4, Multiple matching

1 **Introduction to the topic.**

Use the photograph to show what a typical suburban housing estate looks like in Britain. One house has a built-on extension (a concept that is mentioned in the recording). This is a favourite method of creating more space in one's home without having to move.

2 **Pre-teach vocabulary.**

ANSWERS

1 *keep themselves to themselves*: not socialise
2 *neighbourly*: friendly but not overly so
3 *live and let live*: get on with your life and let others get on with theirs without interference

3 📼 **Listening Task One.**

Students answer questions 1–5 on the first listening.

TAPESCRIPT

Speaker 1: Yeah, I get on with the neighbours very well, with one exception. We live in quite a small area and the neighbours have all been together about sixteen years now, and we've got quite a good relationship and have summer barbecues and things like that. But the neighbour who lives directly above us is not pleased at the sight of me. It all started when we had an extension built and he objected – *he said it was because he didn't want any extra buildings on the estate but … um … I think it was because we had children*, and he'd rather we moved because he didn't want the noise and the disturbance of children. But we had the extension built and it became a continuing source of arguing with him. And he still doesn't like us now. I've never really understood it. I've tried to be friendly with him, but he doesn't want to know.

Speaker 2: Well, you don't get to see most of your neighbours. They're working and you're out working, so it's late evening by the time you're back, but our immediate neighbours are very good. To one side we have Christine and Dave who if we asked them to do anything while we're away or that, they're more than happy – and we do the same for them. To the other side, Rod, Rosemary *and their son Michael. Michael's our son's best friend*, and through the children we have become very friendly with them. We help them with their garden and we look after the cat if necessary, and they would do the same for us, so our neighbours on that side, I cannot fault in the slightest.

Speaker 3: I only have one neighbour right now that I'm sociable with, but I mostly keep myself to myself because I don't know if I have a sense of community. Maybe it's because everybody's working and we don't see each other and I work unusual hours. I really don't get involved with the neighbours much. I stick to my own group of friends now and I don't go outside that. I think you should live and let live. *It was different when I was a kid – you did know your neighbours then*, everyone knew one another. Mothers weren't working back then, they were always at home, and the kids would always go to each other's houses and you'd know the mothers and the fathers. Nowadays when everybody is rushing round and working, you don't get to know people. It's a shame really but that's the way it is and I can live with it.

Speaker 4: Where I live, our neighbours tend to keep themselves to themselves, but I have one neighbour who lives behind me who's very sweet. *She's an elderly lady* and she's lived there ever since we've lived there, and we have what I call neighbourly rapport. We don't go into each other's houses, but we're always there and I know I could always call on her and she, I hope, you know, she would call on me.

Speaker 5: We haven't really had any problems with neighbours, except that we had these horrible neighbours that lived across the street. There used to be an old couple that lived there, but they moved and this young couple moved in and they had this child, and the man would go out every night and sit in his car and just rev the engine, and *it was so loud it would wake us up*. It was horrible and <u>they were always fighting</u>, but we didn't have any problems with them besides that. They still live there now but that guy has gone fortunately, but the little kid's a monster.

ANSWERS

(See underlined words in the tapescript.)

1 H   2 B   3 E   4 D   5 G

4

Students answer questions 6–10 on the second listening.

ANSWERS

(See italicised words in the tapescript.)

6 E   7 F   8 A   9 H   10 C

5 Discussion: response to the Listening text.

VOCABULARY 2 (page 186)

Expressions with *get*

Students complete the sentences.

ANSWERS

1 on
2 got, cross
3 get involved
4 get to see
5 get to know

ENGLISH IN USE 1 (page 187)

Part 1, Multiple-choice cloze

1 Read for general understanding.

The questions check that students have read to the end of the text.

ANSWERS

1 Noisy neighbours.
2 To contact the environmental health office.
3 The title sounds like the same word repeated, *noise a noise*.

2 Multiple choice cloze.

Students can do the exercise individually, then check and justify their answers in pairs.

Ask students to suggest contexts for the options which don't fit here.

ANSWERS

1 A	6 D	11 C
2 B	7 B	12 B
3 D	8 D	13 A
4 B	9 A	14 C
5 A	10 B	15 D

3 Discussion: response to the text.

LISTENING 2 (page 188)

Part 1, Note completion

1 Introduction to the topic.

2 Pre-teach vocabulary.

ANSWERS

1 *doze off:* go to sleep
2 *take a nap:* have a short sleep
3 *a siesta:* short sleep after the midday meal
4 *be deprived of sleep:* not get enough sleep

3 Note completion task.

Give students time to read the questions and make predictions.

TAPESCRIPT

Presenter: Lack of sleep is one of the major difficulties people face in our busy modern world. And it has serious consequences. We know how bad-tempered the sleep-deprived are. But without a good night's sleep, <u>people lose their ability to think creatively,</u> and their use of language becomes restricted to clichés. In repetitive jobs like working in a factory, there is <u>an increase in the number of defective products produced at 3 a.m.</u> There can also be much more serious results: accidents at nuclear power plants, miscalculations on oil tankers leading to them running aground, and even errors in space missions.

This evidence has led some scientists to suggest that people need to sleep more. The argument runs like this: the need to sleep at night seems to reflect the needs of <u>early human beings. Hunter-gatherers couldn't find food at night, and spent the dark hours sleeping.</u> When it was light, they could gather food and were better able to spot predators.

This idea also fits in with what has been found in research studies: when people are allowed to sleep for as long as they like whenever they like, <u>they sleep for about ten and a half hours out of twenty-four.</u> Some scientists argue that a natural pattern was to sleep twice a day, for about eight hours at night and about two hours in the afternoon, which shows how useful a siesta is in societies that have that custom. When you consider that <u>most people are now sleeping between seven and seven and a half hours a night,</u> the difference is obvious.

A major change in sleeping patterns came about through the introduction of electric light. <u>Data collected in 1910 shows that people were sleeping around nine and a half hours a night.</u> But in 1913, Thomas Edison introduced the tungsten filament light bulb, which *produced* provided the bright light available twenty-four hours a day that we are now accustomed to. Edison is himself an interesting case of sleep patterns.

For many years it was believed that Edison slept only four hours, and his inventions were attributed in part to the hard work he put in through the day and night. However, one day, when a visitor arrived to see him in his laboratory in the afternoon, he was told by an assistant that Edison was napping. And he was. <u>He took two naps every day, lasting one to three hours.</u> Together with the four hours he slept at night, this adds up to plenty of sleep each day.

Would we all feel better if we had more sleep? It seems a hypothetical question because today our <u>admiration seems to be for the sleepless.</u> We think our leaders should be tireless, and we regard time spent sleeping as a waste, an unproductive time enjoyed only by the lazy. Maybe it's time for a re-think.

ANSWERS

(See underlined words in the tapescript.)

1 think creatively
2 defective products
3 hunter-gatherers/early humans
4 ten and a half hours
5 seven and a half
6 nine and a half hours
7 (invention of) (electric) light bulb
8 slept/napped
9 are sleepless/do not sleep much/ sleep little
10 wasteful

4 Discussion: comprehension check.

ENGLISH IN USE 2 (page 188)

Part 2, Structural cloze

1 Quiz.

The aim is to give students a reason for reading the text straight through before doing the cloze task. You could introduce the section by eliciting or giving a few facts about Shakespeare:

1564 Born in Stratford-on-Avon, the son of a glovemaker
1583 Married Anne Hathaway
1585 Went to London and worked as an actor
1592 Wrote his first play – 37 plays in total
1616 Died in Stratford-on-Avon

ANSWERS

1 true   2 true   3 true   4 true   5 false

2 Read to check answers.

3 Cloze task.

Have students do the task individually then work in pairs to check their answers. They should be prepared to justify them grammatically.

ANSWERS

1 yourself	6 might/could/may	11 so
2 which	7 up	12 being
3 though	8 including	13 to
4 our	9 become	14 why
5 everything	10 as	15 them

4 Extension activity.

Students can discuss these expressions in pairs.

ANSWERS

1 He gives you a lot of support when you are in trouble.
2 Even though he seems to be behaving strangely, there is a sensible reason for what he is doing.
3 He should not be blamed for what he has done wrong, as he has been badly treated by other people.
4 It's not important.
5 He loved someone very much, but she didn't deserve his love.
6 If music causes love to grow, then I want to hear more of it.

LANGUAGE REVIEW (page 190)

This section revises the major grammatical patterns practised in the course. Let students work in pairs and refer to earlier units and the Grammar Notes. Alternatively you can use this as a test.

1 Multiple choice sentence completion.

Make sure students understand that there may be more than one correct answer.

ANSWERS

1 B, C	7 A, C	13 A, B
2 B, C	8 A, C	14 A, C
3 A	9 C	15 A, C
4 C	10 B, C	16 A
5 A, C	11 B, C	17 B
6 A	12 A, C	18 A, B

2 Error correction.

The errors in this exercise are all ones made by real CAE students in their writing.

ANSWERS

1 . . . I have *a* good knowledge of accountancy. (use of articles)
2 . . . the project I *have been* working on for the last two months. (tense)
4 . . . the train *that* was leaving at 10 a.m. (relative clauses)
5 I don't remember *meeting/having met* this person before. (verb complementation)
6 . . . considered *to be* one of the best (infinitive after *consider*)
8 . . . this *mistake* (wrong word)
9 I understand you need someone to look *after* your home while you are abroad.
10 . . . without spending *anything*. (double negative)
11 I wonder if you could *give me* some information about *how coral reefs are formed*. (verb + IO; indirect question formation)
12 . . . my friend's *advice* that made me *change* my mind about going. (spelling of noun form; *make* + bare infinitive)
14 If you want to *do some exercise* (use of reflexive pronouns; idiomaticity)
15 We didn't succeed *in persuading* our friends (dependent preposition)

WRITING (page 191)

Exam File: Selecting a Part 2 task

Go through the **Exam File** with the class. You can treat this section as a test, and time the students in class. If you prefer, use class time to revise the features of an article, a review, a formal letter and a report. Have students choose a task, plan it in class and write it for homework.

1 How to select a task.

Students should follow this strategy in the exam.

2 Writing tasks.

MODEL ANSWERS

1 Article

Welcome to Melchester!
A Town for Tomorrow
Most visitors are surprised to discover that Melchester is an entirely new town. Before 1990, there was nothing here at all – just green fields and cows! Obviously, this means that the town does not have a museum, as there's nothing to put in it. On the other hand, everything looks new and clean.

Traffic-free
Right from the beginning cars have been banned from Melchester. People have to leave their cars in car parks on the outskirts of town and then walk or cycle in. You definitely need a bicycle in Melchester because there are no buses either. Visitors are often surprised to find locked-up green bicycles everywhere. These can be used by anyone but you have to buy a special card that releases them from the locks. You just ride the bike and lock it up again when you have finished with it. The cards are available from any shop.

A mystery
After a few hours in Melchester, visitors start wondering how goods are delivered to the shops, as there is no sign of any delivery trucks. This is Melchester's great secret! In fact, there is an underground electric railway used for delivering goods directly to shops from lorry parks on the outskirts.

Staying cool
Summers get quite hot here but no building has air-conditioning. No one gets hot and bothered, though. All the buildings and streets in Melchester have been designed to stay cool in a natural way. You'll notice, for example, that we have fountains everywhere, both inside and outside.

Melchester – a model for the future!

2 Review

Eat a lot for a little!

This week we look at three good places to eat which all have something in common: they all offer very large portions at a very reasonable price.

La Perla

This restaurant has been popular with students for decades. When former students, perhaps now rich and famous, return to the town, they usually have a meal here because it brings back such good memories. What's more, the owners, Mr and Mrs Mancini, remember all their customers, even from years ago. The food is Italian, with a definite rustic flavour. It won't cost more than £5 per person and the wine is inexpensive too.

Ahmed's Self-service Curry House

This new restaurant only opened six months ago, yet it's already a favourite with young people who are short of cash. For £3, you can eat as much as you like both at lunchtime and in the evenings – you can just keep going back to the counter for more. It's a real bargain, as long as you like curry that is. You can't get much cheaper than this.

Number One Walton Street

This unusually-named restaurant is the place to go if you have to take your parents out or if you just fancy some really excellent food. It does classic French cuisine and if you go in the evening it will cost you a fortune. The bargain is the set lunch at only £12.50 per person. For good quality food and impeccable service, this is the best deal in town.

3 Letter to a newspaper

Dear Sir or Madam

I was very concerned to read in last Friday's edition of your newspaper about the Council's plans to build low-cost housing in the centre of town on the site known as New Park. I do hope that there is time to raise objections to these plans before a final decision is taken.

In my opinion, the place for low-cost housing is on the outskirts of town where there is plenty of empty land, especially to the east. For example, the site of the former power station, now demolished, has been empty for the last five years. In contrast, New Park is used throughout the day by people walking and jogging, or just relaxing and enjoying the natural surroundings. At lunchtime, it is full of office workers enjoying their break. In the evening, concerts and other events attract large number of people. It is the only green space in the centre of town and it would be a tragedy to lose it.

Moreover, the park is full of wildlife of all kinds, especially squirrels, some of which will eat nuts out of your hand. I have even seen foxes and badgers there. Where would all these animals go if the park is built on? And what would happen to the magnificent trees in the park?

For humans, wildlife and nature the loss of New Park would be a tragedy. I urge the Council to think again and ensure that it remains a place of relaxation and a haven for wildlife.

Yours faithfully

4 Report on a work placement

Introduction

I have recently completed a two-week work placement at Caxton Press as a trainee secretary. The aim of this report is to describe the placement and comment on the suitability of Caxton Press for future student placements.

What I had to do

The daily tasks I had to perform were very varied and interesting. They included:

- answering the phone
- typing up documents
- arranging meetings and taking minutes
- filing
- using a computer database

The people I worked with

The people I worked with, most notably my supervisor, were patient and helpful. I had plenty of opportunities to ask if I didn't know how something functioned.

What I learnt

The most interesting part of the placement was learning how to access and update a computer database. Learning about methods of filing was also useful. In addition, I was given a guided tour of the Press, along with other trainees, which explained the history and day-to-day running of the firm. This gave me a valuable insight into the working practices and goals of the company.

Conclusion

The company has been involved in the work placement scheme for three years, and knows what students need to learn during the time they spend there. The programme is well thought-out, with students being given a range of guided tasks to complete. The fact that each student is assigned a supervisor means that you have someone to turn to for help. I can thoroughly recommend the placement in this company for future students, who I am sure will benefit from the experience.

ENGLISH IN USE 3 (page 192)

Part 3, Error correction

1 Read for general understanding.

2 Error correction task.

Remind students that there is only one mistake per line and between three and five lines are correct.

ANSWERS

1 leather	9 ✓
2 cupboard's	10 forty
3 height	11 ✓
4 ✓	12 kind, goes
5 clearance	13 ✓
6 failed. I	14 played. There
7 page, year	15 reference
8 amazingly, nothing	16 using

3 📼 Spelling quiz.

This is just for fun – let students see if they can beat the native speakers!

TAPESCRIPT

1 allowance – a-l-l-o-w-a-n-c-e – allowance
2 sincerely – s-i-n-c-e-r-e-l-y – sincerely
3 receive – r-e-c-e-i-v-e – receive
4 apologise – a-p-o-l-o-g-i-s-e – apologise
5 unfortunately – u-n-f-o-r-t-u-n-a-t-e-l-y – unfortunately
6 necessary – n-e-c-e-s-s-a-r-y – necessary
7 maintenance – m-a-i-n-t-e-n-a-n-c-e – maintenance
8 immediately – i-m-m-e-d-i-a-t-e-l-y – immediately
9 occasionally – o-c-c-a-s-i-o-n-a-l-l-y – occasionally
10 accommodation – a-c-c-o-m-m-o-d-a-t-i-o-n – accommodation
11 harass – h-a-r-a-s-s – harass
12 embarrassment – e-m-b-a-r-a-s-s-m-e-n-t – embarrassment

Exam practice 3

ENGLISH IN USE

Part 5, Register cloze

ANSWERS

62 take place/go ahead
63 responsible for
64 in business
65 not known
66 are missing/have disappeared
67 contact/touch with
68 every/an effort
69 their enquiries/investigations
70 in advance
71 partial refund
72 unlikely/improbable
73 all our/the
74 apply

READING

Part 3, Multiple choice

ANSWERS

21 B Like everyone else, I used to believe that women were the talkative sex . . . but when I analysed the results . . .
22 C Most of them can't stand up to me so stay silent
23 D But men in a group with women often get bored with what they see as the slow build-up of a topic.
24 A In social situations, this different view of the polite enquiry can often cause bad feelings.
25 B Partly, too, it is a question of giving what Dr Coates calls 'positive face', which means reassuring others about their own value.

ENGLISH IN USE

Part 6, Discourse cloze

ANSWERS

75 I 76 F 77 H 78 D 79 A 80 C

UNIT 1 TEST

1 Multiple-choice cloze

For questions 1–10, read the sentences below and then decide which word best fits each space. Put the letter you choose in the space.

1   You need to be more .... if you are going to save money for a trip around the world.

   A tight   **B** mean   **C** thrifty   **D** miserly

2   Our missing cat was found safe and .... in the neighbours' attic.

   A sober   **B** stable   **C** solid   **D** sound

3   Don't believe everything he says – he likes to lead people up the wrong ....

   A way   **B** path   **C** direction   **D** drive

4   It's not fair to put somebody .... in front of their friends.

   A down   **B** up   **C** through   **D** out

5   Please indicate how useful you found the course on a .... of one to five.

   A rate   **B** scale   **C** grade   **D** rank

6   You can tease him as much as you like – he won't rise to the ....

   A fight   **B** insult   **C** challenge   **D** bait

7   It takes a lot of courage to .... a bully and tell him how you feel.

   A confront   **B** address   **C** encounter   **D** engage

8   It's important to .... your qualifications to use.

   A turn   **B** let   **C** get   **D** put

9   However much he tries to persuade you, please do not give ....

   A in   **B** up   **C** down   **D** to

10   Is there a dress .... at your school?

   A law   **B** rule   **C** advice   **D** code

2 Word formation

For questions 11–17, use the word in capitals at the end of the sentence to form one word that fits in the space.

11   Unauthorised absence could lead to .... from your job.   **DISMISS**

12   Go and ask Jenny – she's very ....   **APPROACH**

13   .... the monarch can dimiss the Prime Minister, but it would never happen.   **THEORY**

14   Sue is one of those people who will do anything to avoid a ....   **CONFRONT**

15   The matter is now in the hands of my .... , Messrs. Grant and Colby.   **LAW**

16   .... is much more effective than aggression.   **ASSERT**

17   You'll love my cousin – he's a very popular, ... boy.   **GO**

3 Structural cloze

For questions 18–25, complete the sentences by writing one missing word in the space.

18   .... a student currently involved in medical research, I would be very interested in this post.

19   It was lucky that you were .... to escape from the fire.

20   You needn't .... written that long letter, a phone call would have been fine.

21   She should have stood up to him .... of meekly giving in.

22   I think we should wait a little longer to start dinner – Basil and Joan .... have got lost.

23   Your fluent English gives you an advantage .... the other applicants.

24   You have enough money so you may as .... buy both pairs of shoes.

25   That car .... be George's, because he walked here today.

4 Error correction

For questions 26–32, find one unnecessary word in each sentence and write it next to the number.

26 .... How long were you being a teacher?

27 .... You must have to been very happy when you found out the good news.

28 .... This is the first time I've never travelled alone.

29 .... I think we last met for two years ago.

30 .... My big brother is always winding with me up.

31 .... You really shouldn't have drive so far when you're tired.

32 .... That's a lot to pay for bed and a breakfast.

5 Writing: register

For questions 33–36, read the first paragraph of this letter of application. Underline the most appropriate word or phrase in each pair for a formal letter.

Dear Mr. Green,

I saw your (**33**) advertisement/advert in the Evening Standard on the 20th June for a part time library (**34**) helper/assistant at your college.
(**35**) I am interested in applying/would like to apply because I plan to (**36**) go in for/train in librarianship in the future.

6 Writing: accuracy (tenses)

For questions 37–40, read the second paragraph of the same letter of application and find and correct four tense errors.

I studied languages at City College for the past year and before that I have spent a year travelling around Australia. I am always very interested in books and reading ever since I was a child. I am also good at dealing with people as I have worked as a hotel receptionist in a big international hotel while I was in Australia.

37 ....

38 ....

39 ....

40 ....

UNIT 2 TEST

1 Multiple-choice cloze

For questions 1–10, read the sentences below and then decide which word fits best in each space. Put the letter you choose in the space.

1 He was horrified to see his feet had become .... in the lines of his parachute.

A jumbled   B coiled   C tangled   D muddled

2 Living so close to the .... for such a long time can be very stressful.

A edge   B surface   C cliff   D point

3 You will not be successful in business if you don't .... risks.

A put   B take   C try   D get

4 He thought he was brave enough to jump out of the plane, but he .... out at the last minute.

A chickened   B swanned   C ducked   D craned

5 I was scared .... when I looked down from the top of the cliff.

A stiff   B tight   C hard   D solid

6 There is no point in continually raking .... past relationships.

A over   B through   C up   D down

7 Your exams are very soon; it's time to .... down to some work.

A finger   B hand   C nail   D knuckle

8 When I got my diploma, I really felt on top of the ....

A earth   B sky   C world   D clouds

9 It should be safe to climb as long as you .... sensible precautions.

A make   B do   C put   D take

10 In late middle age, Sue has suddenly become .... about sailing.

A keen   B good   C mad   D interested

2 Word formation

For questions 11–17, use the word in capitals at the end of the sentence to form one word that fits in the space.

11 Sometimes the desire to do more and more dangerous things can become ....   OBSESS

12 Not many people have the .... to spend months or years exploring remote parts of the planet.   FREE

13 All .... need to have strong persuasive powers.   POLITICS

14 It is .... to take a group of children climbing without their parents' permission.   ACCEPT

15 The singer's .... lifestyle attracts the attention of the press.   CONVENTION

16 Her husband's .... with computers was starting to worry Sue.   OCCUPY

17 You know a lot about setting up a business so why don't you become a .... to help others?   CONSULT

3 Structural cloze

For questions 18–23, complete the sentences by writing one missing word in the space.

18 The boat .... which the first yachtsman sailed around the world is now on display.

19 She promised herself that she would climb Everest .... the age of 35.

20 As .... as I'm concerned, this matter is over and done with.

21 Could you please recall this email from the person you sent it ....

22 It was clear from her diaries that she had .... struggling to survive for several weeks.

23 What actually happened .... that the lorry swerved to avoid the car.

4 Error correction

For questions 24–29, find one unnecessary word in each sentence and write it next to the number.

24 .... The competition in which we entered is very exciting.

25 .... Michael ducked out to avoid being hit by the bullet.

26 .... Tom had been gone out of the door before I could stop him.

27 .... He gave me the book I had always wanted it.

28 .... He has written stories that they have won prizes.

29 .... A few years ago, I had tried to swim the Channel but didn't quite make it.

5 Discourse cloze

For questions 30–34, read the following text and then choose from the list A–F the best phrase to fill the spaces.

My aunt Sandra is a real daredevil who decided at the age of 50 to take up rally driving. It all started when she got talking one day to an old man (**30**) .... The man was so enthusiastic about it, she was persuaded to try it for herself. As a daredevil, Aunt Sandra is the complete opposite of her husband, my Uncle Bert. Long-suffering Bert, (**31**) .... , knew it was too risky and warned her that her reactions would not be as fast as they used to be. He also knew that she was the type of person (**32**) .... , so he hoped she would soon forget all about it.

But Sandra did not forget about it. Instead she looked for an instructor (**33**) .... , and within three years she was winning prizes and beating drivers (**34**) ....

A who was willing to take her on

B who has devoted half a lifetime to trying to curb her enthusiasm

C who attended rally driving events all over the world as a spectator

D who knew nothing about rally driving

E who had 20 years' experience behind them

F who often had crazy ideas but never carried them out

6 Writing

For questions 35–40, join the pairs of sentences using the word or phrase in bold at the end of the sentence. Put the verbs in brackets into the correct tense.

35 He went to Australia. He (want) to explore the Great Barrier Reef. **because**

....

....

36 He was three years old. He (learn) to read. **by the time**

....

....

37 She attended a mountaineering course. She (climb) in the Himalayas. **before**

....

....

38 Tom is very adventurous. His father (prefer) to stay nearer home. **while**

....

....

39 She finished the bungee jump. She (want) to do another one. **as soon as**

....

....

40 He (live) in the USA. He took his pilot's licence. **when**

....

Unit 3 Test

1 Multiple-choice cloze

For questions 1–10, read the sentences below and then decide which word best fits each space. Put the letter you choose in the space.

1 To get to the top you need determination as well as ....

A gift   B talent   C good   D facility

2 She has such .... that she'll work seven days a week if necessary to get what she wants.

A force   B push   C drive   D effort

3 Many married women in the survey said they lacked time to .... an interest.

A chase   B conduct   C proceed   D pursue

4 It is often said that having rich parents is a .... rather than a help.

A handicap   B regret   C failure   D penalty

5 In the long .... you will probably make quite a lot of money out of the business.

A future   B term   C time   D way

6 Because his parents are successful actors, famous people have always figured .... in his life.

A prominently   B prolifically   C proportionately
D properly

7 Your career .... will be much better if you go to university first.

A perspectives   B hopes   C prospects
D developments

8 There were some very strong candidates for the job but none of them .... my expectations.

A took   B made   C gave   D met

9 I really .... that I didn't try to find a quicker way – I wasted a lot of time.

A regret   B wish   C hope   D prefer

10 You should make sure that you get all the money you are .... to.

A owed   B due   C entitled   D promised

2 Word formation

For questions 11–17, use the word in capitals at the end of the sentence to form one word that fits in the space.

11 Although she was told her condition was .... , she remained cheerful.   **CURE**

12 Unfortunately, her degree certificate was a ....   **FORGE**

13 It is unusual to have so many .... at such a young age.   **RESPONSIBLE**

14 Financial analysts are still struggling to find an .... for the collapse.   **EXPLAIN**

15 When she passed 30 Sue became increasingly .... for a baby.   **DESPAIR**

16 Holidays in other countries can be .... as well as fun.   **EDUCATE**

17 It is .... that we didn't buy better quality goods from the beginning.   **REGRET**

3 Structural cloze

For questions 18–23, complete the sentences by writing one missing word in the space.

18 I wish you .... think about things before you do them.

19 I wish I had .... more careful with my money.

20 I regret not .... more helpful when my sister was setting up her business.

21 If you .... read about the company first, you would have had more to say in the interview.

22 Try and predict which company is going to do well and buy shares .... it.

23 I wish I .... afford to buy a new car.

4 Error correction

For questions 24–29, find one unnecessary word in each sentence and write it next to the number.

24 .... If I hadn't have moved to another company, I'd still be at the bottom of the ladder.

25 .... If I would put more effort into my work, I might pass the exam.

26 .... My father regrets to selling his shares just before they increased in value.

27 .... Sue made sure she concentrated on the subjects that were interesting in.

28 .... Your maths needs to be good at if you want to be an engineer.

29 .... I wish you would paid more attention when I explain my problems to you.

5 Register cloze

For questions 30–35, read the text below and replace the words and expressions in italics with the more formal words in the list. There are two extra words you do not need to use.

very reasonable / regrettable / fashionably / regards / celebration / unacceptable / excellent / sophisticated

> We had arranged our parents' 25th wedding anniversary (30) *bash* in a local hotel, which we chose because it was (31) *a bargain*. It was (32) *a shame* that we didn't choose somewhere a bit more (33) *upmarket*. The décor was very shabby and as (34) *for* the food, it was (35) *disgusting*.

30 ....

31 ....

32 ....

33 ....

34 ....

35 ....

6 Discourse cloze

For questions 36–40, read the following text and then choose from the list A–F the best phrase to fill the spaces.

> I'm in a dead-end job at the moment; packing shoes in a factory, and frankly I'm starting to wish I hadn't wasted so much time when I was at school. But I was rebellious in those days. If a teacher told me to do something, (36) .... Although my friends told me to work harder, I just didn't listen, because I was having too much fun. But if I could have my time over again, (37) .... If I'd been more sensible then, (38) .... Last week I reached a real low point, and told a colleague that if I had to spend another day of my life putting shoes in boxes, (39) ....
>
> I really envy some of my friends, who are in high-flying jobs or running their own successful businesses. If I worked for myself, (40) .... , instead of having a supervisor breathing down my neck all the time. I'm going to make this my goal for the coming year.

A I'd be limited in what I could do

B I could make my own decisions

C I'd annoy everybody by doing the exact opposite

D I would go mad

E I wouldn't be in such a boring job now

F I'd try to avoid developing such bad habits

UNIT 4 TEST

1 Multiple-choice cloze

For questions 1–10, read the sentences below and then decide which word best fits each space. Put the letter you choose in the space.

1   Drug-taking is a crime which society simply cannot ....

    A approve   **B** acknowledge   **C** condone
    D consent

2   A good sense of humour is a .... advantage if you want to be a performer.

    A main   **B** most   **C** major   **D** more

3   It is in the .... of the situation that it will attract media attention.

    A feature   **B** character   **C** nature   **D** way

4   She has such a comic expression that it's difficult to keep a .... face.

    A straight   **B** serious   **C** sincere   **D** stiff

5   He was a good comedian but I was rather .... off by his piercing eyes.

    A sent   **B** set   **C** seen   **D** put

6   She is .... to fits of uncontrollable laughter for no apparent reason.

    A likely   **B** prone   **C** open   **D** prompted

7   He comes from a very interesting theatrical ....

    A history   **B** past   **C** life   **D** background

8   Sam took a longer route to .... passing the school.

    A avoid   **B** prevent   **C** stop   **D** deny

9   The picture didn't come out because the .... on my camera didn't work.

    A torch   **B** light   **C** flash   **D** illumination

10 I had to cut down on my .... activities because of my school exams.

    A leisure   **B** hobby   **C** pastime   **D** pleasure

2 Word formation

For questions 11–17, use the word in capitals at the end of the sentence to form one word that fits in the space.

11 The best humour comes from a clever .... of life.   **OBSERVE**

12 He's very .... – you never know what he's going to say next.   **PREDICT**

13 My brother's a comedian who specialises in doing .... of famous people.   **PERSON**

14 Painting gives him the opportunity to express his ....   **CREATE**

15 One often finds a good sense of humour among people with .... qualities.   **LEAD**

16 The comedians of the silent movie era have been very .... in his development.   **INFLUENCE**

17 The vaccination will give you .... for 10 years.   **IMMUNE**

3 Structural cloze

For questions 18–23, complete the sentences by writing one missing word in the space.

18 The performers were told that such poor work was never .... happen again.

19 I definitely remember .... him to meet me here at 6.30.

20 It's .... use phoning again; he's obviously not in.

21 The President is often perceived .... being pro-western.

22 Look, it's really not .... getting upset about it.

23 At last we have succeeded .... getting tickets for the match.

4 Error correction

For questions 24–29, find one spelling or punctuation mistake in each sentence and write the correct form next to the number.

24 .... The best holiday is a combination of siteseeing and relaxation.

25 .... You need to take a brake every couple of hours when you are driving long distances.

26 .... I thought the jokes were clever funny and appropriate for the audience.

27 .... My brother and sister, must know over 1,000 jokes between them.

28 .... His performance is not particularly funny, it is, however, interesting.

29 .... Take my advise and take up a cheaper hobby.

5 Writing: grammatical cohesion

For questions 30–35, complete the text by writing a pronoun or a link word in the spaces.

Laughter is only healthy when people can laugh together. For when (30) .... laugh in this way, our common ground is reinforced, and the uplifting moment is shared with (31) .... (32) .... can, however, be disturbing if one person does not know why others are laughing, because lack of self-confidence may make him think (33) .... is being laughed at for some reason. (34) .... can result in embarrassment and confusion. It is therefore considered insensitive and impolite to laugh without sharing the joke with all (35) .... present.

6 Writing: range of vocabulary

For questions 36–40, read the text below. Replace all the examples of the word 'nice' with a more expressive word from the list. Use each word once only.

tactful / likeable / novel / suitable / inspiring

We thought it would be a/an (36) *nice* idea to make a video to send to my Uncle Charlie in Australia, who is one of the (37) *nicest* people you could ever hope to meet. We went off to a/an wonderfully (38) *nice* location and acted out a scene that told him about our lives. We made sure that it was a (39) *nice* length so as not to bore him. It was a bit amateurish, to be honest, but Uncle Charlie was (40) *nice* enough to send us a thankyou letter, complimenting us on our good work.

36 ....

37 ....

38 ....

39 ....

40 ....

Unit 5 Test

1 Multiple-choice cloze

For questions 1–10, read the sentences below and then decide which word best fits each space. Put the letter you choose in the space.

1 When writing, you should always bear your prospective readers in ....

   A head   B thought   C brain   D mind

2 People who are not familiar with public speaking tend to .... into their microphone.

   A mumble   B grumble   C murmur   D mutter

3 The meeting was .... off at the last minute because the papers were not ready.

   A stopped   B broken   C called   D turned

4 The author managed to buy a new house on the .... of his book.

   A earnings   B receipts   C returns   D proceeds

5 I think you'll like the play – it's .... funny.

   A very   B absolutely   C totally   D entirely

6 No other opera singer has .... the imagination of the public quite like Pavarotti.

   A taken   B caught   C received   D obtained

7 I don't know why he has been so successful – his acting is very ....

   A wooden   B woolly   C worldly   D wordy

8 Clement's new vocation as a novelist is a far .... from working in a bookshop.

   A shout   B cry   C call   D yell

9 She has always wanted to play the .... lady in a Shakespeare play.

   A first   B main   C important   D leading

10 I would .... recommend the new production of Romeo and Juliet.

   A much   B extremely   C thoroughly
   D considerably

2 Word formation

For questions 11–17, use the word in capitals at the end of the sentence to form one word that fits in the space.

11 From the plane, there was a spectacular view over a .... of rivers and forests.   **LAND**

12 As part of the arts festival, some new .... have been put up in the park.   **SCULPT**

13 The poet read his piece very ....   **DRAMA**

14 The children were given a lot of different .... to stimulate their imagination.   **ACT**

15 What are your .... for the literature prize?   **RECOMMEND**

16 The subtle photography and the music make the film very ....   **ATMOSPHERE**

17 Michael Spence's .... novel is likely to be a huge success.   **COME**

3 Structural cloze

For questions 18–23, complete the sentences by writing one missing word in the space.

18 .... the only woman in the play, she felt a certain responsibility to represent women in a positive light.

19 I am quite used to .... criticised in reviews.

20 Those creatures at the back of the stage are supposed .... be ghosts.

21 I envy him; I would love to be able to sing .... that.

22 He was a success, ... having no support from his family.

23 Mike looks as .... he hasn't slept for a very long time.

4 Error correction

For questions 24–29, find one unnecessary word in each sentence and write it next to the number.

24 .... I got used to be a theatre assistant before I started acting.

25 .... Tom worked as if a computer analyst by day and a musician by night.

26 .... This is not the first time that you have broken off your promise.

27 .... Michael went to Drama College, because thinking he would become a very rich film star.

28 .... He sold all his paintings at the exhibition despite of being a complete unknown.

29 .... My brother, who being very self-confident, loves appearing on the stage.

5 Writing: lexical cohesion

For questions 30–34, fill in the space in the second sentence with a paraphrase or synonym of a word in the first sentence.

30 | I feel the storyline is very ordinary. However, the .... is not really the main point of the film.

31 | The film had an extraordinary cast. Most of the .... had been at the top of the profession for many years.

32 | I wouldn't say the play was a comedy. There was, however, a very strong element of .... throughout.

33 | Ask Tom what his advice would be. I would always follow his ....

34 | Some directors rely on special effects. Others seem to .... more on their own creativity.

6 Writing: range of structures (participles and clauses)

For questions 35–40, combine each pair of sentences using a participle. The participle may come from either sentence.

35 I didn't want to offend her. I didn't tell the truth about her work.

....
....

36 He had no hope of selling the tickets. He cancelled the show.

....
....

37 He refused the offer of a job in banking. He chose instead to be a translator.

....
....

38 I was walking around the exhibition. I was looking for a painting to buy.

....
....

39 Many people prefer the old James Bond films. They starred Sean Connery.

....
....

40 He took the play to the north of the country. He thought it would appeal to the people more.

....
....

Practice Test 1

Reading

Part 3

Read the following extract from a book about photography and answer
questions 21–25 that follow. **On your answer sheet**, indicate the letter A, B, C or D
against the number of each question 21–25. **Give only one answer to each question.**

The Photographer

Behind every photograph is an idea. The idea may be mundane: 'This is the way I
looked standing in front of the Eiffel Tower on my vacation;' profound: 'Man's vanity is
surpassed only by his capacity to deceive himself;' or abstract: 'This pattern evokes a
feeling of tension;' but every photograph has its origin in the desire of a photographer
to say something meaningful.

For some people, photography is useful only for preserving memories, or for making a
record of a place or event. At this basic level, most of the photographer's message
remains within his own head. The finished photograph jogs his memory, but means
little to someone else without accompanying clarification. ('Here's one of my
daughter the day she got married. You should have seen her. She was very happy. See
that vase in the background? It was a wedding present. During the reception, it got
broken. It almost ruined the day for her.') The visual content of a photograph in such
cases is very limited, and, consequently, so is the amount of visual communication
that takes place.

Yet the photographer did not set out to produce a shallow photograph, even though
that is what they ended up doing. Had they been asked to put their intentions into
words, they would not have said, 'What I really want to do is create a vague likeness
of my daughter that I can use to discuss her wedding day.' Instead, if pinned down,
they would have said something like, 'My daughter is getting married tomorrow, and I
want to capture her joy, the excitement of the event, and the pleasure I know everyone
present is going to experience.' Never having identified their real intent, however, they
were unable to make the photographic decisions that would have enabled them to
realize their goals.

Thus, the idea behind a photograph must be focused before a photographer will be
able to convey a message effectively. Most people, however, encounter a surprising
amount of difficulty in trying to crystallize their thoughts with sufficient clarity to serve
as the basis for making appropriate compositional decisions. Indeed, if even a modest
proportion of photographers could only convey through their images the fun and
excitement that they had wanted their cameras to capture, the words, 'Why not stop
by this evening and look at the slides I took on my trip?' would not generate such
dread and inspire so many creative excuses.

The reason for this problem lies in the fact that the visual medium of photography is
much less familiar than the spoken and written word. Yet a visual 'language' does
exist for photography, which we define as 'composition', in other words, the controlled
ordering of the elements in a visual work as the means for achieving clear
communication. This 'language' has an identifiable, learnable structure that is
analogous to that of the verbal language with which everyone is familiar, and even

though in today's world the importance of visual forms of communication is rapidly approaching that of verbal forms, visual 'illiteracy' abounds. Consequently, most photographers are unable to exploit the medium effectively, and those comparatively few photographers who can, have as an audience only a limited number of people knowledgeable enough to understand and appreciate the fine points of photography.

Through an understanding of the principles of photographic composition, any photographer can improve their ability to use photography as a form of communication and thereby turn those slide shows into entertaining, engaging experiences. In addition, a knowledge of photographic composition can introduce a photographer to new, deeper, more satisfying dimensions of photography, dimensions of which the casual photographer is completely unaware.

21   What kind of photograph is the wedding picture an example of?

    A One with a subtle, hidden message.

    B One that creates a sense of anxiety.

    C One that only works with an explanation.

    D One that captures an unfortunate incident.

22   In the writer's opinion, a common failing is to take photographs

    A to use as a vehicle for discussion.

    B without having a clear notion of one's aims.

    C about one's own personal circumstances.

    D that do not show the best features of the subject.

23   In the fourth paragraph, what emotion does the writer express?

    A Frustration at many photographers' inability to express their ideas.

    B Surprise at how indecisive many photographers can be.

    C Indifference at the thought of commenting on certain photographs.

    D Dismay that some photographers regard their work as artistic.

24   In likening photography to language, the writer is making the point that

    A photographers have to be able to speak lucidly about their ideas.

    B photography is the most effective form of expression in society today.

    C photography is a discipline with rules that have to be learnt and mastered.

    D a photograph communicates ideas which may be difficult to put into words.

25   The writer implies that people trained in photographic composition

    A will be able to communicate their new knowledge to others.

    B will be more willing to look at the snaps of casual photographers.

    C will appreciate good photographs fully even if they can not take them.

    D will see that photography deals seriously with fundamental issues in life.

English in Use

Part 3

In **most** lines of the following text there is **either** a spelling **or** a punctuation error. For each numbered line **31–45**, write the correctly spelt word or show the correct punctuation in the box on your answer sheet. **Some lines are correct.** Indicate these lines with a tick (**✔**) in the box. The exercise begins with two examples (0) and (00).

Example:

0	ammount
00	✔

Travelling Solo

0	Travelling solo is my life. My work involves a considerable ammount of
00	travel, my weekends are taken up with train trips to remote areas, and my
31	holidays in far-flung destination's are also usually taken alone. I have to be
32	honest and say that given the choise, I probably wouldn't travel alone,
33	however. I am a world-class worrier, not one of those women, who move
34	around without a care. I often want someone to talk to, thought not the sort
35	who invite themselves to join me at my hotel dinning table. But without a
36	doubt you meet more people absorb more, take more memories away and
37	immerse yourself more in the true nature of a country when travelling by
38	yourself. When women say to me, as they often do, that they hate eating
39	on their own in public places, I think its a pity. In such circumstances I
40	indulge myself in a spot of person watching. I come to wild conclusions
41	about their lives and relationships, try to work out where their from or what
42	they do. So if you've never done it before, my advise to you would be:
43	know your limits and plan acordingly. If you don't want to be entirely alone,
44	choose a busy root and meet people. If you're worried about security,
45	take taxis at night and be prepared to pay a bit more, for your hotels.

Part 4

For questions 46–60, read the following two texts. Use the words in the boxes to the right of the texts to form **one** word that fits in the same numbered space in the text. Write the new word in the correct box on your answer sheet. The exercise begins with an example (0).

Example: | 0 | computerised |

TEST INSTRUCTIONS

The driving theory test is (0) .... The
questions will cover a (46) .... of topics
relating to road (47) .... Most questions will
ask you to mark one correct answer from a (48) ....
of four. Other questions will ask you for two or more
correct answers from a (49) .... The aim is to
test your (50) .... of traffic signs and your
(51) .... to spot a hazard. Look at the
question (52) ....

(0)	**COMPUTER**
(46)	VARY
(47)	SAFE
(48)	CHOOSE
(49)	SELECT
(50)	AWARE
(51)	ABLE
(52)	CARE

EXTRACT FROM A NEWSPAPER ARTICLE

(53) .... for jobs amongst new graduates is
always tough. So much so that some candidates are
tempted to lie on their CVs just to get into the
interview. But you can turn your various (54) ....
into (55) .... while still telling the truth.

Start with the basics. 10–20% of (56) .... do not
pay enough (57) .... to the quality and the look of
their CV. These CVs are immediately rejected. But the main
problem is getting enough relevant and (58) .... and
relevant information into the CV.

(59) .... is another weak area so emphasise the
(60) .... skills such as enthusiasm and flexibility.

(53)	COMPETE
(54)	WEAK
(55)	STRONG
(56)	APPLY
(57)	ATTEND
(58)	INTEREST
(59)	KNOW
(60)	TRANSFER

UNIT 6 TEST

1 Multiple-choice cloze

For questions 1–10, read the sentences below and then decide which word best fits each space. Put the letter you choose in the space.

1 For a team to be successful, all members have to .... their weight.

   A take **B** make **C** get **D** pull

2 You really will have to be able to .... down a job for more than six weeks.

   A keep **B** turn **C** take **D** hold

3 It took him a long time to come to .... with the fact that he was homeless.

   A terms **B** acceptance **C** tabs **D** agreement

4 Sue always felt that she was to .... for the burglary because she hadn't locked the door properly.

   A fault **B** provoke **C** blame **D** cause

5 Simon has a very strong .... of duty so he will always carry out his promises.

   A sense **B** idea **C** mind **D** thought

6 The birth of their first child caused a lot of .... in Angela and Ken's lives.

   A uproar **B** upheaval **C** outcry **D** overthrow

7 The interviewer's warm smile soon put Jill at her ....

   A comfort **B** leisure **C** rest **D** ease

8 No .... how long it takes, I will keep trying to find an answer.

   A way **B** matter **C** worry **D** mind

9 I .... to think how you're going to cope all by yourself with two babies.

   A fear **B** avoid **C** dread **D** worry

10 How do they earn enough to .... fifteen children?

   A maintain **B** support **C** hold **D** survive

2 Word formation

For questions 11–17, use the word in capitals at the end of the sentence to form one word that fits in the space.

11 I'm sorry to say I found the people I stayed with very .... **FRIEND**

12 Some .... now have their own nursery facilities for staff with children. **WORK**

13 It was a chaotic .... consisting of parents, children, lodgers and animals. **HOUSE**

14 We wanted to find a nanny who had good .... **QUALIFY**

15 He won't get angry with you – he has a very calm .... **TEMPER**

16 I really must apologise for this little .... **UNDERSTAND**

17 Sam was very grateful to his .... parents for their generosity. **ADOPT**

3 Structural cloze

For questions 18–23, complete the sentences by writing one missing word in the space.

18 I think you should go on this trip of a lifetime in .... of the risks involved.

19 There is now a lot of pressure .... parents to try and ensure that their children achieve well at school.

20 Managers have responsibility .... safety in the workplace.

21 Just drop me .... at the end of the road and I'll walk the rest of the way.

22 The authorities warned parents .... allowing their teenage children to smoke.

23 I lent Joe £20 .... though he still hadn't paid off his last debt to me.

4 Error correction

For questions 24–29, find one unnecessary word in four of the sentences and write it next to the number. Two sentences are correct.

24 .... She succeeded despite of her lack of experience.

25 .... Everyone, even though his girlfriend, was surprised when Tom suddenly left his job.

26 .... I suggest you to get advice from a solicitor.

27 .... Didn't anyone ever warn you of the dangers of travelling alone?

28 .... I never could have done what I did it if I hadn't planned it carefully in advance.

29 .... He always promised that he would look after his elderly parents and he has done.

5 Writing: grammatical cohesion

For questions 30–34, read the text and write one word in each space to complete the sentences.

I spent a year in Australia as an *au pair* for an 85-year-old woman. I did it because I chose (30) .... , thinking it would be less responsibility than looking after a baby. My boss was very charming and kind to me and she expected me to be the (31) .... towards her. That was easy. But I was quite lonely – I didn't go to the playground or the school gates as other *au pairs* (32) .... , so it was more difficult to meet people. When my boss visited her friends, she did (33) .... alone and gave little thought to my social life. I realised that it is difficult for such different generations to live together and (34) .... did my boss.

6 Register cloze

For questions 35–40, use one or two words to complete the second sentence so that it means the same as the first but in a formal style.

35 My sister does nothing to help in the house except to wash the odd dish.

My sister does nothing to help in the house except to wash .... dishes.

36 The problem with holidays is that work piles up in your absence.

The problem with holidays is that work .... in your absence.

37 I bet you'll find it easy to make new friends when you get to Australia.

I .... you'll find it easy to make new friends when you get to Australia.

38 Tom hit the roof when he heard that he was expected to look after the office alone for three weeks.

Tom .... when he heard that he was expected to look after the office alone for three weeks.

39 My boss goes on and on about how important it is to be punctual.

My boss .... how important it is to be punctual.

40 I thought I had cooked enough for two days but Sue and Ellen ate the lot!

I thought I had cooked enough for two days but Sue and Ellen ate ....

UNIT 7 TEST

1 Multiple-choice cloze

For questions 1–10, read the sentences below and then decide which word best fits each space. Put the letter you choose in the space.

1   Many people think that ironing is the worst household ....
    A work   B labour   C chore   D effort

2   I've found someone to clean the house for me so things are .... up.
    A going   B pointing   C turning   D looking

3   After all my complaints, she is .... making long phone calls in peak time.
    A yet   B already   C just   D still

4   When it comes to jobs around the house, my mother and father .... to type.
    A return   B retire   C revert   D reverse

5   He makes a lot of money by buying old houses, ... them up and then selling them again.
    A making   B doing   C putting   D setting

6   My wife and I are jointly responsible for the .... of the house.
    A outlay   B upkeep   C outlook   D onset

7   Don't worry about me – just .... on with what you're doing.
    A stay   B rest   C carry   D hurry

8   After the builders had left, everything was .... with dust.
    A heavy   B thick   C dirty   D over

9   I suggest you .... up a list of things to be done.
    A make   B do   C put   D draw

10 Don't live on the main road unless you have good .... against noise.
    A insurance   B isolation   C insulation
    D assurance

2 Word formation

For questions 11–17, use the word in capitals at the end of the sentence to form one word that fits in the space.

11 My husband's .... around the house never ceases to amaze me.   **COMPETENT**

12 I stayed in a holiday cottage with three very messy ....   **COMPANY**

13 I want a job that has variety – I can't bear .... work.   **REPEAT**

14 My uncle lives in a really .... house with solar-powered heating.   **FUTURE**

15 My mother cleaned the kitchen for three hours, leaving it absolutely ....   **SPOT**

16 We are giving you the job and we'll send you a formal letter of .... in a few days.   **ACCEPT**

17 I need a sweater – it's .... sitting by this window.   **DRAUGHT**

3 Structural cloze

For questions 18–23, complete the sentences by writing one missing word in the space.

18 We'll be .... into our new house on 21 February.

19 We made the .... of the beautiful weather by going swimming.

20 Please bring me the finished report .... this time next week.

21 It's time someone .... the washing up from last night.

22 If you go to court, you'll need evidence to back .... your case.

23 You need a builder quickly – that wall is .... to fall down.

4 Error correction

For questions 24–29, find one spelling or punctuation mistake in five of the sentences and write the correct form next to the number. One sentence is correct.

24 .... When can I expect to recieve the money?

25 .... Whose responsability is it to unload the dishwasher?

26 .... None of my friend's do any housework so why should I?

27 .... Everyone was confidant that Sam would get into university.

28 .... I would recommend her because, although her work is very slow, it's also very thorough.

29 .... Do we have to have the same arguement every day about leaving dirty dishes in the sink?

5 Register cloze

For questions 30–34, use one or two words to complete the second sentence so that it means the same as the first but in a formal style.

30 I really don't mind which job I do – they're much the same.

   The jobs are .... so I am happy to do either.

31 In the end, where you live comes down to how much money you get.

   Ultimately, the area you live in .... your income.

32 When it comes to money, he really has no self-control.

   As far as money .... , he has no self-discipline.

33 This must be the messiest room I have ever come across.

   This is surely the .... room I have ever seen.

34 The police are stepping up their battle against speeding drivers.

   The police are .... their efforts to catch speeding drivers.

6 Discourse cloze

For questions 35–40, read the following text and then choose from the list A–G the best phrase to fill the spaces. Some phrases do not fit.

Somewhere in the great metropolis a strange experiment (**35**) .... for the benefit of TV viewers. A family of four (**36**) .... by living just as their grandparents did. The Epping family from Hampstead in London have had their home specially restored by a team of experts, so that it looks just as it would have done 60 years ago. They (**37**) .... or other concessions to modern living. A film company (**38**) .... in order to make a documentary about it. Quite how they (**39**) .... remains to be seen, but one thing is for sure. By the end of the experiment they (**40**) ....

A will be living in this way

B will have become household names

C will have no mod cons

D is about to be carried out

E will react to life without a TV or washing machine

F will take a step back in time

G is going to be shadowing their every move

UNIT 8 TEST

1 Multiple-choice cloze

For questions 1–10, read the sentences below and then decide which word best fits each space. Put the letter you choose in the space.

1 The police have started to train members of the community in basic crime ....

 A prevention B protection C participation
 D information

2 However at the last training session there was a very poor ....

 A turn-up B turnover C turn out D turn-off

3 To our surprise the burglar came and .... for what he had done.

 A regretted B blamed C denied D apologised

4 The old lady .... on going to court to give evidence.

 A demanded B urged C begged D insisted

5 We all know that you are guilty so why don't you .... up?

 A give B turn C own D say

6 How could we have been so gullible – it was all a .... of lies.

 A pack B heap C bunch D pile

7 They were caught because their sudden wealth gave the .... away.

 A fact B game C idea D match

8 If you continue to .... lies, people will never believe anything you say.

 A give B say C make D tell

9 Kate .... Tim that he had an appointment after lunch.

 A remembered B recalled C reminded
 D recollected

10 Police are trying to .... the stolen goods.

 A trace B track C shadow D stalk

2 Word formation

For questions 11–17, use the word in capitals at the end of the sentence to form one word that fits in the space.

11 The police are convinced that speed cameras are a .... to speeding motorists. **DETER**

12 If you see someone acting .... , please phone the police. **SUSPICION**

13 The way you kept calm in a very dangerous situation was .... **ADMIRE**

14 There has been a .... at the local bank for the second time in a month. **ROB**

15 Mike claimed that he was just an innocent .... and had not taken part in the riot. **STAND**

16 He is too .... to be given the code for the safe. **TRUST**

17 The one thing I will not tolerate from my children is lying and .... **HONEST**

3 Structural cloze

For questions 18–23, complete the sentences by writing one missing word in the space.

18 I can't imagine .... he told so many lies.

19 I'd have .... qualms about reporting a member of my family to the police.

20 That terrible smell must mean that something in the fridge is ....

21 I don't know .... I should believe him or not.

22 Another cause .... concern is the rise in crime in the city.

23 She admitted .... the money out of her mother's handbag.

4 Error correction

For questions 24–29, find one unnecessary word in
four of the sentences and write it next to the number.
Two sentences are correct.

24 .... I really can't believe it what you
told me.

25 .... I don't know what is the motive for
the crime could be.

26 .... Eddie promised me to replace the lost
necklace.

27 .... How many people have you written to
to get all that information?

28 .... It's a good idea to keep up your most
valuable jewellery in a bank.

29 .... I accepted the gift because it was
offered to me as a gesture of gratitude.

5 Register cloze

For questions 30–34, read the informal extract from a
witness statement and then use the information to
complete the spaces in the formal extract from a police
report. Use no more than one or two words for each
space. The words you need do not appear in the first
extract.

EXTRACT FROM WITNESS STATEMENT

We got a tip off that something was up at a
house on the main street. The guy said that
it was up to us what we wanted to do about
it but he didn't want anything more to do
with it. We went to the house, found a large
supply of drugs and arrested two people.
Naturally they wanted to know who had
grassed on them.

EXTRACT FROM POLICE REPORT

We received (**30**) .... from a member of the
public that something was (**31**) .... at 16 High
Street. He said that what we did about it was our
(**32**) .... but he did not want to get
(**33**) .... We went to the house, found a
large supply of drugs and arrested two people.
Naturally they were keen to discover who had
(**34**) .... on them.

6 Discourse cloze

For questions 35–40, read the following text and then
choose from the list A–H the best phrase to fill the
spaces. Some phrases do not fit.

The Smith family didn't know (**35**) .... as
their house had been burgled three times in one
year. The police suggested (**36**) .... but this
would have been very expensive and the Smiths
were fairly sure (**37**) .... They felt it might
actually encourage potential burglars
(**38**) .... and try to break in. A neighbour
advised them (**39**) .... , which they said
would deter most criminals, and the Smiths thought
(**40**) .... After that, they never had any
more trouble.

A to get a guard dog

B in doing nothing

C installing an alarm system

D that it would be ineffective

E what to do

F that it was worth a try

G to accept the challenge

Unit 9 Test

1 Multiple-choice cloze

For questions 1–10, read the sentences below and then decide which word best fits each space. Put the letter you choose in the space.

1 When you have small children, it's much easier if you can work .... hours.

A extendable B negotiable C variable
D flexible

2 Terry is the sort of person who .... on pressure.

A thrives B profits C succeeds D prospers

3 Many jobs that once involved .... physical effort are now being done by machines.

A strong B strenuous C energetic D tireless

4 As an incentive the sales personnel were given 5% .... on every item sold.

A extra B bonus C commission
D compensation

5 So that everybody knows what they are expected to do, we will hold a .... at 9 am.

A lecture B notification C conference
D briefing

6 You must be prepared to work .... hours.

A unsociable B inhospitable C unfriendly
D inaccessible

7 Wait until all the publicity has .... down and then reopen under another name.

A left B let C dived D died

8 You just sit in the office – you can afford to pay someone else to do all the .... work.

A dog B horse C cattle D donkey

9 She passed her law exams without doing a .... of work.

A finger B stroke C speck D dot

10 Many professionals are complaining that their .... is making them ill.

A workforce B workhorse C workout
D workload

2 Word formation

For questions 11–17, use the word in capitals at the end of the sentence to form one word that fits in the space.

11 We don't employ our own writers – we use .... journalists and photographers. **FREE**

12 Sadly, the last decade has been characterised by the .... of many traditional industries. **APPEAR**

13 The problem with jobs in a seaside town is that they tend to be .... **SEASON**

14 The acting world is very .... and you may be out of work most of the time. **COMPETE**

15 If I don't get this article in by the .... on Monday, they won't publish it. **LINE**

16 They won't sack you; they need your .... **EXPERT**

17 Kevin finds his new job more suited to his .... temperament. **ART**

3 Structural cloze

For questions 18–23, complete the sentences by writing one missing word in the space.

18 Surgeons do their first operations .... close supervision.

19 After my first day at work, I was .... exhausted that I went to bed at 8 pm.

20 Don't take the job even .... it pays well initially.

21 Harry succeeded in getting work as a teacher .... his disability.

22 He took very few holidays, and as a .... became exhausted.

23 I would appreciate .... if you could send me an application form.

4 Error correction

For questions 24–29, find one spelling or punctuation mistake in five of the sentences and write the correct form next to the number. One sentence is correct.

24 .... I don't know why they didn't give me the job, I've got more experience than the other applicants.

25 .... Although they say they want qualifications experience is what really matters.

26 .... Why don't you apply for promotion.

27 .... I would be very grateful if you would finish the work by the weekend.

28 .... Many companys are now merging to make very large ones.

29 .... When he retires, his daughter will become the directer.

5 Register cloze

For questions 30–35, read the informal letter and then use the information to complete the spaces in the formal advertisement. Use no more than one or two words for each space. The words you need do not appear in the first extract.

INFORMAL LETTER

Dear Debbie

Yes, the new job is going really well, thanks. I got it partly because I've been out of work for a while, and the company is very good about employing people in this position. I have to work my fingers to the bone, but I don't mind as I really like it. As you know, I did a bit of part-time marketing work when I was in Australia, so it's not new to me. And I have to be good at talking to a lot of different people, which suits me down to the ground! So all in all I'm feeling that I really want to work hard for the company, especially now that I've learnt I'm going to go to other countries to meet up with some customers!

Yours, Becky

ADVERTISEMENT

Z for Zebra – Advertising and Publicity Agency

We are currently seeking to appoint a new person to our busy marketing department. Applications are especially welcome from (30) .... The successful applicant, who must be prepared to work (31) .... , will have relevant (32) .... in this field of work, excellent (33) .... skills, and be able to demonstrate a sense of (34) .... to the company. Some (35) .... will be involved, in respect of liasing with our international customers.

6 Discourse cloze

For questions 36–40, read the following text and then choose from the list A–G the best phrase to fill the spaces. Some phrases do not fit.

Being self-employed can lead to serious overwork (36) .... Statistics show that those who work for themselves take one third to one half as much holiday as the rest of the population (37) .... It seems that they are often very reluctant to turn down work (38) .... There are several reasons for this. One is the fear that if work is refused, it may not be offered again. Another is an underestimation of the amount of time and effort a piece of work will take, (39) .... However, the main reason is probably greed. If there is the opportunity to earn more, it takes a strong will to say no. It is for the same reason that self-employed workers are unwilling to employ others to do some of the work (40) ....

A a fact which leads to a great deal of stress as the work becomes due

B although they would like to earn more money

C as they would have to pay them a share of the earnings

D despite the fact that their average earnings are higher

E because people in this situation often do not give themselves enough time off

F even though they may have more than enough already

G because it is difficult to get work

UNIT 10 TEST

1 Multiple-choice cloze

For questions 1–10, read the sentences below and then decide which word best fits each space. Put the letter you choose in the space.

1 After five years in prison, Hathaway was finally ....

 A disengaged B released C withdrawn
 D loosened

2 Sometimes cases of .... identity go unrecognised for years.

 A wrong B false C misled D mistaken

3 Young schoolchildren are more likely to be influenced by pressure from their .... than from their families.

 A peers B counterparts C equals D colleagues

4 One .... that has been taken is to encourage young people to work with other young people in the battle against crime.

 A act B control C measure D experiment

5 He .... a sentence of 27 years before it was discovered that he was innocent.

 A had B performed C did D served

6 The thief's girlfriend was .... with helping him.

 A accused B blamed C charged D threatened

7 She .... with her child to stop shoplifting.

 A begged B pleaded C urged D argued

8 A small fine is not an .... punishment for someone who is very rich.

 A effective B affected C effectual D efficient

9 The children were .... to clear up the mess they had left before they could watch TV.

 A allowed B seen C let D made

10 None of the men in the identity parade .... any resemblance to the mugger.

 A struck B carried C bore D showed

2 Word formation

For questions 11–17, use the word in capitals at the end of the sentence to form one word that fits in the space.

11 Youth clubs are a good way of keeping .... out of trouble. **YOUNG**

12 Teenage offenders often come from a .... background. **ADVANTAGE**

13 .... is often cited as one of the background causes of crime. **EMPLOY**

14 I didn't want to risk a .... with such a tough-looking man. **CONFRONT**

15 To try and preserve his family's .... , he moved them to a remote part of the country. **PRIVATE**

16 A former criminal, she has now completed her training and become a .... member of society. **PRODUCE**

17 Clothing left at the scene of the crime led to the .... of the thief. **IDENTITY**

3 Structural cloze

For questions 18–23, complete the sentences by writing one missing word in the space.

18 Please collect all the evidence that we have collected .... date.

19 If you give me the work now, it may .... done by tomorrow.

20 The .... of the matter is, prison is the only viable solution we have.

21 The judge had no alternative .... to send Sanders to prison.

22 If America's experience with guns is anything to .... by, I certainly wouldn't want guns to be made freely available in my country.

23 She is said .... have committed 64 acts of burglary.

4 Error correction

For questions 24–29, find one unnecessary word in four of the sentences and write it next to the number. Two sentences are correct.

24 .... Parents are advised not to let their children to wander the streets after dark.

25 .... It is been said that most victims know their killers.

26 .... The goods, which stolen from a delivery van, have been found in a warehouse in the dock area.

27 .... The results of the investigation have yet to be announced.

28 .... Many people spend their early years in the place where they were being born.

29 .... It is difficult to say how many people have been affected by this incident.

5 Register cloze

For questions 30–35, read the following text and then replace the words or expressions in italics with informal alternatives.

Young teenagers wander round the streets in the summer holidays because there (**30**) *are no leisure facilities* nearby. (**31**) *It is alleged* that 60% of the local crime is committed by under 16s. The problem is that there is nothing to (**32**) *deter them from* vandalising, joy-riding etc. The police may arrest them but they usually (**33**) *release them* again after a few hours because (**34**) *of lack of evidence*. If they could (**35**) *require them* to repair the damage they do, it might help.

30 ....

31 ....

32 ....

33 ....

34 ....

35 ....

6 Discourse cloze

For questions 36–40, read the following text and then choose from the list A–G the best phrase to fill the spaces. Two phrases do not fit.

A 24 year old man, James Cooper, (**36**) .... has been charged with the murder of an elderly woman. The crime, (**37**) .... , has shocked local residents. Until the arrest, many local people, (**38**) .... , had avoided the normally popular park. The police, acting on statements (**39**) .... , arrested Mr Cooper at his home. After a confession (**40**) .... , Cooper was remanded in custody. The solving of the case will be a great relief to the whole community.

A worried that the killer might strike again

B given by witnesses of this horrifying crime

C found wandering the streets in a drunken state

D who was taken into custody last night

E made by the accused during questioning

F asked shortly after the murder

G committed in Central Park at 2 o'clock last Wednesday afternoon

PRACTICE TEST 2

Reading

Part 4

Answer questions 31–51 by referring to the magazine article about houses and their owners on pages 150–151. Indicate your answers **on the separate answer sheet**.

For questions 31–51, answer by choosing from the house owners A–E. Some of the choices may be required more than once.

Note: **When more than one answer is required, these may be given in any order.**

Which house owner:			
makes use of things which other people have discarded?	31		
has realistic expectations where valuable objects are concerned?	32		
decided against an immediate large-scale renovation after purchasing their home?	33		
comments on the benefits of their professional circumstances?	34		
has carefully considered the way the layout affects the view?	35		
regards the layout of their house as illogical?	36		
values personal privacy at times?	37		**A** Paula Ross
believes that each new house one moves into should be newly refurbished?	38		**B** Fay Ridgeway
relies on instinct when decorating their house?	39		**C** Shakira Dawes
prevents the house from getting too untidy?	40		**D** Asia Daniki
lives in a house which was built for another purpose?	41		**E** Danny Barnes
does not fall into the trap that many of their fellow professionals do?	42		
likes one aspect of the décor to remain discreet and subdued?	43	44	
appreciates certain historical features which the previous owners seemed not to?	45		
has retained one old feature of the house despite the difficulty it causes?	46		
has a practical application for certain valuable objects?	47		
emphasises choosing a house which one can relax in?	48	49	
bought a house which was in poor condition?	50	51	

Take Five Home Owners

A Paula Ross

Walk into Paula and David Ross's house and you will find a textile designer's gentle approach to decorating. Paula has heaped the house with generous helpings of her own blanket-covered cushions, and coated it in subtle paint colours, both of which serve to soften the edges of a meticulously thought-out interior. Paula says: 'I look at colour from an emotional stance. Flipping through a paint chart, a particular colour will just speak to me. It's totally illogical, not something you can get formally trained in. You've really got to work with, not against a room's light.' Indeed, working with, tuning in and listening to, are all very much part of Paula's vocabulary when it comes to decorating her home. When she and her husband bought it three years ago, they resisted the usual knee-jerk reaction of ripping everything out and whitewashing, instead waiting until they got to know the house properly. This must have taken a fair amount of determination, given the state it was in. The couple knew, however, that beneath the grime was a well-proportioned early nineteenth-century London townhouse. For when the builders moved in they discovered original shutters long since boarded up, and period panelling and skirting boards beneath layers of cheap paint.

B Fay Ridgeway

As a freelance writer for home decorating magazines, Fay Ridgeway was the ideal person to open up her London home to us. The most striking thing about the house is the huge collection of Roman, Greek and Egyptian antiquities. Prints, artefacts and china, almost all purchased from local antiques markets, abound throughout the ground floor. Fay is not precious about them, however: in the sitting-room a Delft bowl stuffed with invoices and bills is her 'filing system'. Fay's daughter seems to have inherited the same collecting gene as her parents, but she prefers disadvantaged soft toys from car boot and jumble sales. Fay, you get the feeling, is the orderly captain of a ship sinking under the detritus of two less shipshape crew members. The house as the guest sees it is as it would be if Fay lived alone, apart, that is, from the mountain of newspapers and books piled up by her husband's side of the bed. Small wonder then that Fay seeks sanctuary in her own office, a tiny purpose-built extension tacked on the back of the house, with a calm, relaxing view of the garden – the envy of her fellow professionals. Over the past 10 years, Fay has repainted the house several times but never changed the restrained palette of bone-white and grey-greens. Does she never get the urge to paint a room in, say, shocking pink? About as often as she thinks of getting a personality transplant, says the look she gives me in reply.

C Shakira Dawes

Shakira Dawes is a make-up artist and her work takes her to many a celebrity home in New York. But expensive price tags and glittery new accessories don't impress her. 'I appreciate best fittings that are low-key and unobtrusive,' she says. Her resistance to expensive furnishings is, she thinks, a hangover from her childhood in France, growing up in an enormous house filled with antiques. 'We had a signed Louis XV dresser and lots of gilded porcelains,' she reminisces. The downside of this fairytale lifestyle was that her mother lived in constant fear of breaking things. Shakira has opted instead for what she sees as peasant chic, where no breakages are ever a tragedy and everything is human scale and cosily livable, even to the extent of being messy.

The house itself is a warren of rooms that, according to Shakira, makes no sense but functions perfectly well. It has been added to several times and Shakira continued the tradition by creating a sunporch downstairs where one can admire the garden without being bombarded by mosquitoes or frazzling in direct sunlight. Two old wrought-iron bedsteads loaded with plump cushions act as sofas, but a wooden dining table intended to create a warm base for candlelit suppers soon disintegrated in the humidity.

D   Asia Daniki

'It never occurred to us to buy a cottage,' says Asia Daniki. Instead she and her husband bought a set of tumbledown agricultural buildings with earth floors and no roofs in south-west England. 'The attraction is having a space with no other history of inhabitation,' says Asia, 'in which you can create a scale of living that is tailor-made. For example, houses from the Victorian era reflect certain proportions, a way of living that we no longer have, and we didn't want to be dictated to by a building. People are informal nowadays, so why squeeze yourself back into a formal way of living?' Miraculously, the building work only took two months. It was a little bit of themselves and an awful lot of everybody else. There was the time when Asia went off to buy the staircase from a reclamation yard and came back with it in pieces in a box. Several carpenters resigned on the spot. But in submission to 'not ruining the atmosphere of the place', they have left the herring-bone brick floor tiles set in sand, 'which is completely mad, because now people walk sand all over the house.' The large barn space is impressive. Once open to the elements, the room is now lined with south-facing windows which let light pour in all year round. Beyond lies the kitchen: a homage to the turbo gas cooker and Smeg fridge carefully concealed by the staircase so that none of the vulgarities of day-to-day living – cluttersome kettles, woks, toasters – can be seen by guests reclining in the living area.

E   Danny Barnes

Just as it is irritating when fashion designers favour T-shirts instead of their own creations, it is equally annoying to discover architects who pontificate on the rudiments of modern design and live in fusty old houses crammed to the gills with surplus stuff. Therefore it is gratifying to discover that architect Danny Barnes practises what he preaches. He bought his four-storey London house six years ago, and has renovated it extensively. Being an architect, he is very sensitive about certain issues. 'One of the first things I learned about houses was to question the validity of ripping one item from a house, only to install it in another,' he says. He takes great pride in completing his home. 'One of the great things about designing your own home is that you don't have to defer to clients' approval. This speeds the whole process up.'

English in Use

Part 5

For questions 62–74, read the following newspaper article about the island of Sark in the Channel Islands. Use the information to complete the numbered gaps in the postcard. **Use no more than two words in each gap. The words you need do not occur in the newspaper article. The exercise begins with an example (0).**

Example: | 0 | a lot |

NEWSPAPER ARTICLE

To the boatloads of visitors who arrive every summer's day, the tiny island of Sark must seem one of the most tranquil places on earth. A ban on cars and lorries means the peace is broken only by the ringing of bicycle bells and the occasional rumble of a tractor. There is also little concern about crime. Cycle theft and drunkenness are the main problems. Sark's original stone prison, several centuries old, is well worth a visit. Theoretically, it remains operative even today, and offenders can still be imprisoned in its two windowless cells, but in practice they are rarely occupied. One fact that never fails to amuse visitors is that an islander can stop anyone doing something that he considers to be an infringement of his rights by reciting the Lord's Prayer in French and crying out for the assistance of the Prince.

POSTCARD

Although (**0**) .... of tourists seem to come here, this island is (**62**) .... place I have ever been to. Cars and lorries are not (**63**) .... and so the only thing (**64**) .... is the sound of bicycles and, (**65**) .... , a tractor.

There isn't much need (**66**) .... about crime either. People have been known to (**67**) .... or have (**68**) .... beer or whiskey to drink, but that's all. In theory, the old stone prison is still (**69**) .... today, but in reality virtually no one ever gets (**70**) .... there. What's very (**71**) .... is that a local person can stop anyone who he (**72**) .... is doing something which infringes his rights by (**73**) .... a prayer in French or shouting for the Prince to (**74**) .... him.

Part 6

For questions 75–80, read the following text and then choose from the list A–J given below the best phrase to fill each of the spaces. Write one letter (A–J) in the correct box on your answer sheet. **Some of the** suggested answers do not fit at all. The exercise begins with an example (0).

Example: | 0 | J |

Time for a change?

Knowing when it is time to replace household appliances is a tricky matter. Manufacturers are constantly trying to persuade us to buy their latest models, (**0**) .... before you can make a decision. Fridge-freezers can keep going for a good 20 years. They change little in appearance in that time, and there's little indication if the temperature is slipping, (**75**) .... However, slight slips in temperature can have serious health implications for food in fridges.

If you find a small fault, isn't it wasteful to replace such a big appliance? Surprisingly it is not necessarily environmentally irresponsible to buy a new freezer. It could be twice as energy efficient as your old one (**76**) .... and be less environmentally damaging. Sometimes, it may be more economical to replace some fridge-freezers well before they break down but this depends on individual models (**77**) ....

The development in dishwasher technology has been interesting. They have roughly halved their energy and water consumption. However, typical programmes take nearly 40 minutes longer and there is no improvement in cleaning performance, (**78**) .... the effect isn't always to improve how well the appliance does its job.

Time doesn't always bring radical changes in technology. Tests have shown that well functioning microwaves typically stay safe and as good at their job as they age (**79**) .... But if it does then decide to pack up on you, where do you take your old faithful to be disposed of? Passing your product on for reuse is often the most environmentally sound thing to do, (**80**) ....

A so it's very difficult to give any general guidance as to when this time comes

B so even where there's been significant technological change

C so you should replace it every five years or so

D so you may be just as well off sticking with the one you've got

E so try not to be influenced by advertising

F so it will pay for itself over the years

G so, if you are replacing an appliance, don't forget that you could buy second hand

H so it's better to repair your old one

I so people rarely replace them before they conk out

J so you need to know how good your current appliance is compared with a new one

UNIT 11 TEST

1 Multiple-choice cloze

For questions 1–10, read the sentences below and then decide which word best fits each space. Put the letter you choose in the space.

1 I think I will miss the sense of .... spirit that goes with living in a village.

  A society   B friendship   C support
  D community

2 She arrived with no home, no job, no qualifications and no money so she has done really well against all the ....

  A chances   B risks   C odds   D predictions

3 We are doing so well that we'll soon have to .... on new staff to help us.

  A hire   B keep   C pay   D take

4 Many women prefer to keep their .... names when they get married.

  A girl   B single   C spinster   D maiden

5 The storm was terrifying, with the .... howling around the house.

  A rain   B wind   C snow   D thunder

6 We had no money for a hotel so we had to .... rough for a couple of nights.

  A stay   B camp   C sleep   D lie

7 I love living in the city centre while I'm young, but when I finally .... down, I think I'll move somewhere quieter.

  A calm   B slow   C settle   D come

8 My plans to travel around the world have .... through because I couldn't save enough money.

  A dropped   B fallen   C given   D put

9 The village is well .... with pubs and restaurants.

  A stored   B supplied   C endowed   D fitted

10 While you're planning, you must take into .... how many people you are expecting.

  A thought   B consideration   C mind   D memory

2 Word formation

For questions 11–17, use the word in capitals at the end of the sentence to form one word that fits in the space.

11 William paid for his emigration out of his .... **SAVE**

12 The Italian Riviera has had an .... lure for me ever since I visited it as a child. **RESIST**

13 People usually work better in pleasant .... **SURROUND**

14 They keep their horse on a .... farm. **NEAR**

15 Sam could not have afforded to go to drama school without a .... **SCHOLAR**

16 I had a .... clash with my new boss, and left the job after just two weeks. **PERSON**

17 The view from the upstairs window is absolutely .... **GLORY**

3 Structural cloze

For questions 18–23, complete the sentences by writing one missing word in the space.

Now, if I can just have your attention, thanks. I'm sure you'll have a fantastic afternoon in Cambridge, as there's something to suit (**18**) .... taste. The Fitzwilliam Museum is well (**19**) .... seeing and most of the colleges should be open to the public today. For those of you who wish to while (**20**) .... the time shopping, the Grafton Centre should provide ample entertainment. But what you really must do (**21**) .... visit the Botanic Gardens. No visit to Cambridge is complete (**22**) .... a trip to this fabulous attraction. As for our evening excursion, there are many things to take (**23**) .... consideration, so please be back at the coach by 5, so that we can discuss what we are going to do.

4 Error correction

For questions 24–29, find one spelling or punctuation mistake in four of the sentences and write the correct form next to the number. Two sentences are correct.

24 .... As a general rule, people in the south are payed more than those in the north.

25 .... We are pleased to say that the operation has been successfull.

26 .... When we visited the village, we were surprised by the general cleanliness.

27 .... What we did then, was to look for a house to buy on the outskirts of the village.

28 .... We didn't see anything very inspiring, it was my father who suggested that we look at the old mill.

29 .... Luckily for us, we were able to move at the company's expense as part of the relocation package.

5 Register cloze

For questions 30–35, read the informal letter to a friend and then use the information to complete the spaces in the formal letter to a school. Use no more than one or two words for each space. The words you need do not appear in the first extract.

LETTER TO A FRIEND

Dear Julie

I'm sure you're well aware that my brother Toby has been having problems for a few years now because there are so few job opportunities in his field of work. Well, just to let you know that he's decided to go and live in New Zealand! The government have said yes to his application. He's got plans to set up his own business out there, and has already managed to rent a flat with a view onto the sea. Lucky him! He's sure it will also be better for the kids too, a better place to bring them up.

Love Sarah

LETTER TO A SCHOOL

Dear Mrs Flintoff

After several years of frustration at the (30) .... of job opportunities here, I have finally decided to (31) .... New Zealand. I am pleased to say that my application for resettlement has been (32) .... by the authorities and that I shall therefore be removing the children (Edward and Melissa Grant) from your school as of May 1. I intend to (33) .... my own business there, and we have already rented a wonderful house which (34) .... the sea! I feel that it will be a better environment in which to (35) .... children. I would like to thank you very much for all your hard work and loving care with regard to Edward and Melissa.

Yours sincerely,

Toby Grant

6 Discourse cloze

For questions 36–40, read the following text and then choose from the list A–G the best phrase to fill the gaps. Two phrases do not fit.

As our grandparents came near to retirement, we needed to help them find somewhere to live (36) .... than their old house. What they needed was a place (37) .... , so that they could keep their independence but still feel that help was close at hand.

What we did (38) .... which we then visited to see what (39) .... Luckily we soon found a small house that was ideal for two people, with wonderful views. The next step (40) ....

A that was close to friends and family

B was to get the old house ready for sale

C that was not expensive

D that was smaller and easier to look after

E was available at a suitable price

F was a difficult decision

G was to ask them to choose an area

UNIT 12 TEST

1 Multiple-choice cloze

For questions 1–10, read the sentences below and then decide which word best fits each space. Put the letter you choose in the space.

1 We took what we thought was the best .... of action at the time.
   A way   B track   C path   D course

2 He .... as a doctor in order to gain access to the hospital.
   A acted   B pretended   C behaved   D posed

3 Well, to .... a long story short, we ended up spending the night in the car.
   A take   B change   C make   D cut

4 Every time she is in a .... , she rings her father and asks for help.
   A difficulty   B fix   C trouble   D hiccup

5 Team sports .... the natural aggression of pre-teenage boys.
   A channel   B conduct   C transmit   D convey

6 He leaves work early to .... his daughter up from school.
   A put   B take   C pick   D collect

7 The first thing she did after her bag was stolen was to .... her credit cards.
   A end   B finish   C invalidate   D cancel

8 During the voyage the passengers sat on the .... enjoying the sunshine.
   A platform   B deck   C outside   D terrace

9 She handled the situation wonderfully and was an excellent .... model for the younger children.
   A role   B example   C copy   D life

10 While the ship was stuck in the ice, the ship's captain knew it was vital to keep up the team .... of his crew.
   A feeling   B co-operation   C spirit   D morale

2 Word formation

For questions 11–17, use the word in capitals at the end of the sentence to form one word that fits in the space.

11 The insurance company may not pay out if you have not taken sensible .... against theft. **CAUTION**

12 So many things went wrong – it was the most .... holiday we had ever had. **FORTUNE**

13 Keep your wallet safe – there are .... in the crowd. **POCKET**

14 Those clouds over there look very .... – we'd better get back to the shore. **THREAT**

15 It looked like a terrible crash but fortunately there were only minor .... **INJURE**

16 In order to claim insurance, you need to report the .... of your camera to the police. **THIEVE**

17 Under the .... of the instructor they made it safely to the top of the cliff. **GUIDE**

3 Structural cloze

For questions 18–23, complete the sentences by writing one missing word in the space.

We faced a long car journey up the motorway to the north, but hardly (**18**) .... we joined the motorway when we hit traffic – a 14 kilometre tailback, to be precise. I realised that we were best off taking the next road off the motorway, no matter where it went, and trying to get north by other roads. (**19**) .... we might be sitting there all day. At first we sailed along nicely, but then (**20**) .... came the first problem: a fork in the road which was not marked on the map. Needless to say, we made the wrong choice and ended up completely lost. After driving round and round for three hours, I was longing for the security of the clogged-up motorway. As (**21**) .... as you're sitting on the motorway, even if you're not moving, you do at least know where you're going. It is not (**22**) .... you've tried, and failed, to create your own detour that you realise the truth of the old saying: 'If you can't beat 'em, join 'em.' Now I never leave the motorway (**23**) .... I'm absolutely sure of an alternative route.

4 Error correction

For questions 24–29, find one unnecessary word in four of the sentences and write it next to the number. Two sentences are correct.

24 .... Had I have known about the risk, I would never have started the journey.

25 .... If you were to be injured, no one would find you for days.

26 .... You can borrow the car on condition that if you stick to the speed limit.

27 .... Go into the garden and pick up some flowers for the table.

28 .... No matter how safe you think it may be, you should still take great care.

29 .... The waiters in this country expect to be tipped off about 15% of the bill.

5 Register cloze

For questions 30–35, read the informal letter to a friend and then use the information to complete the spaces in the formal letter to the Chief Inspector. Use no more than one or two words for each space. The words you need do not appear in the first extract.

LETTER TO A FRIEND

Dear Dawn

I had more trouble from that gang of youths last Saturday – at one point they even got on my roof and started throwing things. I rang the police and told them what had happened, but I wasn't very happy with the way they handled it. I know they're busy and have got much more important crimes to solve, but they said I should absolutely not go outside and try to talk to the youths. They also said an officer would come in half an hour, but it took two hours for anyone to turn up. He did at least say he was sorry for being late, but left me with the impression that he couldn't really do anything, as by then the boys had gone and I had no witness to back up my accusation. I've just written to the Chief Inspector to say if he wants any more details on the case, I can supply them, but I don't suppose he'll be interested either. It's all rather dissatisfactory.

Edna.

LETTER TO THE CHIEF INSPECTOR

Dear Sir

I am writing to draw your attention to an incident last Saturday evening. Some young lads were swearing and breaking glass outside my house, and even climbed on my garage roof. I (30) .... the matter to the policeman on duty, who said that (31) .... should I try to tackle the youths myself. They said they would send an officer round within half an hour, but it was fully two hours before a policeman (32) .... The policeman (33) .... for being late, but said that there was very little he could do, as although I could describe the boys to him, there was no other witness, so it was just my word against theirs. The officer concerned said he would record the incident. However, (34) .... you need any (35) .... information on this matter I am available on 01937 509776.

Yours faithfully

Edna Bryant (Mrs)

6 Discourse cloze

For questions 36–40, read the following text and then choose from the list A–G the best phrase to fill the spaces. Two phrases do not fit.

Advice for lone climbers and walkers:

These mountains can be wild and unpredictable, but it is possible to explore them safely (36) .... For example, always tell someone exactly where you are planning to go, (37) .... if you get lost. If you do have an accident, your chances of surviving will be better (38) .... In cold weather your body temperature can drop very quickly, and you could die (39) .... In recent years, many walkers have used a mobile phone to call for help after an accident; (40) .... , your phone can be a life-saving piece of equipment.

A if you are carrying complete body cover

B as long as it can operate in remote places like these

C unless you're walking by yourself

D otherwise a search party could take days to find you

E unless you preserve your body heat

F provided you have a map

G provided that you take all the necessary precautions

UNIT 13 TEST

1 Multiple-choice cloze

For questions 1–10, read the sentences below and then decide which word best fits each space. Put the letter you choose in the space.

1 Luckily, all of the puppies are .... , even the smallest.

   A thriving   B booming   C gaining   D profiting

2 Most of the birds .... on small mammals.

   A devour   B prey   C exploit   D hunt

3 We had been looking for the nest for hours before we .... lucky.

   A hit   B made   C struck   D came

4 Just take a .... , but you mustn't frighten the mother or the babies.

   A peer   B view   C gaze   D peep

5 We keep the animals .... until they are well enough to go back into the wild.

   A captured   B convicted   C captive   D caught

6 The photographer obtained some amazing .... of butterflies in flight.

   A representation   B likeness   C portrayal
   D footage

7 Remember to .... – the doorway is very low.

   A dodge   B dive   C duck   D delve

8 Ann had to spend the night in a cave, but seemed quite unaffected by her ....

   A affliction   B trial   C trouble   D ordeal

9 He keeps his collection of .... butterflies in tropical conditions.

   A eccentric   B exotic   C domestic   D urban

10 It took four people to .... the piano up the stairs.

   A tow   B tug   C draw   D haul

2 Word formation

For questions 11–17, use the word in capitals at the end of the sentence to form one word that fits in the space.

11 More and more species are becoming .... as the countryside becomes more developed.   **URBAN**

12 Badgers are becoming .... because large numbers are killed on the roads each year.   **DANGER**

13 Children learn a lot about nature from .... programmes on the television.   **WILD**

14 The coastline has been .... developed by the tourist industry.   **INTENSE**

15 If .... continues at this rate, there will be no trees left in 100 years' time.   **FOREST**

16 There's a sign over there saying you have to pay for all ....   **BREAK**

17 The new bird sanctuary will be very .... to nesting birds.   **BENEFIT**

3 Structural cloze

For questions 18–23, complete the sentences by writing one missing word in the space.

I was tired but happy in the evening, (18) .... spent all day in the open air at the nature reserve. In fact I was truly delighted with the results of my labours, for the very good reason that (19) .... long last I had seen a peregrine falcon. All my hard work and meticulous preparation had finally paid (20) ....

The new visitors' centre, along (21) .... the recently opened lakeside look out shelter, has really had a positive impact (22) .... the reserve. I'm not sure, however, about the proposed new lakeside footpath. It will certainly bring more visitors but may also have the (23) .... of disturbing the habitat of animals such as voles and otters.

4 Error correction

For questions 24–29, find one spelling or punctuation mistake in four of the sentences and write the correct form next to the number. Two sentences are correct.

24 .... With new extra tall dustbins having been introduced the urban fox is starving.

25 .... At the beginning of the year, there were only a few geese on the lake now there are about 20.

26 .... People live close to the volcano because the land is so fertile – they don't seem to worry about an erruption.

27 .... By removing the larger alligators from the residential areas, the authorities in Florida have ensured a safer environment.

28 .... Some of the world's best coral reefs are off the australian coast.

29 .... When frightened, a fox might attack, especially if it's protecting its young.

5 Register cloze

For questions 30–34, read the informal extract from a school project and then use the information to complete the spaces in the formal extract from a TV magazine. Use no more than one or two words for each space. The words you need do not appear in the first extract.

EXTRACT FROM A SCHOOL PROJECT

There was a very interesting TV programme the other day about the Scottish wildcat. It said that the wildcat may die out unless something is done to stop the fall in numbers that the species has suffered from recently. The government has declared that anyone shooting a wildcat can go to prison, but it seems that this alone is not enough. Maybe a controlled breeding programme is needed.

EXTRACT FROM A TV MAGAZINE

The Scottish wildcat is in danger of (30) .... Tonight's 'Nature on Two' programme reveals that prompt (31) .... is needed now to bring a halt to the (32) .... in numbers that has hit the species in recent years. The wildcat now has full legal (33) .... but it would seem that this measure is (34) .... and that what is also needed is a controlled breeding programme.

6 Discourse cloze

For questions 35–40, read the following text and then choose from the list A–H the best phrase to fill the spaces. Two phrases do not fit.

It was Friday, the last chance for Dale and Mitch to see the bay's famous dolphins. The two boys jumped into the motorboat and sped out towards the open sea, (35) .... They stopped the motor and sat in silence, (36) .... Then, to their delight, the dolphins came, first one and then several, (37) .... and their possible offerings. One dolphin, (38) .... , lifted its nose above the side of the boat and offered its head to be patted. The two boys slipped over the side of the boat and swam with the dolphins for over half an hour, (39) .... from under the sea. They then sped back to shore, (40) ....

A diving and turning with their new-found friends

B overcome by collective curiosity at the arrival of the strangers

C allowing themselves to be stroked

D hoping desperately to catch sight of the elusive target of their quest

E attracted by the prospect of food

F diving deep under the boat

G feeling elated by what they knew had been the experience of a lifetime

H watching the calm surface of the sea around the boat for any sign of a fin or flipper

Unit 14 Test

1 Multiple-choice cloze

For questions 1–10, read the sentences below and then decide which word best fits each space. Put the letter you choose in the space.

1 At closing time, the customers were asked to .... their drinks and leave.

A end B down C up D sink

2 He didn't want to .... any information about his past.

A show B tell C say D reveal

3 At the beginning of the working day the traffic .... into the city centre.

A strolls B saunters C ambles D crawls

4 As long as he's not harming anybody, it's best to live and .... live.

A allow B leave C let D ignore

5 If you .... a nap after lunch, you'll be able to work until much later in the day.

A sleep B catch C find D take

6 She's such a .... of strength that everyone relies on her in a crisis.

A tower B pillar C post D support

7 It would help me .... if you could go to the Post Office for me.

A totally B absolutely C enormously D largely

8 I told my parents that I had been shopping but they didn't .... it.

A eat B digest C swallow D chew

9 Noise doesn't really .... me because I can just ignore it.

A mind B bother C care D get

10 No wonder she's coughing – she smokes like a ....

A chimney B fire C cigarette D pipe

2 Word formation

For questions 11–17, use the word in capitals at the end of the sentence to form one word that fits in the space.

11 We have had several .... nights caused by loud music next door. **SLEEP**

12 We .... left the window unlocked and the house was burgled. **ACCIDENT**

13 We can't move house until our .... situation improves. **FINANCE**

14 Please take all your .... with you when you leave. **BELONG**

15 A fatal .... was made by air traffic control. **CALCULATE**

16 Looking after their house while they were away was a very .... thing to do. **NEIGHBOUR**

17 We missed the place but it was no .... to stay on the beautiful island for a few more days. **HARD**

3 Structural cloze

For questions 18–23, complete the text by writing one missing word in the space.

From a woman's magazine

Many of the letters I received last month were on the same theme: frustration among women whose menfolk seem unwilling or unable to listen to them. Mrs J Boulton is at the end of her tether, to the extent that she is even starting to regret (**18**) .... married her husband. Well Mrs Boulton, my advice to you is: sit down together and iron things out. (**19**) .... by talking quietly and calmly together will you succeed (**20**) .... resolving the differences between you. Experts agree that men and women converse in different ways: some male partners see conversation with a woman as a way of solving her problems or setting goals. That, I think, is (**21**) .... your husband seems to be interrupting you and imposing his views on you. But if (**22**) .... all your efforts, your husband simply reverts to type, you can at least console (**23**) .... with the thought that you are not alone!

4 Error correction

For questions 24–29, find one unnecessary word in four of the sentences and write it next to the number. Two sentences are correct.

24 .... She is an interesting person but she does talks too much.

25 .... I'll tell you when I will have finished with the iron.

26 .... They do have a tendency to keep themselves to themselves.

27 .... I'll make him a birthday cake if only I have time.

28 .... You really should have take the baby to the doctor.

29 .... The man who I lent to money very quickly vanished, never to be seen again.

5 Register cloze

For questions 30–35, read the formal extract from a magazine column and then use the information to complete the spaces in the informal letter. Use no more than one or two words for each space. The words you need do not appear in the first extract.

MAGAZINE COLUMN

David Cunningham on modern manners

Manners and civility are not what they used to be. An old friend (who shall remain nameless) was a guest in our house for two weeks recently. We used to be the best of friends, so I was pleased at the prospect of being acquainted with him again. As it turned out, he was not the same person. The warm conversationalist I had known was now boorish and opinionated, and as for his manners – he seemed to regard it as his personal duty to consume every bit of food in the house, even some luxury gifts I'd brought back from a holiday in Thailand. Ok, so the food is not really important, but the man's whole attitude as a guest in my house was typical of the lack of manners in society today.

LETTER TO A FRIEND

I (30) .... stay with an old friend recently, the magazine writer, David Cunninigham. We had always (31) .... really well in the past, so I thought it would be a great opportunity to (32) .... know him again. Unfortunately, he'd changed for the worse. He didn't seem interested in what I had to say and easily took offence. He even accused me of eating (33) .... his food, saying I'd eaten him (34) .... house and home, just because I ate some Thai food of his, not realising it was a present. I think it's (35) .... nor there which of his food I ate. What really hurts is the accusation of being a bad guest.

6 Discourse cloze

For questions 36–40, read the following text and then choose from the list A–G the best phrase to fill the spaces. Two phrases do not fit.

A research project into child psychology run by Nottingham University has come up with some interesting findings about the way young children interact and take on roles. In a typical session, groups of 6 primary school children were given a problem solving task to complete and their behaviour was recorded on film (36) .... This process was repeated in 25 primary schools (37) .... Surprisingly, a typical pattern emerged, (38) .... In a majority of cases, two of the children seemed to become the leaders immediately. Another two made helpful suggestions and were happy (39) .... The last two were the most interesting. They merely did as they were told and said very little (40) ....

A as long as their ideas were accepted

B but there seemed to be a similar pattern in many of the groups

C consequently there was a lot of argument

D even though the children involved were selected purely at random

E despite being the strongest personalities

F in order to increase the statistical reliability of the information obtained

G so that raw data could be provided for analysis

Practice Test 3

Reading

Part 2

For questions **17–22**, choose which of the paragraphs **A–G** fit into the numbered gaps in the following newspaper article. There is one extra paragraph which does not fit in any of the gaps. Indicate your answers **on the separate answer sheet.**

Safari in Zambia

We were in the north of Zambia's South Luangwa National Park walking near the Mupamadzi River, where few visitors reach. It is a perfect area for walking safaris, with spectacular scenery and habitats ranging from mature mopane forests to thick bush and open grassland. There are wetlands, too, where the wide meandering river had changed its course and left oxbow lakes and small lagoons. It is a haven for bird life as well as high densities of game. On our first afternoon's walk we hoped the birds would lead us to the game. Vultures and Bateleur eagles were circling near the camp and we were sure they had smelled a kill.

We were about to give up when we caught the pungent smell of a carcass. In long grass we found the remains of an impala. It was the fresh kill of leopards and so well hidden even the vultures had not found it. The leopards could still be close by and might take exception to our intrusion, so it was reassuring to have Collins, the armed game scout from the park authorities, with us.

This was one of two kills we saw over the next few days. The next one we tracked down by sound. For a day and a half we had heard the call of lions in the distance but they, too, proved elusive in the long grass. Then one morning at dawn, we heard them calling not far from the camp and Matthew, our safari guide, had a good idea where the calls were coming from.

We spotted one lioness, and we knew there would be others about somewhere, but we weren't sure where. We tried to get closer by heading in the direction of the lioness, but the long grass closed in around us. There was no way of knowing how close we might have been to those lions.

We retreated to the Mupamadzi River, in search of more open ground. It was early July and the river was broad and shallow as the dry season got under way. Keeping a close eye out for crocodiles, we paddled across. The water was cool and refreshing, ankle-deep most of the way with an occasional knee-deep channel.

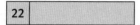

21

Indeed, all the safari staff worked hard for us. This was a mobile camping outfit and every other day, as we took our morning walk, the camp was packed, moved and reassembled – all in time to greet us with cold drinks and lunch.

22

So long as we kept a safe distance, though, they seemed not to see us as a threat and we could walk freely in their environment. This was the beauty of a walking safari, the opportunity to become a part of the landscape; not cooped up in a vehicle driving past the game, but out there with it, walking in the forests and the plains, and paddling through crystal clear waters.

A We had started our walk early that morning, as we did every morning, and when we crossed the river it was time for a mid-morning break. This became a daily ritual, and I felt sorry for Isiki, the tea-bearer, who as a result had to carry a backpack full of tea and cake.

B The best moments however, were always when the game didn't see us. On one walk we were sitting at the edge of a narrow part of the river and heard some impala in the long grass on the other side. We kept absolutely still and they emerged on the shore completely unaware of our presence. They sauntered down to the water's edge and drank, directly opposite us.

C As the anticipation and caution heightened with every step I discovered why this kind of grassland was commonly known as 'adrenalin territory'. Eventually it became impractical, if not a little dangerous, to follow any further.

D Cautiously, we trekked out in their direction, but the grass was high and the woodland thick. Any game or big cats would have heard us coming long before we could get near. Or they could have been within a few feet of us, camouflaged by the thick undergrowth.

E On the far side of the river the grass was shorter and large open areas had been cleared by fire. We always got good sightings of game over there, seeing herds of zebra, impala and puku, the most abundant local antelope. The animals were very wary of us and would sound their alarm calls and run off if we got too close.

F He led us to an open plain known as the garden. Right in the centre was a buffalo carcase surrounded by vultures and marabou storks. We scanned the distance and the shadows for the predators.

G Evidently the animals came back that night and finished off their meal. By the time we revisited the spot in the morning there wasn't a trace left, not so much as a drop of blood.

English in Use

Part 1

For questions 1–15, read the text below and then decide which word (A, B, C or D) best fits each space. Put the letter you choose for each question in the correct box on your answer sheet. The exercise begins with an example (0).

Example:

0	A	

Master the art of being effective

I suffer from a debilitating condition called 'procrastination' – the ability to put off endlessly the things I have to do. Each morning when I wake up, my mind (0) .... into its own decision-making (1) .... Shall I get up or shall I press the snooze button? By the time I (2) .... to what I should wear, the complexity of the decision would need an advisory (3) .... to solve it. I'm already hours behind (4) .... , and I haven't even eaten my breakfast yet.

I have always been a procrastinator. I am tortured by menus and holiday brochures, paint colour (5) .... and satellite television. So much so that I decided to (6) .... in a new book on the subject, which (7) .... it could treat my condition. According to the book, I should identify my weaknesses, then become more productive and develop priorities that (8) .... my personal goals.

My problem, I am told, is that I put off doing something because I (9) .... the outcome. But even (10) .... in a tax form is rarely as dreadful as we think. Apparently, each day I should think of something I don't want to do, (11) .... to it, then use a kitchen timer to (12) .... how long it actually took. If I still can't (13) .... the task, I should visualise newspaper headlines (14) .... my achievement.

So when do I start my new (15) .... ? That's the big problem. I just can't decide.'

0	A launches	B initiates	C commences	D embarks
1	A course	B development	C process	D case
2	A get	B arrive	C lead	D approach
3	A commission	B committee	C community	D communication
4	A timetable	B agenda	C programme	D schedule
5	A charts	B diagrams	C graphs	D maps
6	A spend	B invest	C charge	D insure
7	A challenged	B demanded	C claimed	D pretended
8	A exhibit	B reflect	C display	D imitate
9	A expect	B worry	C fear	D panic
10	A filling	B completing	C writing	D applying
11	A stand	B persevere	C stick	D persist
12	A establish	B authorise	C secure	D institute
13	A head	B back	C face	D shoulder
14	A stating	B notifying	C informing	D announcing
15	A regime	B control	C structure	D management

Part 4

For questions 47–61, read the following two texts. Use the words in the boxes to the right of the texts to form **one** word that fits in the same numbered space in the text. Write the new word in the correct box on your answer sheet. The exercise begins with an example (0).

Example: | 0 | marvellous |

EXTRACT FROM A NEWSPAPER ARTICLE

Technology is a (0) .... thing. E-mail, mobile phones and the internet have (47) .... our lives no end. Yet (48) .... advance has also made life more complicated and (49) .... Gone are the days when you would leave your house in the morning (50) .... by little more than your keys and wallet. By (51) .... , today, many of us head off to the office complete with laptops and palmtops, and almost inevitably a mobile phone in (52) ....

Perhaps not (53) .... , in the last year, there has been a 28 percent increase in street crime.

(0)	**MARVEL**
(47)	RICH
(48)	TECHNOLOGY
(49)	PROBLEM
(50)	COMPANY
(51)	COMPARE
(52)	ADD
(53)	SURPRISE

GUARANTEE

The (54) .... guarantees this product against defects for a period of one year from the date of (55) .... of the product, by the user, from an authorised (56) ....

The guarantee is not (57) .... if any defect is caused by or is the result of any damage or (58) .... of the product. Further to this, it is prohibited for repairs to be made by (59) .... persons.

If you have a question about this product that is not covered in the (60) .... , you can telephone the company by fax or email for expert (61) ....

(54)	MANUFACTURE
(55)	RECEIVE
(56)	DEAL
(57)	APPLY
(58)	USE
(59)	AUTHORISE
(60)	INSTRUCT
(61)	ASSIST

Teacher's Book Tests – Answers

Unit 1

1 1C; 2D; 3B; 4A; 5B; 6D; 7A; 8D; 9A; 10D

2 11 dismissal; 12 approachable; 13 theoretically;
14 confrontation; 15 lawyers; 16 assertiveness; 17 outgoing

3 18 As; 19 able; 20 have; 21 instead; 22 might/could/must;
23 over; 24 well; 25 can't

4 26 being; 27 to; 28 never; 29 for; 30 with; 31 have; 32 a

5 33 advertisement; 34 assistant; 35 I am interested in applying;
36 train in

6 37 I have been studying; 38 I spent;
39 I have (always) been (very interested); 40 I worked

Unit 2

1 1C; 2A; 3B; 4A; 5A; 6A; 7D; 8C; 9D; 10C

2 11 obsessive; 12 freedom; 13 politicians; 14 unacceptable;
15 unconventional; 16 preoccupation; 17 consultant

3 18 in; 19 by; 20 far; 21 to; 22 been; 23 was

4 24 in; 25 out; 26 been; 27 it; 28 they; 29 had

5 30C; 31B; 32F; 33A; 34E

6 35 He went to Australia because he wanted to explore the
Great Barrier Reef
36 By the time he was three years old, he had already learnt
to read.
37 She attended a mountaineering course before she climbed
in the Himalayas.
38 Tom is very adventurous while his father prefers to stay at
home.
39 As soon as she finished the bungee jump, she wanted to
do another one.
40 While he was living in the USA, he took his pilot's licence.

Unit 3

1 1B; 2C; 3D; 4A; 5B; 6A; 7C; 8D; 9A; 10C

2 11 incurable; 12 forgery; 13 responsibilities; 14 explanation;
15 desperate; 16 educational; 17 regrettable

3 18 would; 19 been; 20 being; 21 had; 22 in; 23 could

4 24 have; 25 would; 26 to; 27 in; 28 at; 29 would

5 30 celebration; 31 very reasonable; 32 regrettable;
33 sophisticated; 34 regards; 35 unacceptable

6 36C; 37F; 38E; 39D; 40B

Unit 4

1 1C; 2C; 3C; 4A; 5D; 6B; 7D; 8A; 9C; 10A

2 11 observation; 12 unpredictable; 13 impersonations;
14 creative; 15 leadership; 16 influential; 17 immunity

3 18 to; 19 telling; 20 no; 21 as; 22 worth; 23 in

4 24 sightseeing; 25 break; 26 clever, funny; 27 sister must;
28 funny. It; 29 advice

5 30 we; 31 others; 32 it; 33 She; 34 this; 35 those

6 36 novel; 37 most likeable; 38 inspiring; 39 suitable; 40 tactful

Unit 5

1 1D; 2A; 3C; 4D; 5A; 6B; 7A; 8B; 9D; 10C

2 11 landscape; 12 sculptures; 13 dramatically; 14 activities;
15 recommendations; 16 atmospheric; 17 forthcoming

3 18 As; 19 being; 20 to; 21 like; 22 despite; 23 if/though

4 24 got; 25 if; 26 off; 27 because; 28 of; 29 who

5 30 plot; 31 actors; 32 humour; 33 recommendation; 34 depend

6 35 Not wanting to offend her, … .
36 Having no hope of … .
37 Refusing the offer of a job in banking, he … .
or: … , choosing instead to be a translator.
38 … , looking for a painting to buy.
39 … , starring Sean Connery.
40 … , thinking it would appeal to the people more.

Practice Test 1

Reading Part 3 21C; 22B; 23A; 24C; 25C

English in Use Part 3 31 destinations; 32 choice;
33 women who; 34 though; 35 dining; 36 people, absorb; 37 ✔;
38 ✔; 39 it's; 40 ✔; 41 they're; 42 advice; 43 accordingly; 44 route;
45 more for

English in Use Part 4 46 variety; 47 safety; 48 choice;
49 selection; 50 awareness; 51 ability; 52 carefully; 53 competition;
54 weaknesses; 55 strengths; 56 applicants; 57 attention;
58 interesting; 59 knowledge; 60 transferable

Unit 6

1 1D; 2D; 3A; 4C; 5A; 6B; 7D; 8B; 9C; 10B

2 11 unfriendly; 12 workplaces; 13 household; 14 qualifications;
15 temperament; 16 misunderstanding; 17 adoptive

3 18 spite; 19 on/for; 20 for; 21 off; 22 against/about; 23 even

4 24 of; 25 though; 26 to; 27 ✔; 28 it; 29 ✔

5 30 to; 31 same; 32 did; 33 so; 34 so

6 35 a few; 36 increases; 37 am sure; 38 was angry;
39 keeps repeating; 40 it all

Unit 7

1 1C; 2D; 3D; 4C; 5B; 6B; 7C; 8B; 9D; 10C

2 11 incompetence; 12 companions; 13 repetitive; 14 futuristic;
15 spotless; 16 acceptance; 17 draughty

3 18 moving; 19 most; 20 by; 21 did; 22 up; 23 about/going

4 24 receive; 25 responsibility; 26 friends; 27 confident; 28 ✔;
29 argument

5 30 roughly/very similar; 31 depends on; 32 is concerned;
33 most untidy; 34 intensifying/increasing

6 35D; 36F; 37C; 38G; 39E; 40B

UNIT 8

1 1A; 2C; 3D; 4D; 5C; 6A; 7B; 8D; 9C; 10A

2 11 deterrent; 12 suspiciously; 13 admirable; 14 robbery; 15 bystander; 16 trustworthy; 17 dishonesty

3 18 why; 19 no; 20 off; 21 whether/if; 22 for; 23 taking

4 24 it; 25 is; 26 me; 27 ✔; 28 up; 29 ✔

5 30 a warning/information; 31 happening; 32 our decision; 33 further involvement; 34 informed

6 35E; 36C; 37D; 38G; 39A; 40F

UNIT 9

1 1D; 2A; 3B; 4C; 5D; 6A; 7D; 8D; 9B; 10D

2 11 freelance; 12 disappearance; 13 seasonal; 14 competitive; 15 deadline; 16 expertise; 17 artistic

3 18 under; 19 so; 20 though/if; 21 despite; 22 result; 23 it

4 24 job. I've; 25 qualifications, experience; 26 promotion?; 27 ✔; 28 companies; 29 director

5 30 the unemployed/unemployed people; 31 extremely/very hard; 32 experience; 33 interpersonal/communication; 34 commitment; 35 foreign/overseas travel *or* travel abroad

6 36E; 37D; 38F; 39A; 40C

UNIT 10

1 1B; 2D; 3A; 4C; 5D; 6C; 7B; 8A; 9D; 10C

2 11 youngsters; 12 disadvantaged; 13 unemployment; 14 confrontation; 15 privacy; 16 productive; 17 identification

3 18 to; 19 be; 20 fact; 21 but; 22 go; 23 to

4 24 to; 25 been; 26 which; 27 ✔; 28 being; 29 ✔

5 30 is nothing (for them) to do; 31 People/they say; 32 stop them; 33 let them go/set them free; 34 they can't prove anything/they haven't got enough proof; 35 make/tell them

6 36D; 37G; 38A; 39B; 40E

PRACTICE TEST 2

Reading Part 4   31D; 32C; 33A; 34E; 35D; 36C; 37B; 38E; 39A; 40B; 41D; 42E; 43B/C; 44C/B; 45A; 46D; 47B; 48C/D; 49D/C; 50A/D; 51D/A

English in Use Part 5   62 the quietest; 63 allowed/permitted; 64 you hear; 65 rarely/ sometimes; 66 to worry; 67 steal bicycles/bikes; 68 too much; 69 in use; 70 locked up; 71 funny; 72 thinks; 73 saying; 74 help

English in Use Part 6   75I; 76F; 77A; 78B; 79D; 80G

UNIT 11

1 1D; 2C; 3D; 4D; 5B; 6C; 7C; 8B; 9C; 10B

2 11 savings; 12 irresistible; 13 surroundings; 14 nearby; 15 scholarship; 16 personality; 17 glorious

3 18 every; 19 worth; 20 away; 21 is; 22 without; 23 into

4 24 paid; 25 successful; 26 ✔; 27 then was; 28 inspiring. It was; 29 ✔

5 30 lack/shortage; 31 emigrate to; 32 accepted; 33 establish; 34 overlooks; 35 raise

6 36D; 37A; 38G; 39E; 40B

UNIT 12

1 1D; 2D; 3D; 4B; 5A; 6C; 7D; 8B; 9A; 10C

2 11 precautions; 12 unfortunate; 13 pickpockets; 14 threatening; 15 injuries; 16 theft; 17 guidance

3 18 had; 19 Otherwise; 20 came; 21 long; 22 until; 23 unless

4 24 have; 25 ✔; 26 if; 27 up; 28 ✔; 29 off

5 30 reported; 31 no account; 32 arrived; 33 apologised; 34 should; 35 further

6 36G; 37D; 38A; 39E; 40B

UNIT 13

1 1A; 2B; 3C; 4D; 5C; 6D; 7C; 8D; 9B; 10D

2 11 urbanised; 12 endangered; 13 wildlife; 14 intensively; 15 deforestation; 16 breakages; 17 beneficial

3 18 having; 19 at; 20 off; 21 with; 22 on; 23 effect

4 24 introduced, the; 25 lake. Now; 26 eruption 27 ✔; 28 Australian; 29 ✔

5 30 extinction; 31 action; 32 reduction/decline/decrease; 33 protection; 34 insufficient

6 35D; 36H; 37B; 38E; 39A; 40G

UNIT 14

1 1B; 2D; 3D; 4C; 5D; 6A; 7C; 8C; 9B; 10A

2 11 sleepless; 12 accidentally; 13 financial; 14 belongings; 15 micalculation; 16 neighbourly; 17 hardship

3 18 having; 19 Only; 20 in; 21 why; 22 despite; 23 yourself

4 24 talk; 25 will; 26 ✔; 27 only; 28 have; 29 to

5 30 went to; 31 got on; 32 get to; 33 all; 34 out of; 35 neither here

6 36G; 37F; 38D; 39A; 40E

PRACTICE TEST 3

Reading Part 3   17D; 18G; 19F; 20C; 21A; 22E

English in Use Part 1   1C; 2A; 3B; 4D; 5A; 6B; 7C; 8B; 9C; 10A; 11C; 12A; 13C; 14D; 15A

English in Use Part 4   47 enriched; 48 technological; 49 problematic; 50 accompanied; 51 comparison; 52 addition; 53 surprisingly; 54 manufacturer; 55 receipt; 56 dealer; 57 applicable; 58 misuse; 59 unauthorised; 60 instructions; 61 assistance

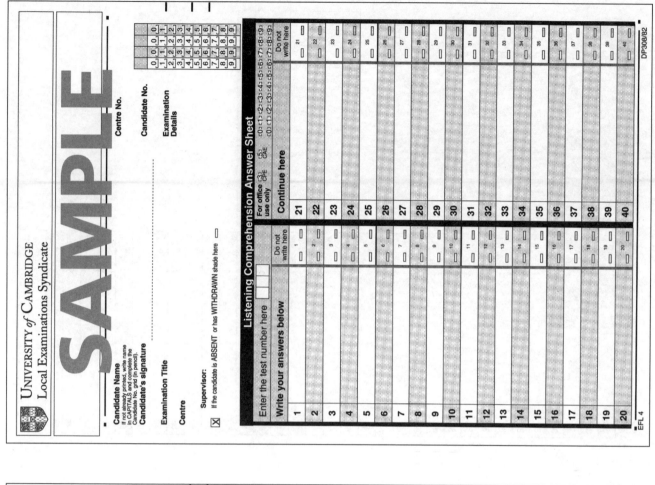

SAMPLE

UNIVERSITY of CAMBRIDGE
Local Examinations Syndicate

Candidate Name
If not already printed, write name
in CAPITALS and complete the
Candidate No. grid (in pencil).
Candidate's signature

Examination Title

Centre

Supervisor:
☒ If the candidate is ABSENT or has WITHDRAWN shade here ▭

Centre No.

Candidate No.

Examination
Details

Listening Comprehension Answer Sheet

For office use only   CPE ▭   CAE ▭

Enter the test number here

Write your answers below

Do not write here

1
2
3
4
5
6
7
8
9
10
11
12
13
14
15
16
17
18
19
20

Continue here

Do not write here

21
22
23
24
25
26
27
28
29
30
31
32
33
34
35
36
37
38
39
40

EFL 4

DP308/82

©UCLES 1999   Photocopiable

SAMPLE

UNIVERSITY of CAMBRIDGE
Local Examinations Syndicate

Candidate Name
If not already printed, write name
in CAPITALS and complete the
Candidate No. grid (in pencil).
Candidate's signature

Examination Title

Centre

Supervisor:
☒ If the candidate is ABSENT or has WITHDRAWN shade here ▭

Centre No.

Candidate No.

Examination
Details

Multiple-choice Answer Sheet

Use a pencil   Mark one letter for each question.

For example:

If you think C is the right answer to the
question, mark your answer sheet like this:

0   A B C⬛

Change your answer
like this:

1–20 A B C D E F G H
21–40 A B C D E F G H
41–60 A B C D E F G H

CAE1

DP306/80

©UCLES 1999   Photocopiable

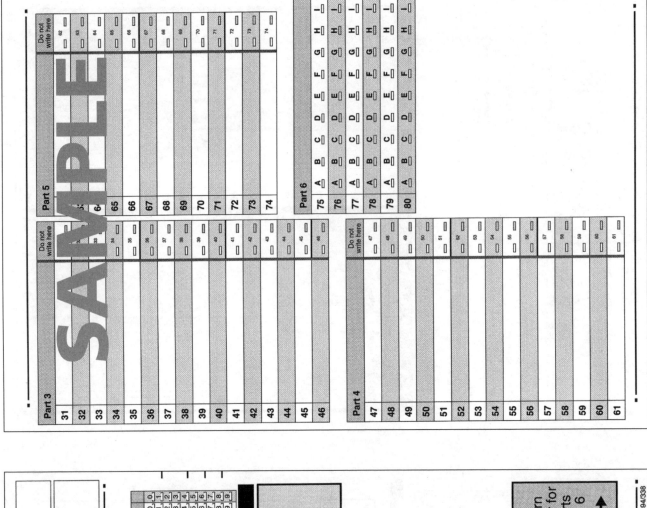

ANSWER SHEETS